Back to Pakistan

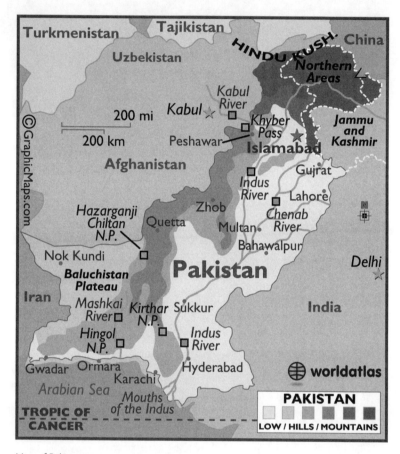

Map of Pakistan

Back to Pakistan

A Fifty-year Journey

Leslie Noyes Mass

ROWMAN & LITTLEFIELD PUBLISHERS, INC.
Lanham • Boulder • New York • Toronto • Plymouth, UK

Published by Rowman & Littlefield Publishers, Inc.
A wholly owned subsidary of The Rowman & Littlefield Publishing Group, Inc.
4501 Forbes Boulevard, Suite 200, Lanham, Maryland 20706
http://www.rowmanlittlefield.com

Estover Road, Plymouth PL6 7PY, United Kingdom

British Library Cataloguing in Publication Information Available

Library of Congress Cataloging-in-Publication Data
Noyes Mass, Leslie, 1940-
  Back to Pakistan : a fifty-year journey / Leslie Noyes Mass.
    p. cm.
  ISBN 978-1-4422-1319-7 (hardback : alk. paper) — ISBN 978-1-4422-1321-0 (ebook)
  1. Noyes Mass, Leslie, 1940—Travel—Pakistan. 2. Noyes Mass, Leslie, 1940—
Diaries. 3. Volunteer workers in education—Pakistan—Biography. 4. Volunteer
workers in social service—Pakistan—Biography. 5. Teachers—Training of—Pakistan.
6. Pakistan—Description and travel. 7. Peace Corps (U.S.)—Pakistan—Biography.
I. Title.
LB2844.1.V6N69 2011
371.10095491—dc23   2011019782

Printed in the United States of America

For George, with me since the beginning,
and
for the children of Pakistan, with us now and in the future

Contents

~

Acknowledgments

Many people are responsible for the creation of this book and deserve more than thanks—they deserve a medal for forbearance, patience, and humor. Among them, I'd particularly like to acknowledge:

Barbara Janes (Taffy) and Nancy Parlin, my Peace Corps friends and traveling mates, for their consistently valuable information, advice, and details about our 2009 return trip to Pakistan;

The Noorani family—Danial, Karen, Sofia, and all of their Pakistan-based relatives—for their superb organizational skills, lavish meals, and gracious hospitality;

Everyone at The Citizens Foundation in Pakistan for sharing their idealism, dedication, and practical experiences with me;

My Dhamke families, for welcoming me when I was young and remembering me so many years later;

Mary and Larry Hasiak, for opening their Florida garret for a quiet place to write; and

My patient and loving husband, George, for his encouragement and wise counsel, then and now.

I thank you with all my heart.

~

Prologue

"Off To Pakistan" read the headline of my hometown newspaper in 1962 and the subject line of some of my email correspondence in 2009. Both times, the first question from my friends and family was "Why Pakistan?" and the next, "Why you?" The third was usually "Do you really want to go so far away from us?" and finally, "Will you be safe?"

In 1962, one month past my college graduation, my answers were glib: Because that's where the Peace Corps is sending me. They need my liberal arts skills. The people want us to come to their villages and schools and work side by side with them as they build their cottage industries, agricultural exports, and rate of literacy. I can keep in touch with you by airmail letters. And yes, of course, I will be safe! I am an American. Our vice president, Lyndon Johnson, and First Lady, Jackie Kennedy, have just been to Pakistan. Pakistanis love Americans! The media tells me so. Why not?

In 2009, a lifetime later, the answers to those questions aren't quite so glib. I really question this time whether I should go off to Pakistan to revisit the country where I had come face-to-face with my own naïveté, youthful arrogance, and inexperience. But I am curious about what has become of the people in my village outside the city of Lahore, and whether the women are still in *purdah*. Do the girls in my village have any better access to education now, I wonder, or has my village become a hotbed of Islamist extremism, further denying books and education outside the purdah wall?

Since leaving Pakistan in 1964, my career has been in education, creating hands-on learning programs for teachers, children, and parents in a variety of school settings. Now, knowing more about education, I wonder what has happened to Pakistani education over the past forty-five years. I have read that Pakistan continues to have one of the lowest rates of literacy in the world, with more than 50 percent of the population illiterate, and I wonder if my work experience with education and literacy as an adult might be of some use in Pakistan now. Can I finally contribute something to the people I tried to help so many years ago?

The question about my personal safety in 2009 is appropriate. The world press reports Pakistan to be one of the most dangerous countries in the world. Will I encounter Pakistanis eager to retaliate against me as an American for perceived foreign policy injustices and disappointments? *Will* I be safe?

I do not know the answers to these questions. But I am eager to find out. Over the course of my life, I have learned the importance of acting on my dreams, however foolish or ill conceived they might seem to others. Returning to Pakistan is a dream I have long held. So with the opportunity to revisit Pakistan in the summer of 2009 presenting itself, I jump at it.

One of my friends, Barbara Janes, a former Peace Corps Volunteer known affectionately as Taffy, has been invited by The Citizens Foundation, a Pakistani nongovernmental education organization, to participate in a project to train science teachers, using hands-on learning activities, and then to supervise these teachers as they work with children in Summer Science Camps in Karachi and Lahore. Taffy calls for assistance from the Friends of Pakistan USA, a group of former Peace Corps Volunteers to Pakistan. Would any of us like to accompany her, she asks?

I would!

Taffy invites me to Chicago to meet Danial Noorani, the chief executive officer of The Citizens Foundation USA. Nancy Parlin, another Peace Corps Volunteer from our era, will also be participating, Taffy says, and Danial will organize our stay in Pakistan. "Danial's wife Karen and daughter, Sofia, will be with us, as well," Taffy assures me. "Danial will know if we are in any danger. We can be sure, if he is in charge, we will be safe."

My husband George and I drive to Chicago the day after Thanksgiving 2008 to meet with Taffy and the Noorani family. They describe the work of The Citizens Foundation and their ideas for a summer project.

I am drawn as a moth to flame. I can't wait to go. And, even though I know our trip might have to be canceled at the last minute because of terrorist activity, I am not afraid. I feel that I have unfinished business in Pakistan.

In 1962, when I first arrived in Pakistan, the country was just fifteen years old. The nation existed in two wings, partitioned from India when British colonial rule withdrew from the subcontinent in 1947. At that time, most of the fifty million people in East and West Pakistan were Muslim and were either original inhabitants of their region or emigrants from India. There was an elite middle- and upper-class minority employed in the civil service, military, and professions, but the majority of Pakistan's citizens were displaced and illiterate farmers, shopkeepers, or landless tenants.

In 1971, when East Pakistan broke away from the western wing and became Bangladesh, West Pakistan became the Islamic Republic of Pakistan, or simply Pakistan. Since that time, civilian and military rule have governed alternately, the population has tripled, and the government has not been able to fully address the social and educational needs of the majority. Today in Pakistan, of the sixty-two million children eligible for school, less than half of them are enrolled.

Entering Pakistan in 2009, I initially view the country through a lens of memory and the current Taliban-focused stories of the Western press. As I travel around Karachi, Lahore, Khanewal, Islamabad, and Hunza, however, I talk with Pakistanis of all ages and every level of education and sophistication. I interview those engaged with The Citizens Foundation, from the original founders and CEO to the humblest school ayahs. I talk with Pakistanis from other philanthropic social and educational organizations and with the descendants of my original village in rural Punjab. I begin to understand that the Pakistan of my young adulthood and the Pakistan presented by the media today reveal an outdated and inaccurate story of Pakistan.

The story of Pakistan I have to tell is a personal one. It is the journey of a twenty-one-year-old volunteer in the earliest days of the Peace Corps, 1962–1964, and as a sixty-eight-year-old volunteer with The Citizens Foundation during the summer of 2009. It is drawn from the journals, letters, and memories of my Peace Corps days and from the observations, conversations, and professional experiences I had with Pakistanis during the summer of 2009.

CHAPTER 1

∼

Arrival in Pakistan, 1962

September 27, 1962
Lahore, Pakistan
Dear George,

. . . After thirty hours in the air . . . we finally arrived in Karachi. The airport reminds me of Harrisburg . . . small and dusty—quite a contrast to our stop in Rome. We were met by a group of reporters and some important Americans and Pakistanis. After some milky sweet tea and interviews they finally let us go to clean up at a nearby rest house. I stood in the shower with all my clothes on and then lay down for what I thought was an all day snooze. In less than an hour they woke me for lunch and a briefing about the next leg of our journey, Lahore. Two hours later I was shaking hands again . . . more reporters, people grabbing my sleeve and slipping a marigold garland over my head, bearers fighting over my suitcase . . . and a long crazy ride from the airport to the middle of the city and Peace Corps headquarters just off the Mall Road. . . . The city is teeming with people, animals, and horse-drawn carriages called tongas, busses, motor scooters, taxis, blaring horns, and confusion. Motor traffic, chaotic and exciting, is directed to the left, but no one pays much attention and everyone seems to drive in the middle of the road.

The Peace Corps office is housed in a former residence, surrounded by high walls with a gate opening to a scraggly lawn, dirt driveway, and clay pots of orange flowers. Behind the offices there are several rooms with rope beds called charpoys and a cement-floor closet with a toilet and showerhead—for transient Peace Corps Volunteers, I'm told. It looks uninviting and dismal—Shudder.

1

Another volunteer and I spent the night with a Pakistani family somewhere in Lahore. The neighborhood is a crowded maze of narrow lanes, shops, and open drains—packed with bicycles, hawkers, beggars, and food stalls. We tried to keep up with Afzul, our host, as he led us to his home, but he walked at least ten paces ahead of us. Some little kids chased behind us and several women, completely covered in black burqahs, bumped into us—on purpose? Afzul missed it all. There were a lot of men sitting in front of shops or on doorsills. They just stared at us—curiously silent. Their eyes were intrusive and made me feel naked.

Afzul's family was welcoming but their bathroom was another surprise: a porcelain footplate set in a corner of their flat roof with a drainpipe leading down to the street. Next to the footplate was a small clay pot of water. No paper. No flush. No shower. The Peace Corps transient room facilities began to look better.

The aroma on the street is an exotic mixture of incense, grilled food, dust, kerosene, sweat, and the most intoxicating flower I've ever smelled—evening jasmine, I think. The air is heavy and wet and hot, even at night. I can't breathe deeply enough to fill my lungs with oxygen.

Tomorrow the Peace Corps is sending me to Sheikhupura—a town about forty miles from Lahore. I think I'll be living alone and I don't have quarters yet. My job is not defined, either, and I'm really uneasy about what I'm supposed to do. We will be going for more training at the Academy for Village Development in Peshawar in another month—but for now, I'll be sent straight to a village.

I've been issued a thermos bottle, a thin mattress, blanket, sheet, and pillow—all bound with leather straps and called a bister—and instructions on how to reach my village. . . .

It's exciting to be here, at last, but I wish you were here, too. I miss you. They tell me it will take two weeks for this letter to reach you—and I'll have to wait another two weeks for your reply. A whole month!! Egads!! Write soon. L

At the University of Minnesota in 1962, we had been given a syllabus describing the Peace Corps Training Program for Pakistan. It explained our duties:

The eighty four Volunteers who will be trained under the current phase of the program fall into two general categories: (1) One group of volunteers will be assigned to the Ganges-Kobadak Irrigation Project in East Pakistan. . . . The second group of Volunteers will fill a number of positions selected from requests made by the Provincial governments of Pakistan. This group of Volunteers will be assigned to the following five projects: (a) Health Project (nurses and laboratory technicians); (b) Education Project (science teachers and librarians); (c) Public Works Project (civil engineers and surveyors); (d) Agriculture Project (agricultural extension workers, vocational agricultural teachers, and agronomists); (e) Community Development Project (community development workers).

My job assignment was to be a community development worker in West Pakistan under the Assistant Director for Basic Democracies.[1] The syllabus went on to detail my responsibilities:

The duties of Community Development workers are to (1) aid specialized workers in health, education, public works, and agriculture in the implementation of their programs at the village levels; (2) assist in carrying out village demonstrations; (3) work with existing local self-government bodies, young farmers' groups, etc.; and (4) perform research in optimal village development programs . . . and to . . . contribute substantially to the effectiveness of other Peace Corps workers in the area and to amass a fund of knowledge concerning the most fruitful direction for the future development of Pakistan.

Helping the people discover their felt needs and then helping them meet those needs was the task of Peace Corps community development workers in 1962. Living in the village, working alongside the people, was the way to accomplish this task.

September 30, 1962
Mirzavirkhan Village, Punjab
Mirzavirkhan is my village home for the next few nights . . . in a one-room brick and plaster schoolhouse, surrounded by a courtyard and high walls. On top of the walls, young children and old women in headscarves are sitting in a line, staring at me. Outside the courtyard gate I hear hammering fists and periodic calling: "What is the time by your watch, Sir." Schoolboys practicing their English I guess.

A Peace Corps jeep dropped me at the village this morning. It was a pleasant surprise to actually be inside a compound—the walls look so formidable from the road. The women and children were very shy, but friendly and eager to talk, though I couldn't remember much Punjabi and they don't know any English. We laughed a lot.

They showed me around the village—very dusty and hot with filthy open sewers. We collected a hoard of raggedy-looking children as we walked, mostly boys and little girls hoisting littler babies on their hips. Everyone was curious and eager for me to visit his house. They were so insistent. One old grandmother kept touching me as though she were blind, trying to figure out if I were a boy or girl—I guess because I have short hair and no headscarf dupatta. She finally shouted at me: "Are you a Village Girl?" The other women laughed. I just grinned and nodded. I'm not sure what it means to be a Village Girl.

At dusk, one of the landowners, a zamindar, took me to his fields outside the village. We walked along a canal footpath through knee-high crops stretching as far as the horizon. It was beautiful and serene. Returning to the village we passed groups of men sitting together on charpoys, smoking hookahs, gossiping and waiting for their dinner. The women and youngest children were behind compound walls patting out circles of bread called chapatis and cooking over smoky dung fires. Young boys walked behind herds of cows and bullocks, prodding them through the narrow lanes, raising the dust to meet the low ceiling of haze. Beyond the village, the sky was streaked with red, gold, and purple.

I feel like I have entered the Old Testament. Dark comes quickly in the Punjab and my life is half the globe away.

After my brief introduction to village life in Mirzavirkhan, I was dispatched to another village in the same district, Dhamke, which had requested a Peace Corps Volunteer. I was told that as a community development worker, my job would be to establish a cottage industry and to begin literacy education with the women and girls in the village.

CHAPTER 2

∼

Work Assignment, 1962

On October 9, 1962, squeezed between chickens, a goat, a woman in a long black *burqah*, three squirming children, and my bister, I tried to sink into the bench seat of the bus bringing me to Dhamke. Every seat was full. Small children sat or stood on bundles on the floor, and all the windows were open. Everyone stared at me. Old men sitting in the front of the bus and young men and boys running alongside and jumping on at the last minute ogled me through the windows. Every available surface of the bus was decorated, inside and out, with tinsel, gold tassels, and bright, garish paint. Even with the windows open and wind rushing in, the smell of so many bodies and so many bundles was ripe. I felt like I was joining a party in full swing, with everyone invited but me.

My bister on the floor beside me was now a bit heavier. In addition to my bedroll, books, and toothbrush, it now held my new village clothing. While in Mirzavirkhan the previous week, one of the tailors had made several *shalwar kameez* outfits for me. The village version of shalwar at the time was white cotton bloomerlike pants, four times the size of my waist at the top, gathered with a drawstring, blousing down and finished at the ankles with a loose band of stiff fabric, topstitched with parallel lines of thread. A kameez was a knee-length cotton dress with sleeves to the elbow and a neckline to the bones just shy of the throat. On my head, I now wore a long, wide white cotton scarf, looped over my shoulders to cover my chest. The headscarf was called a *dupatta*, and everyone, even little girls, wore one. The dupatta was symbolic of a woman's place in society, that of dependence and seclusion.

In traditional society, only prostitutes and dancing girls did not keep their heads decorously covered in public. I found the dupatta to be a nuisance, constantly in my way.

My village clothes did not hide the fact that I was a foreigner. For one thing, at five feet six inches, I towered over most people, even the men. For another, I did not wear a burqah or cover my face when I was in public.

After the onset of puberty, when venturing outside their home compound, Muslim village women wore a burqah—a long, one-piece, tentlike garment of white cotton that fit snugly over the crown of the head and cascaded down to the ankles in voluminous folds of fabric. This covered the entire body and had only an embroidered cutout lattice over the eyes to allow its wearer to see. A more fashionable burqah, worn by Muslim women living in towns or cities, was a garment more like a robe, made of black silk or rayon with loose sleeves and a separate headpiece that draped over the shoulders like a cape. This head covering had an extra piece of fabric that could be drawn across the face so that just the eyes were visible for the outside world to see in or the wearer to see out.

Wearing a burqah signified that a woman was from a family that observed purdah. Observing purdah was associated with the Punjabi concept of *izzet*,[1] and, in the strictest families, women in purdah did not even step outside their own homes. However, for most women, a burqah enabled them to travel beyond the family compound and offered a degree of protection from the intrusive stares or interference from strangers. My understanding was that, except for the women from the lowest social order—the sweepers, midwives, and beggars—and those from the elite educated minority, most Pakistani Muslim women wore a burqah of one sort or another when traveling away from their family home or village.

I opted to skip the burqah and wear just the shalwar, kameez, and dupatta for my everyday attire, and this seemed to satisfy, even please, everyone. My new clothes were comfortable and cool, and they kept off flies and the hard stares of some of the men.

Younas, the secretary of the Union Council,[2] met me at the bus stop by the side of the road near the village of Dhamke. He was a tall, slightly stooped young man, eager to walk me to the rest house where I would be staying, a half mile beyond the village. He instructed several young boys to carry my bister, and I scrambled to keep up as I followed them across the fields.

The rest house was a brick bungalow of three high-ceilinged rooms and a verandah surrounded by tall trees and a rosebush. Behind the bungalow were the former stables and servants' huts used during the time of the British Raj. In my head, I pictured a trim civil servant relaxing on the verandah, looking over the canal and fields, enjoying his afternoon tea. In reality, I was dismayed by the dust, animal dung, and general neglect of the place. Although the rooms were furnished with several charpoys and a table, the rest house had not been lived in for a long time, and it did not look suitable for a social center for village women. It would be a long way for them to come for literacy lessons and a cottage industry, I thought, but it would do as my home.

As I began to settle into one of the rooms, two men dressed in starched white shirts and khaki trousers arrived at my door. They introduced themselves as members of the Tehsil[3] and said they would be staying with me in the bungalow for a few nights. Their bearer and cook would stay in the huts out back.

The presence of these men concerned me. During our Peace Corps training at the University of Minnesota, we were told that women in this conservative Muslim culture were under the protection of their male relatives—fathers, brothers, husbands, uncles. Until they were married, most women did not leave their family compound, and if they did, they wore a burqah and were accompanied by a male relative. Even in their own homes, women were sequestered behind a purdah wall or on another level of the house when strangers entered the family compound. Unmarried women did not fraternize with men anywhere.

Though I was not a Muslim, I was unmarried and had no male relatives or even male Peace Corps Volunteers to protect me. I thought I should follow the local custom and not stay overnight, half a mile from the village, with these men. I was not afraid of the men, but I did not want to stay in the rest house with them and possibly jeopardize my reputation or acceptance with the village women. But I did not know how to avoid the situation.

In midafternoon, Rana Sahib, one of the zamindars[4] of Dhamke and chairman of the Union Council, came out to the rest house to greet me and give me a tour of the village. We walked for half a mile along a narrow canal, then down a dirt path to a maze of many mud-walled compounds that housed extended family units. As we walked, in a mixture of Punjabi and out-of-practice English, Rana told me about himself. He had fought with the British army in Italy during World War II, he said, and owned many of the fields surrounding the village. His wife and children lived in the center of the village with his mother and sister.

According to custom, Rana said, when a man marries, his wife joins him in his parents' home. The bride is supervised by her mother- and sisters-in-law and, until she bears her first child, must submit to the older women's every wish and bidding. If the bride is a second wife, she can be established in a separate household equal to but not better than the household of the first wife. I was surprised by Rana Sahib's conversation and used his explanation of living arrangements to ask about my own. Rana looked embarrassed when I told him that two men from the Tehsil were planning to stay at the rest house with me overnight. I was not sure whether he had arranged their stay or if it was a surprise to him.

We continued our walk through the village, winding along narrow alleys and stepping over open drains and animal dung. Rana told me that most of the inhabitants of Dhamke were Muslim and had emigrated together from a single village in Ludhiana District of India in 1947. The original inhabitants of Dhamke, he said, were Sikhs and had left for India at Partition. Only a handful of Christian families, converts from Untouchable-caste Hindus and living near the bus stop, were original inhabitants of Dhamke.

Eventually our walk took us to the office of the Union Council, where a delegation of village men waited on charpoys in front of the door. They were dressed in white cotton turbans, knee-length cotton shirts, and ankle-length skirtlike wraps called *dhotis*.

I was invited to sit inside at a scarred wooden table on the only available chair. Left alone in the room, I wondered what I was expected to do next. It was hot and dusty. Flies buzzed around my head, landed on my nose and eyes, and bothered my hands. I had an overwhelming desire to put my head on the table and take a nap. But I remained upright, staring around the barren room, waiting patiently for the next event. I remember feeling glassy-eyed and very far from home.

Rana Sahib reappeared, accompanied by Younas and several other Union Council members. The charpoys were brought inside, along with a plate of pale, hard cookies and a pot of hot tea sweetened with sugar, cardamom, and boiled milk. Everyone sat down and stared at me. Younas poured some of the *chai* into a smudged glass and offered me a biscuit from the plate now covered with flies. Politeness forced me to accept both food and drink.

For the next half hour, we drank tea, smoked, and tried to find a common language for conversation. Finally, the tea ritual ended and Rana asked me to tell everyone why I had come to his village. I stumbled and groped for an answer. I told them that I was the Peace Corps Volunteer that the Union Council had asked for. I had come to Dhamke to help the people develop their plans for a cottage industry and for literacy education for women and girls. I understood that they would provide me with a place to live and help me get started with these projects.

I remember being surprised by Rana's question. Didn't he know that I was the Peace Corps Volunteer that he had requested? In a roundabout way, he asked me if there were, perhaps, other volunteers, *male* volunteers, who could come and work in the village with me. His need, he said, was for help to increase the yield in the fields and for electricity. Cottage industry and literacy for women and girls had apparently not been his request, though he was too polite to say this. The men in the Union Council did not know what I, an unmarried woman, would be able to do in Dhamke, he said. However, he assured me that he would provide food, shelter, and protection for me and that I was welcome.

I looked around the assembly of disgruntled Union Council members and village elders and wondered. I naively had expected to step into a well-defined job in this village, with a coworker to show me the ropes and a private place to live. Instead, there was no real job for me in Dhamke, no place to live, and no coworker to help me get started. And as a single woman, I had little credibility with the men in charge of my destiny.

Somewhere in the bureaucracies of the Peace Corps in Lahore and the Basic Democracy in Sheikhupura, my gender and qualifications, and the needs of Dhamke, had been miscommunicated.

Now what? I had no idea. And I was mad at the Peace Corps for botching up my assignment. But I was determined to figure out a way to work in this village.

CHAPTER 3

~

The Vision, 1962

October 19, 1962
Academy for Village Development, Peshawar
Dear George,

   After ten days in Dhamke, I am back with my Peace Corps friends for a week of further training in Peshawar. I'm no longer mad at the Peace Corps, but I still don't have a real job.

   The Volunteers here seem to be living pretty well and though some are equally disgusted with the lack of job definition, I am the orphan of the group. No other woman is alone in a village; everyone else has, at least, a place to live and a real job. The teachers have already started teaching and the men assigned to agricultural extension and engineering projects all have co-workers. But we Community Development workers are on our own. No one really knows what we are supposed to do.

   At this academy there is plenty of talk about community development, but no one has any concrete suggestion about how to get started. I can see that the villagers need a lot of help—just simple hygiene and a closed sewer system would be a start—but I am told to just observe and offer suggestions only when asked. First they tell me that the program must come from the women and then, in the next breath, say I should outline a plan and jump in and get it started. But the women are behind the purdah wall and I don't know what they want—and I really don't know how to reach them, much less how to get started. I feel completely at a loss and out of my depth. It's so hard to be a woman—much less a change agent—in this culture.

11

At least I didn't have to stay in the rest house in Dhamke with the two men from the Tehsil. That would have been a disaster. Somehow I convinced Rana Sahib that it would be better for me to stay somewhere in the village. His solution was to put me in the Union Council office in a storeroom next to the men's meeting room, with only a chair, a rope bed, a candle, and a door that would not close. As in Mirzavirkhan, outside the compound the village boys amused themselves by elbowing and shoving each other to get my attention, and from morning to night, the rooftops around me were lined with staring brown eyes—dozens and dozens of children and the Christian women—all watching to see what I would do next.

A young girl from Rana's compound brought me food every day, and Rana Sahib himself came to visit me several times in the evenings. I do like him. He seems to be trying to figure out what to do with me—even though he wasn't really expecting me. I guess he feels he is stuck with me because we have begun to talk about what I might be able to do in Dhamke. I spent some time visiting with the village women in their compounds while I was waiting to come to Peshawar, but the Muslim women were not allowed to visit me in the Union Council office.

I think Rana sees his responsibility is to protect me from the village men—and to protect the village women from me.

The lecturers at this Academy for Village Development mean well, but they don't have much experience with village women. And, I'll bet none of them has ever spent the night in a village—at least a village like Dhamke. They tell me I'm supposed to "change the social patterns of village life." I guess I first have to figure out what those patterns are.

I wonder what will happen when I go back to Dhamke? I can't imagine being there for two more years!

I really miss you. It is so dark with only the stars keep me company. But they are bright overhead—and they are the same ones you see—just ten hours earlier.

Love,

L

Two weeks later, I was back in Dhamke, refreshed from speaking English with my friends and eating hot dogs and fries at the nearby U.S. Air Force base in Peshawar. I still had only a fuzzy understanding of my job assignment, but while I was in Peshawar, Rana Sahib had found a space for me to live, not far from his own family compound in the center of the village. He proudly led me to an old stable of two small rooms separated by a courtyard and walled off from the street. He said I could turn one room into my home and use the other for a social center. Some women and girls could come to the social center in the afternoon, he said, to sew, knit, and embroider.

I was surprised, relieved, and grateful for this turn of events. At least it was a beginning, though I did not know how to teach sewing, knitting, or embroidery. But, I had some books with good diagrams, and in my own home, I thought I could create a place where women could gather. At last, I could begin my job as a community development worker.

I set about making the stable my home. With the help of Younas and two Peace Corps Volunteers living temporarily in Lahore—Bill Lorah and Dick Smith—we cut two windows and rebuilt the walls of the stable using a mixture of cow dung, mud, and water. We dug a latrine under a small tree in the courtyard and walled it off from the prying eyes of neighbors on the roof next door. In the corner of one room, we cemented a four-foot square on the floor and cut a drain to the street. I purchased a fifty-gallon tin drum from the bazaar in Lahore, fitted it at the bottom with a hand-cranked paddle wheel, and placed the refitted drum on the concrete square to serve as a water barrel cum washing machine.

One room of the stable became my kitchen/washing/eating area. I furnished it with a counter-cupboard made from a three-foot-high wooden packing crate, a kerosene Primus stove and lantern, and a large tin trunk in which I stored my clothes, books, and writing materials. I whitewashed the walls, spread jute mats on the baked-mud floor, and hung bright cotton fabric over the doorway, window, and front of the packing crate. The room was dark, even in the daylight. But it was mine.

The room across the courtyard, where I slept in the coldest weather, doubled as the women's social-center-to-be. I furnished it initially with my charpoy, a hand-cranked sewing machine, a tin trunk filled with Village Aid homemaking books and sewing supplies, and a table made from a square of wood balanced on my suitcase. I covered the baked-mud floor with woven mats and draped lengths of bright cotton over the doorway and the window. This room was also very dark, but it was private and out of public view for the women in purdah who would visit me.

I planned to use embroidery, sewing, and knitting lessons as the hook to bring the women to me. Once they began to trust me, I thought, we could move on to other topics, like hygiene, family planning, and literacy.

Open sewers, flies licking the corners of babies' eyes, sores festering on old women's hips, dirty hands preparing food, and the ever-present dirt, dust, and dung did not seem to bother anyone but me. I saw the women and girls around me as poor, illiterate, and ignorant. I saw my job as teaching them how to keep a cleaner home, cook more nutritious meals, bear fewer children, learn to read and write, and have a better life. Eventually we would start a cottage industry and the women would begin to make a little money of their own. The social center I envisioned would become a school. I had big plans.

What I did not realize was that the women and young girls in Dhamke knew how to turn cow dung into mortar and fuel and how to organize their households while squatting by the fire patting chapatis, nursing an infant, and tending to toddlers in the cold predawn and after-sunset dark. These young mothers worked all day mending clothing, bathing children, pleasing their mothers-in-law, and keeping flies and animals at bay. These women knew how to embroider, sew, and knit far better than I did. They just did not have time for it. Their lives were already full.

The plans I had for the women at my social center were all *my* plans. They were based on *my* ideas of development and on my dismay at the living conditions I saw all around me. The need for better sanitation, family planning, and knowledge of the outside world through literacy, though obvious to me, were of little concern to the village women or to their men.

Meanwhile, Bill and Dick, the Peace Corps colleagues who had helped me rebuild my house, were staying at the rest house just outside of Dhamke. For them, the rest house was the solution to their housing needs; it was on the bus line to Lyallpur[1] and Lahore and central to the engineering and agricultural extension projects they had been assigned to carry out in Sheikhupura district. By staying in the rest house, the three of us could share household food expenses and Bill and Dick could, perhaps, help Rana Sahib with some of the agricultural projects he had in mind for Dhamke. It was easy to convince Rana of this plan. Bill and Dick were the male Peace Corps Volunteers he really needed and the male "relatives" I needed to give me credibility with the village women.

With Rana's help, the three of us persuaded the Peace Corps and our supervisor, Ikram Mohyddin, the Assistant Director of Basic Democracies in Sheikhupura, to allow my two "brothers" to live in the rest house. I was happy to have their company, especially during the long dark evenings when the villagers tucked into their compounds, smoking and eating around their campfires, talking about their day. With Bill and Dick to share meals and conversation, I could have the same companionable experience. And with three of us eating together, we could afford to splurge on vegetables and meat for our evening meal.

We enlisted the help of a village shopkeeper, Ata Mohammed, to bring us food from his many suppliers; our menu expanded beyond oatmeal, pancakes, boiled eggs, and tea. None of us really knew how to cook, but we managed

to learn the rudiments of soup, curry, and boiled undercut (beef). We nicknamed Ata Mohammed "Jerry" after Jerry Lewis because of his unfailing good
humor and antics purchasing our daily fare. Jerry, his sister Envir, and their
mother, Bivi-gee, would become good friends and our surrogate family in the
months to come. They were the first family, outside of Rana's compound, to
accept us and include us in their everyday lives.

Within weeks of the loneliness I had experienced in the Union Council
office and the despair in Peshawar, I had acquired my own home in the village and my own male family to help me gain the confidence of the village
men and women. Could a social center for the women and girls be far behind, I remember wondering?

Every day, with renewed energy and enthusiasm, I dressed in my new
shalwar kameez and dupatta and visited the village women who were not
yet allowed to visit me. I wound my way through the narrow village lanes,
collecting small children and dogs as I walked, and knocked randomly on
compound doors. To my surprise, the women opened their doors to me,
welcomed me into their homes, and graciously pulled out a bed or chair
for me to sit on as I tried to talk with them. My Punjabi was improving,
but I was still a long way from fluent. None of the women spoke English.
We usually laughed a lot while I stumbled along, trying to answer their
questions.

In each household, I was offered a smudged glass jar of buttermilk, water,
or lemonade to drink. I began to recognize the glass jar and wondered if it
were passed from one household to another when I came to call. I always felt
obliged to accept, however, and often suffered the consequences of nausea
and dysentery from the untreated water or the well-traveled jar. Occasionally I was offered hot tea and a boiled egg. These were safer and easier on my
system, but much too expensive for any but the wealthiest family to spare.

Like Rana, the women I visited were curious about why I had come to
their village. They wanted to know about my children, my husband, and my
brothers. They handed me their babies to cuddle and quizzed me about my
underwear. Occasionally, my underwear would disappear from my courtyard
clothesline, and I suspected that my questioners knew more about its construction and style than I did. I sometimes wondered if any of my bras and
panties were under the shalwar kameez of my hostesses or hidden in one of
their tin trunks.

The women were talkative, friendly, and interested in my life. But try as
I did to persuade them to come to my home, the Muslim women would not
visit me. They did not understand the idea of a social center and told me they
would not be allowed to participate.

It was not only the village women who were puzzled about me. Their menfolk were also very uncertain about my place in their traditional Muslim village. As a young, unmarried woman, I had no credibility with them. I was not, nor did I want to be, part of the authority structure. My understanding of the Peace Corps modus operandi was to wait for the people to tell me what they wanted and then to help them form a plan of action. I still expected to facilitate rather than dictate their plans. But I also expected that their ideas would match mine, and that we would all come up with the same plan.

I was so impatient to begin. In addition to removing the surface differences of dirt, flies, open sewers, and the odor of dung everywhere, I wanted to change the lack of privacy and the submissiveness of women to the men in their families. I thought that narrow lanes and high walls separated households from each other and that the women were completely excluded from the outside world.

I felt that I was responsible for helping the women change their ways and become more productive, healthier, and less impoverished. I blamed the women for accepting their imprisonment and the men for imprisoning them.

> November 14, 1962
> Dhamke
> Taking Rana Sahib's mother to the doctor in Lahore makes me wonder, again, about my role here. . . . She is so sick and so frail. Although she was confused by the city and the hospital and the doctors and nurses, she really held up well. I tried to calm her by showing her picture books about the hospital while we waited. She was like a child, really, but cooperative even though she was scared. The bus and taxi ride were hard on her—she's nothing but jutting bones under her clothes. With every jolt of the bus I thought she would break in two.
>
> We finally made it back to Dhamke by early evening. All her male relatives were waiting at the bus stop. One of the boys lifted her onto his bicycle and wheeled her home while I tried to explain to Rana that she might have cancer. I gave him the ten-day supply of pills the doctor had given me for her. I hope she'll get better but I really have my doubts. Sixty years of living in these conditions . . . what can I possibly do to change this?
>
> Is this really what I'm supposed to be doing here???

My role, living in the village, creating a model home, visiting women, and being kind to elderly parents did not satisfy my impatience for what I perceived to be my real work with the women. I wanted to begin to educate these women. Basic education, I thought, was the only way to change the pattern of village life, and I desperately wanted to effect the social change I considered to be my community development responsibility. But Rana seemed really grateful for my help.

At the time, Pakistan had a literacy rate of only 12 percent. In the entire country, only 42 percent of the children were enrolled in any kind of primary education, fewer than ten thousand students were enrolled in secondary schools, and the overwhelming majority of students, either primary or secondary, were male. Although educational reform was part of his current Five-Year Plan, President Mohammed Ayub Khan admitted that compulsory, universal primary education for Pakistani children was many generations away. Most villages had no primary school for boys, let alone for girls. If they could afford education at all, families sent only one son to school; other sons went to work at an early age and never learned to read or write. Boys who did attend school usually went to the nearest village school for two or three years and learned, at most, basic mathematics, how to read and write the national language, Urdu, and perhaps a bit of English. Religious training with the village *maulvi* or imam was often the only education possible for the poorest boys.

Village girls fared even less well. Daughters were kept at home to learn the homemaking skills that would be expected of them by their future mother-in-law. Girls were lucky to learn to write their own name, much less to read or write in Urdu or English. Village families who might value education for girls were often hard pressed to find a nearby girls' school. In 1962, in the entire country there were fewer than 127,000 primary school teachers. Furthermore, these teachers were mostly male, and Punjabi families would not allow girls to be taught by men. The observance of purdah prevented many women from entering the teaching profession, so few women were being trained as teachers, and the teacher-training institutes or junior training colleges that did exist were few in number, inadequate, and poorly attended.

Most girls learned to recite the Quran at home, were married at an early age, and often lived with their husband's family by their midteens. I wanted to change all this. But to accomplish my plans, I had to break through the purdah barrier that prevented the village women from visiting me in my home.

So far, my only visitors had been a few young boys wanting help with English. I tutored them in the evening and lent them simple books on American culture, politics, and literature.[2] Eventually, these boys began to bring their younger sisters with them when they came for a visit. With even younger children on their hips, the girls all wanted to look through my tin trunk of books and clothing. They were very curious and eager to learn a few words of English. I taught them the English alphabet, and together we learned the Arabic letters used to write Urdu.

So, as I continued to visit the older women and girls in their homes and to invite them to visit me in mine, I began to feel a slight quiver of progress. Even though the women in purdah still did not come, they entrusted their old women and young children to me.

CHAPTER 4

~

Living Village Life, 1962

At the end of December, after I had been in the village for almost three months, a fellow Peace Corps Volunteer asked if his fiancée, an American graduate student working on a thesis about women in purdah, could stay with me occasionally and study the women in my village. I agreed with an enthusiastic yes. Even though Bill and Dick spent many evenings with me, sitting on the floor around my suitcase/dining table, eating by the light of a kerosene lamp, gossiping, and playing word games, I was lonely for an American woman's friendship and welcomed her company.

Rana Sahib found another charpoy to squeeze into the sleeping/social center room in my tiny compound, and Carol arrived, in due course, to begin her village study. A stately five-foot-nine-inch blond, the village men could not take their eyes off of her when she walked through the narrow lanes with Benny, her smaller and darker fiancé from the Philippines. By this time, my Punjabi was fluent enough to understand, and respond to, the many questions the village women had about the couple.

If they were engaged, Envir and Bivi-gee wondered, why were they allowed to be together before the wedding? Envir was engaged to her cousin and would be married within a few months, but she had not been allowed to be in the same room with her betrothed or even to be seen by him since their parents had arranged the nuptials.

And how was it possible for Carol to be in the same house as Bill and Dick in the evening when we had meals together? It was all right for me to eat with my putative brothers, but the women could not understand Benny and

19

Carol's relationship nor Carol's position in our household. The women had other questions as well.

During the three months that Bill, Dick, and I had been in Dhamke, our living quarters had become a favorite stopping place for many other Peace Corps Volunteers and staff members as they traveled the road between Sheikhupura, Lyallpur, and Lahore. Several times a month, two or three extra people would stop for tea or dinner or just to see the village. My compound had become an interesting showplace for visiting dignitaries, and often, as I escorted my visitors around the village, I found doors that were usually open to me firmly closed. I thought that my parade of visitors might somehow jeopardize the very fragile relationship I had been trying to establish with the village women, and it worried me. Still, I welcomed Carol's expertise and knowledge of purdah and thought she might help me understand how to better reach the women behind their purdah walls.

Using village census records supplied by Union Council secretary Younas, Carol designed a survey to find out more about the families in Dhamke. She joined me on my household visits and, with the help of an interpreter, interviewed the women and recorded as much information about their lives as they were prepared to share. I began to suspect that many of the women were eager to visit me, but needed a reason to do so.

One day, Rana Sahib surprised me with the news that he had dismantled the cooking area in his compound and wanted help building a new kitchen just like mine. The next Friday afternoon, a small group of burqah-clad women from his compound knocked on the door to my courtyard and briskly demanded to look at my house. They were curious, it seemed, about the kitchen that Rana was planning to replicate.

The women inspected my concrete slab on the floor, my washing machine, the curtained packing crate I used as a cupboard and counter, the septic tank, my books, and my clothes and underwear. I showed them the room for the social center with the sewing machine and homemaking books, and we swatted flies together as we sat on my charpoys sipping tea. We talked, haltingly in Punjabi, of the cold weather. When I asked them if they could help me sew a *rezai*, a village cotton quilt to keep me warm on the chilly winter nights, they nodded and several agreed to come again and help. My hopes for a women's social center cum school began to rise again.

After that Friday, a small coterie of women began to visit my home from time to time to sit and chat and watch me go about my daily chores. Everything I did was new and different for them. I cooked on a Primus stove, boiled water before I drank it, scrubbed and agitated my clothes with hot water and soap in my washing machine, brushed my teeth with a toothbrush and toothpaste, and used the latrine in my courtyard rather than make the daily trip to the fields at sunrise and sunset.

The women were amused by my inability to embroider a lazy daisy and grabbed the knitting from my hands to pick up the stitches I invariably lost, but they were impressed with my prowess on the sewing machine. I had watched my mother create a wardrobe of new school clothes for me on her antique foot-treadle machine during the hot summer evenings of my child-hood. Doing without electricity in our summer cottage when I was ten had been exciting and mysterious. I had loved the long, dark evenings of talking, reading, and playing games by lantern light. Now, in a Punjabi village, I real-ized how important those experiences had been as preparation for my new life.

Eventually, the women in Dhamke began to accept that I spent many hours by kerosene light, reading the books from my tin trunk and writing in my notebooks. In a small way, I became a nonthreatening model for them for the possibility of something different. And even though I still did not have a concrete job to do, I was busy every day sewing and talking with the women who visited me, cleaning and keeping house in my small compound, teaching young children to write numbers and letters, cleansing and ban-daging cuts and sores, and trying to make friends and be helpful to everyone who asked me.

During the month of February, Bill, Dick, and I observed the long days of fasting during the religious observance of Ramadan and celebrated at its end the culminating feast of Eid-ul-Fitr with the village.

February 25, 1963
Dhamke
We saw the sliver of new moon in the sky tonight. Tomorrow we'll celebrate Eid with the rest of the village. There has been so much excitement in the air all day. The children have been milling underfoot, their heads freshly oiled, their hands painted red, and, for the girls, new glass bangles. I have a new outfit to wear tomorrow, as well—a silky kameez of shocking blue dots on a background of shimmering gold, peacock blue shalwar, and a gauzy blue dupatta. Bill has a long blue coat with a Nehru collar, called an ashkan, and Dick will wear a new vest embroidered with gold stitching over his white kurta shirt and shalwar. We'll be very fancy tomorrow—and up at dawn, receiving bedangled and bedazzled visitors, eating sweet rice and vermicelli, pay-ing Eid greetings, and handing rupees all around.

The excitement reminds me of Christmas morning when I was little—getting up before dawn and racing downstairs to find our stockings and Christmas tree full of gifts, dressing up for church and a big dinner with all our relatives afterwards. I don't really understand the customs of Eid, but the traditions—gifts, new clothes, prayers, special foods, and relatives' visits—are movingly familiar. I do know it will be a time of celebration, fun, and gifts for children and the poor. The men will pray in the Union Council office and the women, for once, will pray in the mosque.

I'm glad the village is including us in the celebration.

Bill, Dick, and I began to be invited to family celebrations as well, and when she was in the village, Carol joined us. In early March, we attended the marriages of Jerry and Envir to their first-cousin counterparts in a village one hundred miles away. The negotiations and gift exchange leading up to the nuptial ceremonies usurped our attention for several weeks as we accompanied Bivi-gee to the villages of her extensive family. Carol and I spent many hours drinking tea, holding babies on our laps, and admiring bridal clothing as we chatted with the female relatives of the extended clan.

March 1–4, 1963
Dhamke
Envir's Wedding
Carol and I have been visiting Envir's house every night to dance and sing with the women. At the beginning of the week, only her sister and mother were there but as the wedding day drew nearer, more and more people began to arrive. The dances and songs got pretty raunchy—a lot of swaying and hip-thrusting and knowing giggles. Thursday night there were dozens of women and little girls crammed into Bivi-gee's small compound. They painted each other's hands and feet with red henna and squabbled over who would paint mine. It took about two hours for my feet to dry—but the design is pretty and I feel very much a part of the festivities.

The day before Envir was to leave for her mother-in-law's compound, I went to help Bivi-gee spread long prayer rugs across their courtyard. As soon as the big pots of rice arrived, we began to set out the food for the wedding guests. The women have been cooking for days—all kinds of chicken and mutton and vegetable curries—but the sweet rice mixed with saffron, currants, and almonds is, by far, everyone's favorite.

While we were working, we ate some of the sweet rice we had pilfered and hidden in our dupattas—another use for the ever functional dupatta—and then went to the door of the compound to hang Envir's dupatta across the opening. The band arrived, then the male guests. Finally, the groom was announced and Envir's sister tried to bribe him to go away. No luck. He entered, but we couldn't see his face because a headpiece of long strings of flowers and sparkling glossy paper covered it. We women were pushed back inside the house, away from the men.

I stayed with Envir in the farthest corner of the room. She was dressed in her oldest clothes and had not had a bath all week. We stayed there, pressed in by all the women guests while the men sat on the prayer rugs in the courtyard for their meal. When the men finally left to smoke and gossip in their own quarters, Carol and I went home. Exhausted.

Early the next morning, a group of female relatives woke us to come to breakfast with the bride. Envir had bathed by this time but she was still in her oldest clothes and didn't know what time she would have to leave. We helped Bivi-gee and Envir's older sister spread the dowry out for display in the courtyard—beautiful shalwar-kameez, colorful quilts, brass plates, glassware, and gold jewelry. The groom arrived, again in his flowered headpiece, and threw paisa for the children. There was a lot of confusion as the children scrambled and tussled for the coins.

Finally it was time for Envir to get dressed in her wedding clothes and jewelry. Bivi-gee began to braid and oil Envir's hair and they both began to sob. Envir's sister and girlfriends helped her into a pink silk shalwar kameez, gold nose ring, filigreed gold earrings and a modern brown burqah. The burqah is a sign of her new status as a married woman. Seeing it cover Envir's pretty face made me want to cry along with them.

When she was fully dressed, Envir began to sob louder but her cries and moans could not compare to Bivi-gee's. All the women hugged and cried and sang a mournful song about leaving as they began to pack up the dowry. By the time the band arrived, Envir was ready to go, still sobbing. The groom's representative helped her into a covered doli (palanquin) carried by his friends, and the groom, band, and bridal procession swayed out to the bus stop.

We left them at the bus stop. The men will take one bus, the women another. Envir is coming back tomorrow, and then we'll all leave with Jerry, on a chartered bus, for his janj wedding ceremony. Envir will spend eight days at home and then return to her new home with her new mother-in-law.

Envir's wedding was not that fancy. Bivi-gee never did change from her old clothes and the house, though newly whitewashed on the outside, was none too clean on the inside. To me, it seems that Envir is not getting married at all—she's just changing girlfriends. Her life will be with women and children, all relatives. Her husband seems more like a new male sibling, the marriage an arrangement to keep family lands and possessions all together.

March 5–6, 1963
Sialkot
Jerry's Janj

Carol, Bill, Dick, and I put on our best clothes Sunday morning to join Jerry's wedding party. First we went to his parent's house. Envir was there, radiant. The courtyard was crowded with friends, relatives, and the band. Jerry was all dressed up in a long silk kurta (shirt) with flashy decorations on his wrists, garlands of flowers around his neck, a white turban on his head, and strings of flowers covering his face.

The wedding party paraded to the bus stop passing rupee notes over Jerry's head to the band in front, and tossing coins to the children behind. It was colorful, confusing, and exciting. Dust, kids, clamor, and dogs were everywhere.

We changed busses in Lahore, boarded the chartered bus for Sialkot, and arrived in the late afternoon. We had to hike three miles into the village and wait for the men to perform evening prayers and then waited longer for a new band to meet us. We didn't arrive at the bride's house until almost dark. Again, rupees were passed over Jerry's head, "In the name of Allah, for the marriage of Ata Mohammed, given by (name of donor) a rupee" to the band ahead of us as coins were tossed to the children behind us.

In the village, Carol and I were sent directly to the women's quarters where *we* were the main attraction. We sat on a charpoy and answered questions, suffered pokes from curious fingers, and swatted flies while the bride's mother and sisters set out the wedding feast. As part of the groom's wedding party, we were honored guests and not allowed to help. After the long bus ride and maddeningly slow walk to the village, the wait seemed to drag on for hours.

When the food was finally ready, the band and men reappeared and went up to the roof to eat in the cool evening breeze. We women ate on the floor of the bride's room in stifling heat, amid crying babies and toddlers careening into our shoulders and stepping on our plates.

After dinner, the women cleared the food away, made a space in the middle of the floor, and commanded us to dance. I thought the Twist might be a little silly without any music, so resurrected the Hokey Pokey and taught the women and girls how to "put your right hand in and shake it all about. . . ." They loved it and wanted more—but I was exhausted and wanted to end the day.

We all went out to the fields and then back to someone else's dark house to sleep. Carol and I shared the same narrow charpoy in a room with three other women and too many crying babies and small children. The women talked and giggled and kept the kerosene lamp burning all night. . . . We didn't get much sleep . . . and at four thirty everyone got up to go to the fields and begin the day anew.

We sat around for hours with the women, answering questions shouted at us in a dialect that combined Hindustani, Urdu, and Punjabi into a hodgepodge neither Carol nor I could understand. We never did see the bride, off somewhere in the corner of her room, being oiled and dressed, we assumed, for the journey back to Dhamke with Bivi-gee, her new mother-in-law.

After a few more hours and more sweet rice, the band and men arrived carrying the doli for the bride. She was crying quietly into her fine wedding dupatta but was pulled forward anyway by her sobbing mother and sisters. Her doli was hoisted on the men's shoulders and we all began the three-mile walk, behind the band, to the bus back to Lahore and, finally, to Dhamke.

On the way back, the heavens opened and it began to pour. Carol and I let the rain splash onto our grimy skin and best dupattas, blur our vision and smudge our red-dyed hands. Bill and Dick were right behind us, laughing at the sky and soaked.

This time we left the bridal party when they changed busses in Lahore and headed straight to the shower in the Peace Corps transient room. I'll never badmouth that shower again—it is another kind of heaven.

Day by day, week by week, our volunteer team became part of the village family, trusted—or at least tolerated—strangers who seemed no longer quite so strange. But the pace of village life, to me, seemed very slow. And much as I enjoyed village feasts and customs and appreciated the friendship and acceptance of the women who now visited me, it was hard for me to see that my efforts had made any progress toward significant social change.

When Carol finished her research and left the village to return to the United States, I was once again alone in my mud home. However, by this time, I was established enough with the women to be able to act with more confidence.

One of the results of our village survey was that several women had expressed a desire to earn money of their own and were willing to work for it. I concluded that they were ready to begin a cottage industry and made several trips to Lahore to visit tourist shops specializing in Pakistani handicrafts and investigate a market. I talked with members of several cooperative boards, who suggested that I organize the women to work in their own homes, doing the kind of work in which they were already skilled. Several shops in Lahore asked if we could supply cloth-lined basket handbags and gave me a handbag sample to show the women of Dhamke. Since sewing and basketmaking were two of the many skills in which the women excelled, I thought we might give the project a try.

When I showed the handbag prototype to the women and to Rana Sahib, all agreed that it was a good idea and said that they would help. The details were vague, but Rana pledged to supply the straw for the baskets, and several women volunteered to weave the baskets and attach them to drawstring cloth handbags for the tourist shops on the Mall in Lahore.

March 22, 1963
Dhamke
Dear George,

Something exciting has finally happened! At last!!!!

We went to a village council meeting this afternoon to tell the elders about my cottage industry project with the women. Dick told them about his idea to raise chickens. It went pretty well and the men seemed receptive. At least they didn't say NO.

Rana was here for a long visit tonight. He is all set to get started on the cottage industry—but he's not so keen on the chickens. But he promised to supply the straw for the women to strip and weave into baskets. I can show them how to attach the baskets to the handbags with my trusty sewing machine. At last! Something is finally happening! Maybe the women will actually begin to make some money and not be so dependent and poor. I can't wait to get started. I hope we can find enough women to help with the straw. I'm too excited to sleep!

Oh! And one other kind of strange thing happened. When Rana came to visit, he was sort of stumbling around with something to say that, at first, I couldn't figure out. Then he asked me to marry him! That is, to be his SECOND wife! He already has one very nice one—and several children.

But don't worry. I whipped out your picture and told him that I was "already promised to someone else. Sorry." Hope you don't mind being pre-engaged—but it takes the pressure off. Rana took the news well—I'm not sure he was serious anyway.

On that note, gotta get to bed—but I'm too excited to sleep. Write soon.
Love,
L

My next task was to find a Pakistani coworker to help set up the cottage industry. In Peshawar, I had learned about government Village Aid projects organized in rural areas by the Basic Democracies in each district. Young Pakistani men and women with some education had been hired and trained to work in these projects, and a young woman might be available to work with me. I approached the Union Council, my district supervisor, and the Peace Corps and begged for one of these workers to come to Dhamke and help me with my fledgling social center and potential cottage industry. I asked for, and eventually received, the name of a trained "lady worker" living in Lyallpur, a city known for its textiles industry about twenty-five miles from Dhamke.

One afternoon in late April, Saroya, a sturdy young woman in a black burqah, and her father came to visit me in Dhamke. Using a smattering of English and Punjabi, we sat in my courtyard, drank tea, and talked about the possibility of Saroya coming to live and work with me to develop a cottage industry at our social center. In addition to her training as a lady worker in Village Aid, she had completed eight years of primary education and could understand a little English. Although she did not have any experience organizing cottage industries, she had worked with women in village social centers and was eager to work with me.

It was agreed that the Assistant Director of Basic Democracies would post Saroya to Dhamke and pay her salary, Rana Sahib would include her under his protective family umbrella, and the Cooperative Development Board would lend us four hundred rupees (about one hundred dollars) to begin our straw purse project. Saroya's father gave his blessing, and Saroya moved in with me. We began to make plans for the cottage industry and secured an order for thirty drawstring basket purses from a shop on the Mall in Lahore. I couldn't believe my good fortune. I had a coworker and a real job to do, at last.

~

CHAPTER 5

The End of the Beginning, 1962

Saroya and I became good friends as well as housemates. With her rudimentary English and my village Punjabi, we managed to communicate well with each other, and together, we enlisted help for our cottage industry from some of the younger girls at the social center. We taught the girls how to use the sewing machine, made several designs for cloth drawstring purses, and experimented with ways to attach our platter-shaped baskets, called *chengheras*, to the purses. Eventually we came up with a pattern that suited everyone. Then we went out to the fields to harvest straw.

May 7, 1963

Dhamke

Saroya and I spent all morning in the fields with the girls, gathering straw and sweating. The work is hot and backbreaking. My fingers are on fire with splinters and blisters. Maybe we should have organized the women first—or set a price per bundle of straw and spread the word that we were paying or something. No one wants to work in the hot sun. I don't really blame them, but we can't wait for their help forever. The straw has to be done *now*, the rains are coming and time is so short. I guess we have to do it ourselves, like *The Little Red Hen*. We'll never get enough at this rate!

May 14, 1963
Dhamke
It rained all yesterday morning and was so muddy in the afternoon, we
couldn't pick straw. Couldn't go to the fields today because Saroya is
sick. Our straw pile is pitiful. I spent my time yesterday bandaging a
little boy's hand, then went to his village, Mirpur, to talk to his mother.
She makes baskets and knows how to strip straw. Maybe she can help
us. We need more straw and women to work with it.

The straw supply for our basketmaking grew very slowly, even though
Saroya and I and a few little girls continued to go out to the fields to pick
and strip it every morning. In the afternoons, we visited women in Dhamke
and tried to convince them to help us. We showed the women the drawstring
purses that we planned to attach to the baskets and gave them a choice of
jobs to do—sewing or basket weaving or straw gathering—to be part of the
cottage industry.

But the lethargy of summer had begun. The temperature hovered above
100°F every day, even when it rained, and the oppressive heat and ever-
present dysentery sapped everyone's energy. I was worried about our straw
supply and knew that once all the straw was gathered and stripped, it would
take several more weeks for the women to weave the baskets. Our progress
was very slow. And I seemed to be the only one with a sense of urgency
about meeting the order for basket purses that we had promised to the shop
in Lahore.

By this time, Bill, Dick, and I had decided to hire a man from the Christian section of Dhamke to cook our evening meals for us. James and his family moved into one of the outbuildings at the rest house and, at the end of
our long hot mornings in the fields and long hot afternoons visiting village
women, Saroya and I would walk out to the rest house to eat under the trees
with Bill and Dick. It was cooler and quieter there, with the early evening
breeze off the canal and only the shuffle of bullocks returning to their stalls
to break the silence. And though having a cook was more expensive, James's
meals far surpassed anything Bill, Dick, or I could manage. Besides, it was just
so hot!

Our new eating arrangement did not please Rana Sahib, however.
Whether it was because James was a Christian or because Rana really was
worried about Saroya's well-being, he began to admonish me for tarnishing
Saroya's reputation and to scold Saroya for "mixing up" with Bill and Dick
at the rest house.

May 20, 1963
Dhamke
Today was just plain confusing! Saroya's father arrived before breakfast, and the Peace Corps staff just after. We told Peace Corps about
our progress with the cottage industry and my worries about getting
enough straw. Dr. Sill, our Peace Corps liaison, suggested that we
ask the Christian women to help us—but doing that would circumvent
Rana's sister who is in charge of storing the straw. Not a solution Rana
can live with, I fear.

At the meeting Rana mentioned our new eating arrangements
at the rest house and said that Saroya was joining us, "mixing up"
inappropriately with Bill and Dick. Dr. Sill told him Saroya's father was
very pleased with our project and our living arrangements, so Rana
backed off. I'm not sure what is really going on, but before he left
this morning, Saroya's father invited Bill, Dick, and me to their home
in Lyallpur next week. But I can see that Rana is still not happy.

May 25, 1963
Lyallpur
We left for Lyallpur about five o'clock this afternoon. Saroya's family
lives in a company-town textile mill kind of neighborhood like the ones
I used to visit with my father in New England. What a nice family!
And scads of kids. We had dinner, went for a walk, and then came
back and talked—all in Punjabi—and understood each other! Saroya's
mother is really nice.

Next morning we paid a visit to the girl's school and then toured
the mills with Saroya's brothers. As we traveled through the various departments, the workers in that section would stop working
to greet us. It was all very formal and friendly but I was worried that
we stopped production everywhere we went. Later we bought some
fabric—it's gorgeous!—then went back for lunch with the family.

I had a wonderful time—probably the best time with a Pakistani
family since I've been here. Saroya's parents seem to like us a lot and
are proud that she is with us.

So there, Rana!

By the end of May, the time for harvest and our energy for stripping straw
had come to an end. We still did not have enough straw for the number of
purses we had promised to the shop in Lahore, so we decided to visit the

woman basket weaver in the nearby village of Mirpur to enlist her help. Saroya bargained with her for some straw, and the woman and her sisters agreed to join our cottage industry enterprise and help supply us with baskets. Their help might possibly save the project, I thought; my bandaging her son's hand a few weeks ago might have been "grease" on her palm.

But help from the Mirpur women did not please Rana Sahib. When he discovered that we had talked with women outside of Dhamke, he was furious. He scolded Saroya again for her inappropriate behavior with Bill and Dick and then abruptly withdrew his support for our cottage industry project. The straw that we had stored with his sister mysteriously disappeared, and the women in our social center began to whisper among themselves that Saroya had been "mixing" with my brothers when we had our meals together. Rumors, jealousies, and hard feelings raced from one compound to another, and our plans for a straw purse cottage industry unraveled and disintegrated in the blink of an eye.

I never did discover why this happened. Rana may have had second thoughts when he realized that he could not supply enough straw for the baskets needed for the purses that had been ordered. His disapproval of Saroya's behavior seemed overblown to all of us at the time, particularly after we had stayed with Saroya's family in Lyallpur and received her father's enthusiastic blessing. Our solicitation of help from women in the next village may have angered Rana, but that solution could have easily been averted with more cooperation from the women in Dhamke, which he could have insisted upon. Or Rana may have felt that he would lose face if a cottage industry run by women succeeded. Whatever his reasons, however, without his support, our drawstring purse cottage industry in Dhamke could not go forward.

In retrospect, I think that our cottage industry failed because it was really my idea—an American solution to a Pakistani problem. But at the time, I was devastated and very frustrated with Rana. Our relationship was such that we could have heated discussions—and we did. But he did not yield.

It seemed that I was right back where I had started, with an on-again, off-again women's social center focused on sewing and gossip, no cottage industry, and no real job in Dhamke.

Without the cottage industry project, Saroya's assignment in Dhamke was in jeopardy, as well. To bolster it, we decided to branch out and visit nearby villages to extend the idea of social centers to their women. To pique interest, Dick and I borrowed a movie projector and a generator from the United States Information Agency (USIA) office in Lahore and spent many hours previewing and choosing Urdu films from their library. On a sheet strung between two trees, we showed Disneyesque cartoons about hygiene, nutrition, inoculations, and healthy living to audiences of all ages. TV, air conditioning, and electricity had not yet come to Dhamke and its neighboring villages, so our outdoor theater was a huge success. Rana Sahib took the credit for this success and was mollified.

In late July, Dick was able to secure an electric line for Dhamke and bring electricity to the village shops and wells. Rana was one of the first to have electricity in his home, and my house, down the lane from his, soon followed. I now had a forty-watt lightbulb and small electric fan to brighten and cool the dark and sultry nights. And Rana's face was saved.

By August, the social centers that Saroya and I had begun in two nearby villages became places for a handful of women and girls to gather in the late afternoons and early evenings. While the women sewed, we talked to them about maternal and child health, modeled appropriate home sanitation and hygiene, discussed safe ways to cook, gave them new ideas about clothes washing and soapmaking, and demonstrated new ways to dry and store food. But these social centers were not the formal schools for female literacy or cottage industry that I had envisioned. They were merely places for women to meet, learn some new skills, and expand their horizons beyond their own compound walls.

My model home, with its latrine, washing machine, strange customs, and "brothers," was only a modest start at changing the patterns of village life in Dhamke and a few nearby villages. I was restless and eager for something more.

At the end of August, the Basic Democracies posted Saroya to a new project in Sheikhupura. Her assignment was to train lady workers to establish social centers in villages throughout the district and to supervise and support these women with periodic visits and retraining once their centers were established.

I wanted to join this project. It seemed to me that training Pakistani women to run their own social centers and then supervising and assisting them with further training could become a legitimate Peace Corps project for women's basic education. "A project planned and run by Pakistani women," I remember arguing, "could be continued after my two-year commitment in Pakistan ends. This project would make all my experience in Dhamke, so slowly and painfully acquired, worth it. It would be a more realistic way to help the people help themselves."

With some hesitation and reluctance, the Peace Corps agreed to let me move to Sheikhupura, join Saroya and her lady workers, and try.

I left Dhamke with mixed emotions. Dhamke had been my home away from home. The villagers were my friends and Pakistani family; Rana Sahib was my protector and entrée as a community development worker. But I felt I had done all that I could do in his village.

The village women were content with things as they were. Those who met at the social center had learned to use the sewing machine. They had been exposed to a different way of doing their household tasks. Some had even adopted water barrels and septic tanks in their compounds. Many young boys and their sisters had learned the English and Urdu alphabet and could now read and write a bit in both languages.

I had made a stab at social change and had grown up a bit in the process. I was disappointed that I had not been able to start a cottage industry or a real school for girls, and suspected that I had not made much difference in anyone's life. But I had tried, with all my heart, enthusiasm, and naïveté.

In the middle of September 1963, I moved my bister, books, and household goods to Sheikhupura, the seat of the district and then a small city thirty-eight miles from Lahore. I left behind my model house, washing machine, concrete slab, septic tank, electric fan, and lightbulb, along with Rana Sahib and social centers for women in Dhamke and two other nearby villages.

I had learned a lot in Dhamke—much more than I had taught. My eyes glistened with unshed tears for the women who had befriended me and for Rana Sahib, the man who had accepted me and kept me as safe as I was prepared to let him.

When the women gathered to hug me and wish me well in my new home, however, there was no wailing or sobbing as at Envir's wedding. My friends pressed embroidered napkins, handkerchiefs, and a tea cozy in my hands and begged me to come back soon and often. I fully intended to do just that. I did not know that it would be forty-five years before I would return to Dhamke to see any of them again.

My eyes were wet, as were theirs, but my spirits soared with the possibility of making a new start in changing the patterns of village life in a real job, in Sheikhupura.

CHAPTER 6

~

Arrival in Pakistan, 2009

Flying into Abu Dhabi on June 30, 2009, I watch the bright sun become a red line on the horizon, fade to twilight, and then plunge us into darkness, mirroring the simulated image on the TV screen in front of me. With the ten-hour time difference, it is evening again, but we have been in the air for only twelve hours.

We disembark to a waiting bus, cross the tarmac, and file singly past an infrared camera measuring our body temperature for the presence of swine flu. We all pass.

My colleagues Barbara Janes—"Taffy" to her friends—and Nancy Parlin and I find ourselves in an ultramodern circular terminal under a domed ceiling of oversized tiles. With streams of well-dressed Middle Eastern men murmuring into cell phones and hijab-scarved women carrying babies and small children, we walk past a small mosque; Bulgari, Cartier, and other high-end shops; and several fast food cafés. The glare is blinding and bright. No one seems to notice us as we climb the spiral staircase, though we are the only women in Western clothing, blonde- and silver-haired, in our golden years. It is a relief to feel invisible and to be ignored.

We make our way to the gate area for a connecting flight to Pakistan. Here the sense of order is markedly different. Instead of forming a queue, the would-be passengers push and elbow their way forward, all trying to be first through security. The uniformed gate attendants look on impassively and do not attempt to order the flow. We women have a separate curtained security check. Our bodies are patted for weapons and contraband by stern young women, their faces circled in tight scarves, their voices brusque. My friend Taffy does not want to be touched, but her resistance is met with rude hands on her breasts. We take our places in the waiting area and watch the confusion around us. I am bemused by this system and reminded of teenagers trying to surge through the doors of a rock concert, everyone waving a ticket and elbowing their way forward.

On the plane, I am seated next to a woman physician who works for the Aga Khan Health Services, the largest nonprofit health care system in Pakistan. We have a long conversation about professional opportunities for women in Pakistan. She is concerned that the conservative atmosphere of the Taliban and the restrictions they impose on women's education might adversely affect her teenage daughter. I am surprised by her candid political comments; she is surprised that I am traveling to Pakistan. She expresses appreciation for my courage and concern for my safety while in her country, and we exchange email addresses and cell phone numbers.

Our plane arrives in Karachi at four in the morning. Instead of the dusty scramble across the airfield I remember, we disembark into long hallways linked to the main terminal for international arrivals. I am surprised at the elegance of the Jinnah International Complex. Gone is the large black hangar, Kala Chapra, constructed for the British R101 airship in the 1940s and used as a visual marker for planes landing in the 1960s, the last time I was here. In its place is the sprawling Quaid-e-Azam International Airport housing several hangars and three terminals, for domestic, international, and hajj[1] operations.

We walk past a string of bank and ATM counters, commercial offices, departure lounges, shopping facilities, and McDonald's and KFC franchises, through the main terminal, and into the heavy predawn air. Several drivers from The Citizens Foundation (TCF) are waiting for us, holding small signs of identification and welcome. They escort us to the parking area and quickly load our luggage into a small white van and us into a smaller car. The air shimmers under tall poles of yellow, red, and orange light. My breath mingles with the dense humidity and fills my nose and mouth with moisture. As we leave the airport complex, our driver flips a switch to condition the air.

We slip through the slumbering streets. For the next week, Taffy, Nancy, and I will stay at the Defence Club, a residential hotel built on a former military cantonment named, appropriately, the Defence Society.[2] The other members of our team—Karen Noorani and her daughter Sofia—have already arrived and are staying nearby with Karen's husband Danial's relatives.

The drive to the Defence Club is detached and uneventful. The streets are tree lined and quiet, as are the houses behind their closed gates and tall cement walls. At our gate, two uniformed sentries check our driver's papers and then wave us through to a large compound of buildings and lawns. There is a clubhouse with a dining room and verandah, an Olympic-sized swimming pool, a gymnasium, and a hint of elegance from the days of the staid British Raj.

Taffy, Nancy, and I are assigned to two large rooms, each with en suite bathroom, small refrigerator, TV, and heavy drapes at the windows. The rooms are dark and musty until the bearer pulls a cord attached to an overhead fan and flips a switch on the window air conditioner. We will soon discover that these switches create a wind tunnel of frigid air when the electricity is on and a cave of cloying humidity when the electricity unexpectedly shuts off. But to my jet-lagged and weary body, this hardly matters. I have six hours to unpack, shower, and sleep.

Welcome back to Pakistan.

I awake to the insistent rapping of a polite young man bearing a tray of boiled eggs, cold toast, and strong black tea, the breakfast we had ordered at dawn, just a few hours ago. It is now almost noon Karachi time, but my senses proclaim midnight of the night just missed. I cannot sleep any longer, however. I am too excited being back in Pakistan. I want to break out of our darkened rooms and explore the Defence Club. But first, our team of five needs to meet and decide on a plan of action.

Taffy Janes is our team's curriculum leader. She has a master's degree in education from the University of Chicago and is an adjunct professor of student teachers at Illinois Institute of Technology. She has spent the past twenty-five years teaching inquiry-based science to middle school students in the Chicago area. Since her initial Peace Corps teaching experience at Frontier College in Peshawar, Taffy has returned to Pakistan several times, most recently in 2007 when she presented a series of hands-on science workshops to TCF teachers as part of their in-service training.

Karen Noorani is the second in command of our teaching team. Karen is a professional violinist and a teacher with the nonprofit Music for Youth program. She has an MA in violin and is a recent MA graduate in education from Roosevelt University, where she studied curriculum design and small group experiential teaching. Karen has traveled to Pakistan many times in the past twenty years to visit her husband's family and to perform in fundraising concerts. Her daughter Sofia, a sophomore at Beloit College, has come along to work with the Pakistani college students who have volunteered their vacation time to help in the Summer Science Camps.

Nancy Parlin and I are the teaching team gofers. Nancy has a PhD in sociology and is a veteran of thirty-five years as a university professor and administrator. As a Peace Corps Volunteer with a master's degree, she worked on research projects at the Academy for Village Development in Peshawar and then assumed responsibilities as the director of a community development project in the Khanewal district of the Punjab until the Peace Corps left Pakistan in 1965. Nancy has traveled extensively throughout the world and has returned to Pakistan twice since her initial Peace Corps experience. She has a keen interest in the country's infrastructure and progress and has the perspective of a seasoned social scientist.

My career as an educator began after I left the Peace Corps, earned a doctorate in education, and became a teacher and administrator for early literacy and education programs in various stateside venues. Although I have traveled internationally as a consultant during my thirty-year career, this is my first trip to Pakistan since 1964. In addition to assisting with the Science Camps, I want to become familiar with the current education system in Pakistan. I hope to interview as many personnel from TCF as I can to more fully understand their vision of education in Pakistan and our mission, as volunteers, to help them.

Among the five of us—Taffy, Karen, Sofia, Nancy, and I—our team represents a depth and breadth of teaching experience and knowledge of Pakistan not shared by many educators in our position. We are eager to begin the work that has brought us back to the deserts of Sindh, the plains of the Punjab, and the mountains of Hunza, even though it is the middle of the Pakistani summer, the most grueling time of the year.

To call a team meeting with Karen and Sofia, we use a cell phone. In the old days, I reflect, we would have dispatched a bearer with a chit, a written message, and waited several hours for him to return with a reply. Now, of course, our conversation is immediate. Karen tells us that our first task will be to shop for summer-weight shalwar kameez. The heat and humidity are brutal, she says, and we will roast in the cotton shirts and pants we have brought with us. She and her sister-in-law, Uzma, will pick us up in an hour.

While waiting for Karen and Uzma, I take another shower in a bathroom decidedly different from the one I had used on my first night in Pakistan so many years ago. At that time, I stood in a corner of a flat roof, poured water over my head from a small pail, and watched the wastewater cascade to an open drain on the street below. Now, I stand on marble tiles in the bathroom adjacent to my room, lift my face to a streaming flow, and collect the overflow water in a pail at my feet. The wastewater collects at my ankles before emptying into an underground sewer system.

The porcelain footplate next to the shower is also gone, replaced by the familiar commode we know in the West. These are welcome changes.

Another welcome change is the ease of shopping for shalwar kameez in 2009. In 1962, purchasing a new outfit consumed both energy and time. First was a two-hour bus ride to the city, then a horse-drawn *tonga* ride to the cloth bazaar, another tonga ride to the tailor, an uncomfortable fitting process in full view of other shoppers and shop assistants, and a waiting period for the garments to be sewn. Ready-to-wear clothing then, if available at all, was of poor quality and much too small for my Western-sized body. A shopping expedition from the village in the 1960s could take up to a week, with return visits to the tailor by repeated tonga and bus rides along city streets crowded with animals, bicycles, taxis, pedestrians, and ox-drawn vehicles and many unexpected delays.

On this day in 2009, Uzma's driver takes us to three separate shopping areas in Karachi, along divided highways streaming with motorized traffic. I stare at private cars, small business vans with Arabic and Chinese lettering, colorfully painted buses crammed with passengers, riotously decorated trucks carrying goods from all over the country, and motorcycles with entire families perched atop them. When traffic backs up or slows for any reason, the drivers just honk their way through to even more congested side streets and steadfastly ignore other vehicles wedging in front of them or narrowly brushing their side mirrors.

Gone are the tongas and bullock carts, private rickshaws, bicycles, yellow taxicabs, flocks of sheep, goats, dogs, and the ever-flowing mass of pedestrians swaying and nudging to the middle of the street.

Karachi's motor traffic has quadrupled since the early 1960s, I'm told, and animal-drawn vehicles are no longer permitted on major city streets. Pedestrians are confined to the sides of the road and must dodge the traffic as best they can when a broken sidewalk or pavement in need of repair forces vehicles off the main street. Traffic lights and uniformed police attempt to direct the confusion, but many drivers ignore their signals or brush them aside as superfluous. I am stunned by this change.

Parking is a nightmare contest of its own. Leaving our driver to the camaraderie of other drivers similarly engaged in the parking competition, we join a flow of women shoppers, some in black burqahs reminiscent of the 1960s, and enter a boutique of shalwar kameez beautifully displayed in every color and fabric. I am delighted to discover that outfits in my size are now represented plentifully in the middle of each rack. Pakistani women are larger than they once were. Gone is the mortification of a large Western-sized body. The fashion choices today are dazzling.

We American women dive right into the melee of trying on, discarding, and deliberating over the beautifully sewn cotton, linen, and silk shalwar kameez "suits" at our disposal. Although I had brought several tunics and white cotton pants with me to wear until I could replace them, my home-made outfits are pale and boring compared to the array of ready-made outfits of vibrant colors and soft lawn[3] available now. No male tailors or curious young boys lurk behind the fitting rooms in today's modern shops. We model our selections in front of full-length mirrors in the privacy of other women only.

By the end of our first afternoon back in Pakistan, Taffy, Nancy, and I have each purchased several new shalwar kameez suits and have experienced the same kind of gracious courtesy from the shop attendants we remembered from our earlier days in Pakistan. This time, however, we pay our bills by credit card and retrieve our purchases in plastic and paper bags emblazoned with store logos. In 1962, there were no plastic shopping bags, and parcels, if encased at all, were trussed with string and wrapped in flimsy brown paper that would be reused many times and discarded only when completely tattered.

That evening, still catching up with the time difference, Taffy, Nancy, and I sit on the verandah of the Defence Club, showered and feeling spiffy in our newly purchased Pakistani clothing. A bit disoriented and tired from our afternoon's shopping spree, we watch a parade of small cars enter the Defence Club compound, stop at the foyer, and release well-dressed families arriving for dinner. Dinner in the Pakistan of 2009, we soon discover, never begins before 8:30, and the only predinner drinks available are soda, tea, or fruit juice.

In the soft glow of outdoor garden lights, an evening sea breeze whirs tiny no-see-ums above our food. I am distracted by the late-night scene before me: young men talking into their cell phones while they supervise their children on nearby playground swings; women seated in groups by themselves, gossiping and laughing together. In the 1960s, I muse, the women would have been supervising the children, and the men would have been sitting together, gossiping, smoking, and waiting to be served. But back then there were no playgrounds that I ever saw, and there were certainly no cell phones.

Still, I feel at ease in this setting even though we are the only Western-ers, and the only foreign women, in attendance. It surprises me that no one has approached us to ask who we are or why we are in Pakistan. And I am astonished by the popularity and ever-present use of cell phones. It looks to me as though every adult in Pakistan has one and uses it frequently.

In 1962, a curious crowd of onlookers eager to engage with us would have interrupted our dinner, and bearers in white turbans carrying handwritten chits would have assisted conversations with those not present. Telephone conversations then took place by booking a trunk call on overland telephone wires available to only a few private citizens and civil servants. During the two years I lived in Pakistan in the 1960s, I never once used a telephone. I did, however, write and receive many chits.

CHAPTER 7

~

Work Assignment, 2009

Our work for the first few days in Karachi is to become acquainted with our colleagues from The Citizens Foundation (TCF), visit the TCF school designated as the Karachi teacher-training site, organize the supplies we have brought with us and that the staff in Karachi have assembled, and prepare the classrooms for the teacher-training phase of the Summer Science Camp project. After the Karachi teacher training, our team will fly to Lahore and repeat the teacher-training sessions with Lahore teachers and staff in that region.

At the end of the teacher-training sessions, the Summer Science Camps for children from TCF schools in both Karachi and Lahore will begin, and our assignment will shift to that of assisting the Pakistani teachers as they implement our science curriculum with the children at the camps.

The Summer Science Camps will be divided into two age-appropriate sessions: first, a one-week primary level for grades five through eight, and then a two-week secondary level for grades nine and ten. The camps will run concurrently at two TCF school sites in Karachi and three in Lahore. In addition to training the teachers for these camps, we will also train a group of student volunteers recruited from colleges in Lahore and Karachi. The student volunteers will assist the teachers as they work with children in the camp sessions.

During the camp sessions, Taffy, Nancy, and I will support the teachers and student volunteers at the Lahore school sites, and Karen and Sofia will return to Karachi to support the teachers and student volunteers at the sites there. Over the course of the summer, we expect to be working with approximately fifty teachers, fifty student volunteers, and a thousand TCF primary and secondary schoolchildren.

The method of instruction we will use in the teacher training will be new to most of the teachers and student volunteers. The method is based on ideas from inquiry-based learning. We hope that once the teachers have experienced this method of learning and understand the method of instruction, they will use it to teach the children in the Science Camps.

The science lessons that Taffy and Karen have designed will be presented in a series of activities or projects. While engaging in the activities, the teachers, student volunteers, and children will be called upon to ask questions, conduct experiments, and record the evidence that will lead them to solve problems posed in each activity.

Inquiry-based instruction is a departure from the traditional way of teaching science in Pakistan. The method was developed in the United States and Britain during the 1960s in response to a perceived failure of more traditional forms of instruction in which students were required to simply memorize fact-laden materials. Inquiry is a form of active learning where progress is assessed by how well students develop experimental and analytical skills rather than by how much knowledge they possess. In a science curriculum, this means that students are presented with a problem to solve and the teacher guides them to solve it without making the solution explicit. This requires students to work together, to think critically, and to search for solutions based on the evidence rather than the predefined "correct" answer.

The primary-level inquiry-based science camp activities will be:

- Seeds: Growing and observing bean plants
- States of Matter: Discovering the physical properties of gaseous, liquid, and solid matter
- Spool Racers: Designing spool racers to meet specific parameters
- Clay Boats: Creating clay and aluminum shapes that will float best in water
- Newspaper Towers: Building towers within the parameters of strength and balance, using newsprint

The secondary-level inquiry-based science camp activities will be:

- Mystery Powders: Using a variety of physical and chemical tests to describe the properties of five common substances

- Measuring pH: Investigating the common characteristics of acids and bases
- Newton's Laws: Experiencing, understanding, and applying Newton's Laws of Motion
- Electric and Solar Energy: Identifying, understanding, and using series and parallel circuits, batteries, and solar cells
- Solar Cookers: Designing, building, and testing solar cookers
- Water Testing: Testing water for the presence of coliform bacteria
- Speed and Acceleration: Understanding and testing speed and acceleration using drip timers

After breakfast on our second day in Pakistan, a TCF van arrives early to transport Taffy, Nancy, Karen, Sofia, and me to the site where the Karachi teacher training will be held. En route, we stop to pick up Shameem Jahangir, the manager for secondary science education for TCF Karachi. Shameem is a sophisticated woman of indeterminate age, dressed in an immaculately starched and pressed shalwar kameez. I notice that she has draped her dupatta across her chest rather than over her stylishly cut black hair and that her handbag and sandals are fashionably chic. Most of the women we meet at TCF headquarters will be similarly attired, that is, in colorful well-pressed shalwar kameez and coordinated dupatta draped over their shoulders rather than their hair. They all look stunning to me.

Shameem's bearing and English are as impeccable as her style and gracious manners. As our van bumps along through the chaotic streets of Karachi, she explains the transportation system vital to the TCF school system: "We have a fleet of two thousand white Suzuki vans which seat eight passengers and a driver. The size of the van is deliberate and insures that all of our teachers and principals are in their classrooms every day of the school year."

"TCF school buildings are limited to no more than thirty children per classroom," Shameem continues, "with no more than six classrooms in a school unit. Every day, each teacher and principal is transported from her home to her respective school free of charge. You can imagine what a logistical feat this is, especially when the government calls for schools to be closed on a particular day, sometimes as late as midnight the night before.

"But our transportation system assures that our teachers and principals are present in their classrooms every day. The vans also transport supplies, textbooks, and visitors to the schools. They are essential to our overall success as a school system."

The van we're in is equipped with windows that open, three bench seats, and seat belts for the driver and passenger seated next to him. The logo painted on the back and the sliding side doors proudly proclaims in bold green lettering: *The Citizens Foundation. Quality Education for the Less Privileged.* I think this system of transportation is brilliant, and I say so.

I feel very privileged to be escorted to our destination by a TCF driver. My knowledge of public buses is that they are crowded, hot, unreliable, and, in 2009, probably risky. As we zoom along the road, I notice several signs in English and Urdu: "Go away, America. Go away!" and feel doubly grateful to be riding in a TCF van.

Our destination this day, and for every day of the week of Karachi teacher training, is Goth Dhani Bux, one of the poorest slums in the city. The streets of this small neighborhood are lined with shops, vegetable stalls, small mosques, tire dealers, sagging electrical wires, and doorways leading directly into crowded homes and courtyards. Some of the streets are paved, but most are surfaced with hard-packed dirt or crumbled cement, mounded in the center to accommodate an underground sewage ditch. Circular manhole covers protrude above these mounds in the center of the streets, in some cases several feet above, and force vehicles to swerve and dodge around them as they maneuver past the pedestrians and animals shambling by.

Outside the gate of the TCF school training site, the street is littered with trash, broken paving stones, piles of dirt and cement, and small heaps of debris. However, inside the walled compound, the school is an aesthetic oasis—a well-maintained two-story structure of airy classrooms set around a tidy courtyard of polished tiles and potted ferns.

We are greeted by the ayah housekeeper and *chowkidar* gatekeeper with warm smiles and salaams and are ushered up several steps to classrooms full of the boxes of supplies that have been purchased for the Summer Science Camps. Assembled in the teacher's staff room, a team of young women from the TCF Karachi headquarters is waiting to help us unload the boxes and sort the supplies.

Karachi is hot and humid in July. During the day, temperatures range between 91°F and 104°F with a relative humidity between 73 and 88 percent. Air conditioning in offices, hotels, shopping malls, and private homes is available, but subject to the vagaries of load shedding.[1] In an overly air-conditioned room, when the electricity cuts out, the heat and humidity inside can become even more oppressive and intense than outside, and when load shedding occurs, many workers just stop what they are doing and wait for the electricity to come back.

TCF schools are not air conditioned, but because the classrooms are deliberately arranged around open courtyards and have many windows for cross-ventilation, the inconvenience from load shedding is limited to interruption of service for computers, electric lights, and overhead fans. When load shedding occurs in a TCF school, the students and teachers continue to work. Sometimes there is a breeze.

With the help of the Karachi-based TCF volunteer coordinators and teacher-training staff, we begin to sort through the boxes and divide the supplies and equipment into piles for different classrooms. We need to sort hundreds of items gathered in both the United States and Pakistan—everything from rubber bands, spools, and wooden drip cars to hand lenses, balance scales, and litmus paper.

With the windows open to the air from the ocean, the heat is sticky and wet. By midmorning, we Americans are soaked with perspiration and grimy with dust. We look and feel wilted. Our Pakistani colleagues, more accustomed to the high temperatures and humidity, still look fresh and unfazed by the morning's work.

We break for a lunch of egg salad sandwiches, biryani,[2] and soda and eat around a large table in the teacher staff room. Our conversation is about the materials we have been unloading and their curious purpose in science education.

Taffy and Karen have spent the previous three months designing the hands-on activities for the inquiry-based curriculum that is planned for the science camps. Making full use of the Internet and cell phone conference calls, they and the TCF education managers have already begun a dialogue about the supplies and materials we are unpacking.

The traditional way of teaching science in Pakistan requires specific, often expensive, laboratory equipment for the teacher to use in a lecture and demonstration format. Students are expected to observe, take notes, and memorize the procedures and formulas in order to understand the concept being presented. In inquiry-based science teaching, however, students participate actively in every lesson by using materials at their own desks. Materials for this kind of science exploration are not necessarily designed for the laboratory and can usually be found in the marketplace or local business for little or no cost.

Initially, there had been some confusion about the nature of some of these supplies and the importance of having so many materials, enough to ensure that each student could make use of his or her own. The everyday items that we are unpacking to use in the science lessons are a new idea for some of our Pakistani colleagues. Locating some of these supplies in the bazaar had been an enormous effort in patience, cross-cultural understanding, and trust for both educational teams.

Taffy discovered early in the lesson-planning process that some items were not available at all, at least in the form that she knew them. For example, one lesson—to design a racing toy that would travel a meter (three feet), using a spool of thread, a rubber band, a toothpick, a pencil, and washers was almost aborted for lack of clarity about spools. After several confusing email messages, Taffy learned that sewing thread in Pakistan is packaged on small squares of cardboard rather than on round wooden or plastic spools; spools of thread are unknown in Pakistan's bazaars. She had asked the Pakistani team to purchase spools of thread in bulk, not realizing this packaging difference. Once this issue was clarified, the Pakistani team was easily able to locate a supply of small spools—used to wrap electric wire rather than thread—and the projected lesson was saved.

Being able to clarify this and other minor issues quickly and easily in cyberspace was a tremendous aid to both teams as they planned the Summer Science Camps. Had the Internet and Skype conference calls been available to the Peace Corps and Basic Democracies planners in 1962, I thought, our jobs would certainly have been better defined and more easily implemented once we volunteers were in-country. But *Masha Allah*, as they say in Pakistan— "God willed it" that way in 1962. *Insha'Allah*—God willing—it will be different this time around, in 2009.

CHAPTER 8

~

A Clearer Vision, 2009

After lunch, while my friends continue their labors with supplies, Amar, a TCF driver, arrives to escort me across town to meet with Ahsan Saleem, one of the founders of TCF. Although still a little dazed from the heat, morning's chores, and jet lag, I am full of questions about TCF and hope Ahsan can begin to answer some of them.

Once again, the chaos of city traffic astonishes me. Familiar driving etiquette of turning, changing lanes, and obeying traffic lights seem to be only haphazardly observed. As we drive by the U.S. Consulate and the Marriott Hotel, Amar explains the presence of the concrete security barriers and armed guards that detour our car. Both buildings had been sites of terrorist attacks in recent years, and, security barriers notwithstanding, I close my eyes and envision tomorrow's screaming headline: "Bomb Kills American Woman on Karachi Highway."

I have not yet had enough experience in the country to feel completely safe, and the kidnapping and beheading of the *Wall Street Journal*'s Daniel Pearl in 2002 and the more recent *Economist* and *Time* magazine descriptions of Pakistan as the most dangerous place in the world, travel with me. We are only a short distance from the place where Benazir Bhutto, the former prime minister, narrowly escaped an assassination attempt in October 2007. I am sobered by the unfortunate reality that a similar attempt on her life was successful several months later in Rawalpindi.

We reach the high-rise office building of my destination without incident thankfully, and Amar accompanies me onto the elevator. I am the only woman in a small lift, surrounded by perspiring Pakistani men, and I am mindful that load shedding might interrupt our ascent. It does not, though, and I breathe a sigh of relief when we reach the top and I am met by Ahsan Saleem's polite young assistant. He ushers me into a well-appointed office of leather couches and highly polished tables and chairs.

While I wait, I set up the recording devices I have borrowed to tape my interviews. I have not yet mastered the audio function of the iPod and am fussily adjusting the microphone when Ahsan enters and greets me with a formal handshake and broad welcoming smile. He is younger than I had expected and, at first glance, reminds me of the stateside Pakistani instructors in my Peace Corps training. I am circumspect as he offers water, coffee, or juice to slake the thirst from my journey across the city and am only too aware of my wrinkled shalwar kameez and inelegant appearance.

I quickly discover that Ahsan is nothing like the Pakistani playboys of my youth, but instead a thoughtful, well-spoken man of middle age. His good manners ignore my disheveled appearance and soon we are speaking freely, as comfortable acquaintances. I tell him a little about my Peace Corps experience in Pakistan and my interest in Pakistani education. He tells me that he was educated in Pakistan between the mid-1960s and mid-1980s and is one of the six founders of TCF. He is still a member of TCF's Board of Directors, he says, but his full-time occupation is as CEO of the private steel company where we are meeting.

I ask him to tell me about education in Pakistan and his experience with TCF.

"Let me tell you what happened before TCF started," he begins. "It was 1995. Some friends often used to sit around and think about how things in Pakistan could be improved. There were a lot of fires. Not a lot of people were interested in putting out the fires . . . nothing concrete. That is what put us all together. We were frustrated with the way things were moving . . . but knew if we just sat around and said what was wrong, things would never be corrected. We wanted to be part of the solution instead of part of the problem. So we decided to do something to correct the situation.

"We sat down and said, 'What do we do?' We decided to take a pad and write down the ten most burning issues: intolerance, poverty, health, . . . overpopulation. . . . Actually, [for] all the questions we posed, the solution was education. So we decided to tackle education. What did we know about education? Nothing. But we thought most of the problem in education was the education system itself . . . that it was a managerial problem."

From my reading, I knew that at Partition in 1947 the purpose of education in Pakistan had been to prepare citizens for government or military service. The educational system at that time was often described as a three-tier structure serving the rich but not the poor. The first education tier was formed by the elite Western-style private schools for the children of the wealthiest; the second tier by the state-run government schools, supposedly free to all children but in reality too expensive and inaccessible for most families; and the third and smallest tier by the Islamic religious school system, the madrassas, which had been operating on the subcontinent since the mid-nineteenth century.

Initially, the elite private schools of the first tier followed a British system of examination, used their own curricula and textbooks, and brought in teachers from outside the country. The languages of instruction in these schools were Urdu, the national language, and English, the official language of government and business. Graduates of these schools often went abroad to complete their education.

The government schools in the second tier were administered by each province but reached only a small portion of the population. The language of instruction in these schools was Urdu, and English was taught as one of the subjects. In the early years after Partition, the standard of instruction at this tier was adequate for this system's graduates to be able to provide the workforce for Pakistan's public sector as well as the rapidly growing private sector of the economy. Some of Pakistan's better-known scholars and professionals, including the Nobel Prize–winning physicist Abdul Salaam and the well-known economist Mahbub ul Haq, were the products of the early government system.

Graduates of the elite private schools and the provincial government schools found employment in civil and military service and became the Pakistani establishment.

The religious schools in the third tier, run exclusively by the Islamic organizations before the 1980s, were at the lowest end of this three-tier educational spectrum. The majority of students in the madrassas came from families who could not afford to send their children to government or fee-based private schools.

In the early years of the country, most of the young boys in the madrassa system memorized the Quran in Arabic and went no further in their schooling. Madrassa students completing the higher levels became the imams for the mosques, teachers for the madrassa system of religious education, or political workers in the Islamic parties.

Inevitably, the two systems of education—one to develop a Western-style military and civil servant establishment, and the other to provide preachers and political workers for mosques and Islamic parties—produced two very different social classes with very different worldviews and ideas about the way Pakistan should be managed.

In the early 1970s, Prime Minister Zulfikar Ali Bhutto nationalized the elite private schools to provide Pakistan's students with a more equal opportunity for education. However, Bhutto's views of equality and equal opportunity were considered godless by many of the Islamic religious authorities in the country. The two groups began to clash in the political and social arena, and many of their political battles were fought on the government-run college and university campuses. For a number of years, the agendas of the competing political parties took precedence over education on the campuses of the nationalized colleges and universities.

In the 1980s, changes began to take place in some Pakistani madrassas, as well. During the Soviet occupation of Afghanistan, some educational institutions were established in the refugee camps along the Pakistan-Afghan border to train mujahideen[1] to fight the Soviets in Afghanistan. These schools were given the cover of madrassa to Islamically legitimize their operations and to solicit funds from all over the Muslim world. To these schools, the United States provided equipment and training, and the Saudis provided money and a curriculum with a more conservative interpretation of Islam than the relatively liberal view of Islam traditionally taught in the mainstream Pakistani madrassa. The primary function of these new madrassas was to train young men to fight a jihad against the Soviets in Afghanistan.

After the death of President Muhammad Zia-ul-Haq in 1988, government schools worsened significantly as Pakistan plunged into a period of political instability. From 1988 to 1999, four elected governments and three interim administrations governed the country. The elected governments, preoccupied with retaining their power, paid little attention to the economic development of the country in general or social and educational development in particular. The 1990s are often cited as the lost decade for education and social services in Pakistan.

In 1995, the year that Ahsan Saleem and his friends began meeting, education in Pakistan had been deteriorating for some time. For many decades, the federal government had allocated only a small percentage of gross domestic product to education. During the 1990s, although the government enlisted the assistance of various international donors in the education efforts,[2] the programs failed because of the corruption, inefficiency, and dysfunctional operation of the government itself. Corruption, incompetence, bloated payrolls, ghost schools, and financial malfeasance plagued the government schools. My conversation with Ahsan reiterated my understanding of the problems of education during these years.

"We looked around," Ahsan says. "Half of the Pakistani children never saw the inside of a school. There was no moral authority of the government to enforce that children go to school. For those who did go to school, the teaching was terrible. In the 1960s, children coming out of the government schools could go to university. In 1995, that was no longer true. If we left these children out on the street, we were robbing them of their childhoods . . . of the possibility to work in the future. We were making them unemployable, yet we were expecting them to become good citizens. No wonder they grudged people like me. Why should they have anything to do with people like me?

"We saw that education to create good citizens was gone. It is extremely urgent to get this back. Even if people don't get jobs . . . if they are in a school program they will learn to not spit on the roads, they will not be intolerant, they will be civil, and they will have a good spot at getting a job in later life. The other thing is, if we can move their aspirations one notch higher, their focus will change. If we can help them to make informed choices, things will change."

He continues: "My friends and I looked at another issue: What is the answer to the education problem in this country? There was not just one answer. *Any* answer was the right answer, so we had to choose which answer we would try. Nonformal? Technical? Mobile vans? Nonprofit?

"We said, 'What do we want from the children?' We want them to compete with children of people like us and have more success. Just learning to read and write is not enough. . . . You must be in the system of the formal school."

A "system of the formal school" meant, for Ahsan Saleem and his friends, schools that were accessible and affordable to both boys and girls in their own neighborhoods, staffed by trained teachers instructing in Urdu *and* English. It meant schools where learning to be a good citizen and becoming an agent for positive social change was as important as becoming literate or learning an employable skill.

"Formal schools have to have a building," Ahsan explains. "They can't be under a tree. They should be something people would be attracted to. A sanctuary. Like a lighthouse. And the teachers and principals need to show up. The children cannot be left without a teacher or crowded into classrooms with only one teacher and fifty or sixty other children.

"We said we would pick up the children from the poorest community and put them into school. That's all."

In short, they wanted to create for Pakistan's poorest children schools that could provide the same quality of education that was available to their own children. So Ahsan and his five friends set out to build such a school system.

"We thought if we tackled education from the paradigm of management, we could use our strengths as managers. . . . We were all CEOs of our companies. . . . We all brought to the table a little madness, passion, empathy for people, . . . and managerial skill . . . to help solve the problem. These were the things we had . . . no other skills. All of us were naive . . . but not being part of the existing education system became a strength.

"We decided that we would be a professional organization. We went out and hired one of the best managers in the business to run this organization and restricted our board to oversight and fundraising—the things we could do. The responsibility for running the schools was for the professionals.

"We chose to structure . . . as a nonprofit. We could have chosen other options, but we chose a not-for-profit company which requires you to report your earnings to the SEC [Securities and Exchange Commission], etc. We put a structure to it, incorporated the company. We called ourselves The Citizens Foundation—no apostrophe because it is for all citizens.

"In the first year, we chose five corners of Karachi and built the first five schools. We wanted to put our own money into the first schools before we asked others to risk their money on the venture. We wanted to debug the company. We knew we could ask for more money after we were successful with the first five schools. Groundbreaking was 1995. All five schools opened at the same time in 1996."

Ahsan elaborates on some of the initial challenges of building a system of formal schools. "We did not want to address children who had another choice. The model here was that children had to go to school, but for the poorest children it was not easy because of transportation, because their parents were not at home to get them off to school, because the schools were too far away. So, we said, we will take the schools to the children rather than the children to the schools.

"We discovered that people did not send their girls to school. Why not? We were not ready to believe that people did not *want* to send their girls to school. Children are children. We found out that people cannot afford to send *all* their children to school. So they chose for themselves. The boys would stay in the family when they grow up. The girls would get married and leave. So, if you have limited resources and can invest only in one, you invest in the boy.

"As I said, these families don't have the money to go to the free-school government school. It costs ten dollars per month for books, uniform, stationary, spending money in the 'free' school. We made a study of all of our parents and discovered they earned about 2,500 rupees per month, fifty dollars. Out of that, they were already spending ten dollars on education, but most people were spending it on just one child. What they were doing was sending one child to school, the other child to work. That money paid for the child going to school.

"We wanted to take the choice out of their hands—which child to send. So we fixed a fee of 5 percent of the family's pay for education. They could send not just one child, but *all* their children, for the same amount as they could send one child to the free school. Now they did not have to choose which child to send to school and which one to work. And it also worked for girls. Now parents could afford to send their girls to school, too.

"Then we discovered that people were not comfortable to send their girls to school where there were only men teachers. That gave us another idea. We need to take away the need for this choice and remove this reason. So we have 100 percent of our teachers as female teachers. That works for everybody: (a) families can't say they are uncomfortable with only male teachers; (b) families will equally send all their children; (c) we are now showing in those underprivileged areas a role model for girls to do something else . . . come back to teach in the school where they can walk to. So we have 100 percent women staff.

"It is very strange, but a fact, that now everybody wants to send their children to school. *Everybody* wants an education for their children. Especially now. So what happens?

"Ten, twelve years ago we used to see that in the urban slums there were a lot of children on the streets, but there were three powers: the local mullah, the local bully, and the local corrupt police official. Now comes the school. It challenges all three. Now we know that when these children come to school, they actually take back much more than our own children take back from their school. When these less privileged children take back something, they take back some of the power of education to their homes. Although their parents are not educated, the children are educating them—washing your hands, covering your food. . . . Eventually there is a change. And they know that the school there is headed by a woman. She is giving advice to our children. Maybe she can give the parents some advice, too. So the local mullah, the bullies, are no longer the only ones to give advice.

"We have a unique system. We stumbled upon it. We said we would go into a community. How do we get the trust of the community? How do we get them to send us the girls? We wanted to enter into a dialogue with people in the community.

"To be able to open doors, we hired one woman from the community to do hygiene work. She is the ayah. She teaches the children how to use the toilet, wash their hands, comb their hair, brush their teeth. She is the door opener to the homes of the children in our communities. Every school also has a guard/groundskeeper type person, the chowkidar. Part of his job description is to sit around in the evening smoking and talking with the fathers, convincing them to send their children, their girls, to school. We had to go into the community to scout for the right persons for these jobs."

I am sardonically reminded of my Peace Corps days in Dhamke, trying to win the trust of the community for my women's social center. I wish I had had the services of an ayah or chowkidar, or the prescience of these six friends who understood the Pakistani social structure and knew how to make it work.

"These were the fundamental issues," Ahsan concludes. "We chose a very difficult model. We were not in it for ourselves . . . to venture out and do a project just to do the project. We were apolitical. We focused on fighting illiteracy. We wanted to reduce the number of children on the streets, put them into schools, do teacher training. We knew we couldn't do everything. We were nibbling at the problem. Where would the money come from?

"In Pakistan, there is the most per capita contribution to charity in the world. People in Pakistan are a giving people. We knew they would give to our schools. . . . We said, yes, we can raise this money and build and sustain these schools. So we decided our project would be a macro project. We would build a thousand schools all over Pakistan."

Whew! I sit back on my leather couch, amazed. Ahsan's words are a lot to process in one afternoon.

We break for coffee and Ahsan suggests that I meet with other founders, staff members, managers, trainers, teachers, students, family members, ayahs, chowkidars, drivers—all members of the TCF family. He will open the door, he says.

I rise to leave and walk through his door to talk to this new generation of citizens in Pakistan, educated to address the problems of their country rather than to grab the spoils of their own education and disappear. I am eager to meet them.

CHAPTER 9

~

An Introduction to The Citizens Foundation

My third morning in Pakistan, Nancy, Karen, Taffy, and Sofia return to sorting dusty supplies at Goth Dhani Bux, while I am whisked downtown, starched and pressed, to begin meeting the people Ahsan Saleem has told me about. The early morning traffic has subsided and I can actually see the buildings and read the billboards as we speed along the highway. When we reach our destination, Amar, my driver, again accompanies me to an elevator that takes me swiftly to the office of Ateed Riaz.

A tall, distinguished gentleman dressed in a gray, well-cut business suit, Ateed Riaz is a man of many talents. He holds a postgraduate degree in international relations from the University of Karachi, is associated with the Imrooz Group of Companies in Pakistan, is one of the six founding directors of TCF, and served as the CEO of TCF for three years from 2000 to 2003. His neatly trimmed beard, piercing, alert eyes, and exquisitely polite manner give the impression of gracefully harnessed kinetic energy.

As we begin our conversation, I discover that not only is Ateed Riaz a businessman interested in social reform, but he is also a poet, a philosopher, and a deeply committed Muslim pragmatist. We talk in a quiet air-conditioned office away from the buzz of telephones and computers. I tell him about my earlier Peace Corps experience and my interest in the Pakistan education system, past and present.

"In the past," Riaz says, "we had dedicated teachers and successful students in the government schools. I know of a government school student who went on to get a Nobel Prize . . . a good example of the successes of the government system. . . . And our parents went to government schools.

"We used to have good teachers in our schools . . . people designed by God to be teachers . . . and environments for magic to happen. . . . [There were] strong bonds between the teacher and student. But the government simply did not have the capacity to run the education system it nationalized in the 1970s.

"Many administrations talked about the need for education reform, for money for schools, for girls' education, and for serving the poorest of the poor . . . but the reform programs of these administrations never fully addressed the problems nor succeeded in healing the educational wounds. . . . While the population of the country tripled, the number of schools with trained and competent teachers and administrators did not.

"Some public schools don't even really exist. These are called 'ghost schools.' There are at least thirty thousand ghost schools in Pakistan today. These are school buildings that exist on paper but in reality were never built . . . or are staffed by principals and teachers who either do not show up or are not actually qualified to teach."

The World Bank and many other observers have corroborated the existence of ghost schools in Pakistan. In these schools, young children are often left to the supervision of older students because the teachers are absent. The classrooms are overcrowded and dark. There are not enough books, paper, chairs, or tables. Money allocated to building schools and to paying administrators and teachers often never reaches the children, who remain uneducated either by dropping out[1] or by failing the year-end examinations.

The quality of education in the majority of government schools is poor and relies on learning by rote and repetition. Continuing professional development for teachers is limited, and teacher salaries are low. Teachers and administrators in the government system cannot be fired, and they are not held accountable for student failures.

"Today the people coming out of government schools cannot go into the mainstream," Riaz continues. "There are some schools . . . technical schools where they are teaching wiring, etc., that are doing the job . . . but less than 5 percent of seventeen- to twenty-three-year-olds receive any vocational training, and less than 8 percent of Pakistan's workforce has any formal vocational training at all.

"Bureaucratic red tape and political interference drove the education system into the ground. Though there were over a dozen high-level commissions on how to fix the system, few, if any, of the recommendations were ever implemented."

And so, in the 1990s, private charities and nongovernmental organizations stepped in to fill the void.

"We thought, Why not get together and actually sow the seeds of a large nongovernmental organization or civil society organization?" says Riaz. "We thought this organization should not be for profit and our endeavors should not be paid for. Initially, we were six founder-directors, and one of us has now retired. . . . We took the primary education into the heart of the less privileged areas . . . the *katchi abadis*. We went and physically built schools there. . . . One of the founding directors is an architect, so his firm designed the school buildings without any charge.

"We built five schools in the first year, and we had the teachers trained from outside. Teachers Resource Center gave the training the first year. This is how we started.

"In the second year, we built ten schools and then fifteen and so on. *Alhamd'Allah*, God Willing. . . . After the first three or four years, we needed a space for those children who were passing primary education, so we started opening up secondary schools. Now we have built six hundred school units across Pakistan and enrolled eighty thousand students. Seventy-two percent of our graduates go on to higher education."[2]

Remembering my struggles getting a cottage industry started in Dhamke in 1963, I ask Ateed Riaz about the funding sources and organizational structure of TCF.

"When we went out looking for money," he replies, "we got very good support from the Pakistani community and Pakistani diaspora. We only focus on Pakistani community. There is no one donor or organization. Today we have maybe eight or ten thousand donors. Our philosophy is very simple . . . we just go out sending messages and telling people that this is what the organization is all about—come and see our work. We go and show them the schools; they see and like them. We ask, Where do you want to fit in?

"Since we founders are all coming from a corporate background, there is only one method that we know . . . the corporate method. That is why we have instituted the company as a nonlisted public limited company, limited by the guarantee. We know only one method: put transparency, audit, accounting procedures, monitoring and evaluation, accountability into the organization and make job descriptions.

"We have not sought money from government. We do not have any terms. We have schools. We teach children in our schools. If some donors say they want to support X number of schools, the board will look at the offer. We have not gone out seeking support. But we focus only on Pakistani individuals, corporations, and businesses. There are many corporate organizations that are supporting us. It is their project as much as ours. They know us from businesses; they know we are running a good business and what we say we mean—there is no underhand deal."

Suddenly, Ateed Riaz the social reformer becomes Ateed Riaz the poet-philosopher: "The situation in education is very burning, so to say. Whenever we lift the lid from the bucket, there is a fire, because there are millions of children who don't go to school. I can only address my immediate target of 360,000 children. But there are millions of children in the bucket. So every solution is a right solution. Therefore, whatever anybody is doing for education, even under a tree, in a tent, or in one room, I salute him.

"But here the question arises, why are we doing all this? We do this to develop people. On that side, at the end of the day . . . we get as the net result the number of children, who are bright, graduating from our schools, talking good, working well, and showing good manners. That is our bag, and every year we have a bagful of such children, which we then let go into society and we take a new batch of children. That is our pot of gold, which we get at the end of the day.

"We follow the regular national curriculum, but we try to improve it. We try to teach science and math in bilingual terms. We have some small unusual practices, like all our teachers come to our summer training program every year for four weeks. This is held everywhere. We talk to them about their own subjects. We divide them into groups and . . . we could be talking to them about anything from physics to creative and lateral thinking to astronomy to anything to develop and open minds of the children. So we devise our own courses. We are really pushing for children to become more confident in the way they approach things."

"Our philosophy is very simple," says the deeply committed Muslim pragmatist. "Our philosophy is that, God forbid, if one day a war erupts between India and Pakistan and it is perceived as a Hindu-versus-Muslim war, I want the child who has studied in a TCF school to protect his Hindu neighbor from anybody who may want to harm him.[3]

"The human being carries the software that I have not written; I have not designed the human being. The software has been designed and written by God. So I would like to teach our children to look for the software manual so that they can decide what role they want to play. But our children have to think and then come to that level. What is best for them: paan shops, the ever-present kiosks that sell cigarettes and the betel nut leaves that Pakistanis love to chew? Looking after parents? Doing PhD? Given a chance, our children will be able to make decisions.

"If education is doing that, then I think education is successful, because it is making people think and arrive at a good conclusion. If education is not doing that, then it has failed. Our model is formal education. Our model is to open doors in the mind of a child, so that he or she can make good decisions."

Ateed Riaz is very hopeful about Pakistan.

"In Islam, you cannot be pessimistic. We are very thankful and always positive. If we move forward, we hope that everybody makes it polite, soft, standing up to whatever they think is wrong. Not being aggressive but just telling their minds in soft tones. . . . We feel that the human being is very superior, with the potential of flying very high. In Islam, we say, 'If you find someone in the gutter, you probably put him there.'

"I'll tell you a real story. A friend of mine went to the city of Medina and went to a woman squatting on the floor selling something. He negotiated with her, but she would not sell to him. She said, 'If you like it, buy it from that other tradeswoman. I will not sell it to you.' So he got a local to come and talk to her in her own language. She talked to the local and explained that she had already sold enough that day and that other woman had not yet sold any, so I should buy from her. The message is clear: We need to help each other.

"Most of our children, once they've graduated, will mix and mingle with the rest of the population. . . . And once they mix and mingle, their voice should be a voice of reason, a voice of peace. I hope the children coming out of our schools are good, caring children, looking after their neighborhoods, their societies, and are more tolerant."

"This project belongs to the people of Pakistan," he concludes. "It is for us to sustain. We have to learn to stand up and solve our problems. It is a very simple work. Our head office in Karachi is the nerve center. Here, everything is open, our cupboards are open, curriculum and syllabus are open, our doors are open."

At the end of our interview, Ateed Riaz says, "I think you should talk to some of the people who see the project from an insider's view. Get some stories from the students and teachers. Let me organize this."

We leave the air-conditioned sanctuary of Ateed Riaz's office and walk to the elevator. I look over the banister to the open courtyard several stories below. It is laid with long prayer rugs, and I remember that today is Friday, the Muslim Sabbath, when everything stops in the early afternoon for prayers and worship. I apologize to Ateed Riaz for possibly delaying him from his Juma prayers. "No, no," he assures me. "We will all stop at one o'clock for prayers, and then everyone will return to his work."

We shake hands and I am turned over to Amar, who has been waiting to escort me back to the TCF office on the other side of the city. I trade the dark, cool office building for the hot noonday haze and follow Amar through a throng of men, small cars, and motorcycles, all coming toward me. I step carefully over pieces of concrete and street debris and try to avoid the groups of men heading to their Juma prayers.

In the old days, I muse, I would have been stepping over animal dung and open drains and dodging tongas, ox carts, and bicycles; I would have been hurrying to find a rickshaw to take me to a bus so that I could reach my village before prayers began. In the old days, the sun would have been just as blazing hot, but the haze in the air would have been from animals and dust rather than gasoline-powered generators and automobiles. Away from the bazaar, the air would have been clear, the light dazzling.

On this day, all around me, the air is dense and muggy. The sun is hidden behind a scrim of exhaust fumes. Everything looks gray. And I am being driven across a city that merely *interrupts* its work for Friday prayers and goes back to work on Friday afternoons. I take in these changes and wonder what will be next.

When I reach the building of the TCF headquarters, load shedding has also contributed to the early afternoon grayness. The electricity is off, and I am obliged to walk up seven flights of stairs to the TCF office suites.

The TCF central offices are unadorned and unassuming. The central reception area at the top of the stairs opens at each end onto a large room full of desks, computers, stacks of papers and books, windows on three sides, and only a few partitions. The desks and tables in the center of the room face each other and are grouped, loosely, into departments. Around the perimeter of the room, several glass cubicles with doors that can be closed are separated from the general hub and are the domain of senior staff. Nancy tells me later that this openness is the "Microsoft model," designed to facilitate communication among workers. It reminds me of the open classroom concept of education popular in the progressive and informal schools of Britain and the United States in the 1960s and 1970s.

I walk in and am greeted with nods and smiles of welcome by men and women associated with donor giving, marketing, volunteer support, human resources, curriculum development, and teacher training. It is a colorful mix of young and not-so-young Pakistanis. The men are dressed in casual shirts and khaki pants, the women in bright shalwar kameez. I will talk with some of them, as well as with the senior managers and CEO, in the days ahead.

Dr. Ahson Rabbani, one of the vice presidents, offers me a cold drink, and we sit down to chat. "We recently reorganized," Dr. Rabbani tells me. "The CEO is now a three-person job: the general manager is one job, the vice president for input—fundraising, marketing, supply chain management, volunteers, publishers, and so on—is another job, and the vice president for output, the education product, human resources, volunteer programs like your Summer Science Camps, teacher training, and so on, is the third job. My job is vice president of input . . . the financial sustainability of the organization . . . to raise funds for the short term and the long term.

"TCF has had a certain strategy and a track record of raising funds. The first strategy is that this education mess is a *Pakistani* problem. We got into this mess. So we Pakistanis are responsible for getting out of it."

I am beginning to recognize this phrase: "This is a Pakistani problem" and its underlying commitment, "We Pakistanis are responsible for getting out of it." Both the phrase and the commitment are new for me and very different from what I assumed and experienced in the 1960s. Back then, I remember, the assumption was that we foreigners had deep pockets and would show the way and facilitate the social change necessary to move the country forward. The problems might have been Pakistan's problems, but we Americans had the means and thought that we had the expertise to solve them.

I share these thoughts with Dr. Rabbani and ask him to tell me more about Pakistanis taking responsibility for Pakistani problems.

"This is a cornerstone of TCF's foundation," he said. "The founders began by putting in their own money. Then they asked friends and family to look at what they had done and to also contribute. We are very proud of that."

"There is a lot of philanthropic emphasis in Pakistan," Dr. Rabbani explained. Our second cornerstone is the Islamic system of *zakat*: one-fortieth, or 2.5 percent, of your assets every year must be spent to help the poor. We go after mass giving from zakat. For one thousand schools, we need one thousand donors. Our major donors support one school or more. You don't have to be a millionaire to build a school.

"We have built schools all across Pakistan. We are in all four provinces, in sixty-two different cities, plus in Azad Kashmir.[4]

"We also have zakat donors of just one hundred rupees or less. We do fundraising activities, walkathons, dinners, etc. We are just beginning to look for international grants and donors, etc. . . .

"The magic of TCF is that today we are the largest nongovernment educator of children, but there is no one person known as TCF. In TCF, people of different backgrounds and temperaments have come together, not one person for any glory, no political angle.

"It is a challenge to know how to sustain our organization, however. When well-intentioned people start projects . . . very few are able to sustain it. We are concerned, but not worried, about sustainability.

"Part of the board direction is that there is a lot of faith in God as long as we are doing the right thing, not for our own glory, and if we work hard, we will be successful. We have seen help coming from so many places. You coming to help us are an example. Your family and friends will be worried about you coming to Pakistan. Who puts that in your heart? God. You being here add quality to the education that is intangible.

"We have many volunteers. . . . Our organization runs on volunteers.

"We have a very simple focus, motivated for just one purpose: to educate children, get them off the street. We give these children hope. After ten years, what will they do? Become skilled workers? Higher education? It's up to them and their hard work. We can't play God and decide for them. We give them a fair chance.

"We have an optimism and hope, but we cannot do everything. We focus on one thing and do it well."

Dr. Rabbani takes me across the room to meet Neelam Habib, the manager of donor relations. An earnest young woman in dark-rimmed glasses and headscarf, Neelam has been with the organization since its beginning.

Neelam describes her job to me: "I greet any potential donor and then I take donors to school visits . . . to meet the teacher, see the children, to show them how we work. I work independently. I help the donor choose whether they want to build a school or support an existing school. When a donor chooses a project, another TCF department entertains their proposal and then marketing becomes involved to promote their gift.

"Our donors have been our best ambassadors and our supporters. That's how we spread the word around, rather than anything else, like advertising. There are some women who do fundraising from their own homes, working themselves to organize a walkathon, or a dinner, and all the proceeds come here and everything goes to making the schools.

"We used to do one big event, but we now do four events. Every quarter we do a manageable event. Some events will end up maybe with enough money to run ten schools, some for three schools. . . . So now our biggest challenge is our running expenses, which are pretty high."

She continues: "For the first time, we have touched granting. Up to now, we have not taken any money from any grant organization, but we are starting to look into that, and my responsibility is to approach some grants. We have approached three organizations locally and internationally, and we are hoping to hear from them. We fulfill the requirements of many grants—they all want to give money, and they are asking the same kinds of questions. If you are running a competent organization, you will be very open with what you are doing and you will have no problem in filling out grant applications. Sure, we can do it. Because we have been doing it by ourselves up to now. . . .

"So we've opened a lot to new donors. We put their name as signage on the school or inside on a plaque, depending on how much they give. A donor who pays to build a school gets the right to select the name of that campus and the wording/message on a marble plaque in the foyer."

My conversation with Neelam is interrupted when my teammates return from their unpacking endeavors at the teacher-training site in Goth Dhani Bux. Neelam, I think, is ready for her workday to end as well. We have all been invited by the senior TCF staff to a Pakistani seaside barbeque at one of the most popular restaurants in the city.

I make a note to find out more about the financial infrastructure that supports TCF schools in future interviews. But for now, everyone is ready for the weekend to begin, and I am ready to trade my microphone and tape recorder for the respite of more casual conversation by the sea. It has been a long, intense day, and I am happy to put away my gear and clatter down the stairs behind my teammates.

CHAPTER 10

~

Setting Up Training, 1963 and 2009

The next morning, a Saturday, Taffy, Nancy, and I again journey to the teacher-training site at Goth Dhani Bux to put the finishing touches on the classrooms and supplies that we will use on Monday, the first day of training. When we arrive, only the ayah, Lateefa, is present. Her warm smile of welcome and eagerness to please embraces us all. She looks so much like Bivi-gee, Jerry and Envir's mother, I instantly feel at ease—right at home back in Pakistan.

While we wait for the others to arrive, Taffy, Nancy, and I decide to explore the neighborhood. We draw a crowd of excited children, mostly boys, and the curious stares of men and women who are attending to their morning chores in the dusty marketplace. I am surprised to see a maze of electric wires overhead, spliced and attached to each other and to buildings, all sagging toward the street.[1] There are piles of trash and plastic bags in the alleyways, and graffiti is scrawled on walls everywhere I look—not so different from a slum anywhere in the world, I suppose. The smell is distinctly Pakistan, however—a mixture of spices, open fires, hair oil, sweat, animals, dust, and incense; it is unforgettably familiar.

Although we are dressed in shalwar kameez, we three blond- and silver-haired pale women obviously do not belong to this neighborhood. At one point, an older man approaches us, tells us that he is a retired professor, and begins to bombard us with questions: "Where are you from?" "Why are you here?" and our least-favorite question, "What is your age?" The professor invites us to his home to meet his female relatives, who are beckoning from their rooftop several houses away. We are about to accept his invitation, when Lateefa calls from the corner; Karen, Sofia, and Sanobar Javeed, the school principal, have arrived at the school and are waiting for us.

As we begin to walk back to the school, two officious young policemen on a motorcycle come up from behind and demand to know "our business." Their English is not up to our explanation, and our Urdu is not helpful for them. They follow us all the way back to the school gate, where Lateefa explains our business sufficiently well that they vroom away, apparently satisfied. To my knowledge, no baksheesh[2] is involved, and this is the end of the exchange.

But the incident makes me uncomfortable and wary. In the 1960s, checking in with the local police had been mandatory before entering or leaving your town of residence for more than two weeks. Back then, however, a policeman following me on a motorcycle, demanding to know my business in another village or town, would have been unthinkable.

Today's encounter brings to mind yesterday's conversation with Ateed Riaz about the power of corrupt police, bullies, and mullahs in the slum neighborhoods. I wonder if it is Lateefa's enhanced status in the community as a TCF ayah that has persuaded these very brusque policemen that we foreign women are harmless.

We spend the rest of the day organizing supplies and setting up the classrooms. Two additional ayahs, Zakia and Noor Banu, and their children also join us. Sofia quickly enlists the help of the young children and keeps them busy counting out washers and spools. Karen's superb organizational skills keep us all focused. By the end of the afternoon, we have boxed up all the materials to be sent on to the Lahore training site, arranged a supply room for the Karachi teachers, and set up the training classrooms for Monday morning's teacher-training session.

The work is hot and tiring, but our spirits are high and I am amazed and pleased by how well everyone works together. This day has been an extra workday for the ayahs and school principal, a day they usually have free. But they have worked with us all day, without grumbling or shirking.

How different this day has been from my days in Dhamke and Sheikhupura in the 1960s. I remember how hard Saroya and I labored to gather straw for our cottage industry in Dhamke, often completely on our own, and how difficult it was to prepare the lady workers' training program in Sheikhupura without any outside help or official cooperation. In the early 1960s, even though many promised to help us, few ever followed through, and to get the job done, we usually had to wait and wait and eventually do it ourselves.

October 14, 1963

Sheikhupura

Dear George,

I've been in Sheikhupura for over a month now, trying to arrange meetings with all the officials in charge of approving our Lady Workers Training program. I can't tell you how many times I've gone to someone's office at the appointed time only to find the person away for a week, or no longer working there. Our training program is supposed to start at the end of this week, and I hope it won't be postponed, again. My last stumbling block was the District Commissioner. I sat for two days in his outer office and finally met with him—at the window of his car as he was leaving the Tehsil office. I shoved the proposal of the training program under his nose—and he glanced at it and said we could go ahead—so I guess that we can begin.

I have several lecturers from the College of Home and Social Science, the Vocational Training School, and Planned Parenthood lined up to talk to the Lady Workers next week. I hope they all will actually come. It is really hard to get everyone together. So often when someone tells me they will come, they really mean "yes, I hear you and know you want me to come." They aren't really agreeing to show up— and that is so frustrating because I continue to count on them and they continue to disappoint me. O well, I guess that's just Pakistan—but it is hard to accept.

Saroya and I have spent a lot of time visiting all the Lady Workers in their villages and looking for a place for them to stay during the training. We finally decided to put charpoys in the training room so the Lady Workers can bring their bisters and sleep, cook, and learn all in the same place. The compound is surrounded by high walls and our recruits are excited about coming into town for a week. I have some films from USIA to show them and Saroya and I will do some nutrition and hygiene demonstrations. The Basic Democracies Director told me yesterday that I was *very serious* and that I got many things accomplished in a very short time. He said that Pakistanis would not be able to do so much in such little time. To me it feels like a very long time and that I have not done very much—or had much help from him.

I've been in Pakistan for over a year now. It hardly seems possible—so much has—and hasn't—happened. Keep your fingers crossed that all will go well with the Lady Workers Training and that everyone actually will do what they have promised to do. I can't wait to get started.

Love, L

On this Saturday in 2009, reflecting on the help we have had preparing for the Summer Science Camps in Goth Dhani Bux, I am grateful that the days of noncooperation and unhelpfulness of the 1960s have passed. I am encouraged that our experience today represents a meaningful change at the grassroots level in Pakistan.

This evening, Taffy, Nancy, and I are invited to the home of Seema Chhapra, the director of human resources for TCF Karachi. Sitting on her rooftop patio, sipping fresh mango juice, and listening to the evening call to prayer from a nearby minaret, I feel as though I am on a movie set. We are only a few miles from the slum of Goth Dhani Bux, but the breeze here is sweet, the air clear, the heat bearable. Looking down at the parklike setting of Seema's manicured neighborhood, I watch three teenage girls stroll by. One is dressed in blue jeans, one in capri pants, the third in a long Western-style skirt. Their younger sisters play jump rope nearby. Here again is another side of Pakistan.

At the end of the evening, Seema and I agree to meet again early Monday morning before the Science Camp teacher-training program begins. I am eager to hear her story.

Early Monday morning finds me on Seema's patio once again. This time, we are alone in the thick morning air. I am intrigued to see that Seema is not wearing the hijab around her hair and is dressed in Western-style jeans and cotton blouse. Before we begin our formal interview, she tells me a little about herself.

"First, I want you to understand my background," she says. "I am now an American citizen and a Canadian citizen; I travel on my American passport, but I am from Karachi.

"I had an arranged marriage to my first cousin. . . . I had just barely finished my twelfth grade. We went to Canada for one and a half years, but we didn't like it too much because in 1974 people did not accept outsiders. We moved to Dubai for a year, but then moved to the U.S. I had two kids by the time I was twenty-three. When my kids were twelve or so, I got a divorce and joined a bank at the entry level.

"I had really good role models, and they encouraged me to go back to school, and I went back and finished my BA in business studies. I kept getting promoted until I became vice president. It took me eight years to finish my degree, because I was working and doing it in the night.

"The kids were growing up. I married again, this time to a Christian from Pakistan. At that time in my life, I became more interested in my religion, Islam, and I think my husband felt a little threatened. I got a divorce and decided to go to Dubai to live with my niece.

"In 2002, just before I was leaving for Dubai, I decided to have a medical checkup, and the doctor called me to tell me I had cancer. So I couldn't leave. Uterine cancer. My life was saved by going to the doctor for the checkup.

"My brother, one of the founding directors of TCF, convinced me to come home to Pakistan. I just didn't want to be away from family, so my brother said, 'Come to Karachi and stay with us. . . .' So I moved back to Karachi."

This move brought Seema to TCF. "At the end of 2002, my brother told me to come on vacation with him to the mountains. The first day . . . back, he called me to come to TCF to meet Ateed Riaz Sahib. I gave [him] my resume, and Ateed Riaz said, 'When can you start?' I said I am still very weak from cancer, and he said, 'You set your own hours.'

"At first, I did only general things part-time. . . . When they asked if I could do some teacher training, I said, 'Sure, why not? It can't be that different from the training I did with the bank.'

"At that time, TCF was very small," Seema explains. "There was no Education Department, no Human Resources Department, only a small Finance Department, a one-person Donor Department, a one-person Marketing Department, an administration person who looked after operations, and a CEO.

"TCF had a small teacher-training center donated by Ardeshir Cowasjee, a journalist for *Dawn*.[3] He's a donor for one of our larger schools, called the TCF Mauripur School, Cowasjee Campus. Cowasjee's family owned a lot of property in Karachi, and he gave us a beautiful piece of property in the old city to run a training center. It is a very valuable piece of property.

"My job was to go and work with five or six people and decide what kind of training to do. At that time, the new hires would come in January, we would train them in February, and then in March send them into the schools to observe to see how a teacher should be. In April, the beginning of the new term, we sent the new teachers into their own schools. So that is how the whole teacher training began. We used to teach a lot of content knowledge, like English, science, grammar concepts, because our teachers were weak in them.

"The teachers that we attract are right out of school. They are raw. When they come from other teaching positions, there is a lot of *de*-learning involved. We talk about creativity—don't like rote learning—so we would rather have teachers without any previous teaching experience.

"The number of teachers we train depends on the number of new schools we open. Generally when we open a school, we hire four classroom teachers, kindergarten through grade three, one teacher for English language, and one teacher for pre-kindergarten. One year, we opened sixty new schools, another year, eighty.

"The preservice training is for new teachers. This year we did a one-week preservice training in March and the rest in June. Teachers get a month off, and then train for one month in the summer.[4] The experienced teachers have their training in June and July.

"From 2003 to 2005, I did all the preservice and in-service training," Seema continues. "But because the academic staff was growing very fast, . . . we developed a methodology of training the trainers. Our initial training team became the 'trainers of the trainers,' or TOT. We took the brightest teachers and principals, and they became the trainers. The trainers get a stipend, and there is prestige involved.

"For two years, we trained the trainers in Karachi. . . . But TCF became so big, we had to divide Karachi into two regions, and Lahore into two regions: Moulton, Khanewal on one side; Sheikhupura, Faisalabad on the other side. . . . Now we have four regions and try to group our trainings to be cost-effective. Each region has to develop their own trainers so that each region can be self-sufficient."

At this point, I must interrupt our interview because the teacher-training session for the Summer Science Camp is about to begin, and I have promised to be there. As I wait for Seema's driver to arrive to take me to the training site, I tell Seema about my recent encounter with the policemen in Goth Dhani Bux and about how Lateefa, the TCF ayah, had diffused the situation. I am curious about the role of ayahs in TCF schools and communities and intrigued by the industriousness of the ayahs that have been helping us at Goth Dhani Bux.

Seema tells me that ayahs are typically sweepers from the lowest class of society and have access to many families often walled off to outsiders. "When TCF builds a school in a slum neighborhood," she says, "one of their first hires is an ayah from the community. Part of the ayah's responsibility is to tell others about the new school and invite them to join. The ayah provides credibility about the teachers and confidence in the school and is the entrée into the neighborhood for the TCF principal and area manager when they come to invite families to send their children to the school."

"I would have loved you to meet one of our ayahs from Karachi last year," Seema continues. "We have an adult literacy program.[5] . . . This ayah came on the stage. In front of two thousand people, she said that when she was growing up in her village, there was no school for girls, only for boys. When she married, she came to Karachi and had six kids and no time to study.

"This woman became a TCF ayah, and they came to her door and asked her to join the adult literacy class. She was so excited to join. So she asked her husband, and he said OK, if you can still do all your work at the house. So she began, and TCF let her bring her baby to class. She said, 'What this has done to me is that when I go to the hospital, I know which room to go to. I can read how much medicine to give. I can go to parent-teacher meetings.' She was so confident telling her story. Her confidence to become literate came from being a TCF ayah."

Seema's driver appears, and I exchange Seema's hospitality for a trip back to the neighborhood of Goth Dhani Bux. The same dusty, trash-laden landscape slips by, but I am impervious, lost in thought about the impact of education at the simplest level of society: Lateefa, an illiterate ayah gaining the self-confidence to challenge the police in her neighborhood; an uneducated mother of six learning to read and write as an adult after her household and ayah cleaning duties are finished. Both of these women were empowered by the presence and accessibility of a TCF school and their involvement with it.

As we pull up to the school gate, Lateefa greets me with a smile and salaam, and I impulsively ask her if she will meet later in the day and tell me about her work. She nods enthusiastically, and I do not doubt that she understands my request.

Inside the gate, I hurry through the outer courtyard, now crowded with small TCF vans and drivers, and ascend several steps to the inner courtyard where twenty-five TCF teachers and principals, five central office training staff members, two central staff volunteer coordinators, and twenty college-student volunteers are waiting for the first day of Summer Science Camp teacher training to begin.

Taffy and Karen have decided to team-teach the entire group in one room on this first morning so that everyone will have the same orientation to inquiry-based learning and to the goals for the Summer Science Camps. The classroom is crowded and hot. Large library tables have been pulled together to accommodate five groups of nine learners at each. The principals, area managers, and other visitors from the central office staff sit around the perimeter of the room to watch.

We have deliberately set up the classroom so that small groups can work together to explore the equipment in the center of each table, to ask questions of each other, and to form hypotheses and test for answers to the questions they have posed. There is enough equipment for everyone to be engaged as an active participant. We have designed the classroom this way to model the classroom arrangement for the children in the Summer Science

Camps. At the end of the morning's lesson, Taffy and Karen will articulate this classroom management strategy as they discuss the principles of inquiry learning with the teachers, student volunteers, and visitors from the TCF central staff.

In the afternoon, the teachers will be divided into groups based on the grades they will teach. Karen will work with the primary-level teachers; Taffy, the secondary-level. The classes will be conducted in English, and Shameem Jahangir, our curriculum liaison with TCF Karachi, will translate troublesome concepts or words into Urdu. Nancy and I will be the gofers in each classroom and will assist wherever we are needed.

The air shimmers with dust motes stirred by ceiling fans overhead. The buzz of conversation hushes to a murmur. It is hot, and the electricity, predictably, shuts off almost as soon as Taffy begins to speak. The teachers listen attentively to her delivery and take notes. There is laughter and keen interest as the training program for inquiry learning and Summer Science Camps begins.

This first day of training in 2009 is a sharp contrast to my first day of lady workers' training in Sheikhupura in 1963.

October 24, 1963
Sheikhupura
Our training started today. Rather, the Lady Workers assembled and we waited for the important inauguration ceremony—the dignitaries from the Basic Democracies and District Council office to come and give us their welcome and blessing—and waited, and waited. No one ever came. So we began without them.

Two lecturers from the College of Home and Social Science came to talk about nutrition. One of the women was English and has been in Pakistan for many years and speaks Urdu beautifully. The other, a young Pakistani woman, has probably never been to a village and seems a little too grand to actually work with village women. But both women were really interesting and jolly and the Lady Workers were polite and attentive to everything they had to say.

After the lecturers left we gathered in a circle and talked about what we wanted to accomplish in the training. The Lady Workers asked for practical demonstrations. Tomorrow Saroya and I will do just that. We'll present some nutritious meal planning and everyone will cook. Mohyddin [the Assistant Director of Basic Democracies in Sheikhupura] probably won't understand this kind of teaching and will probably think we're having a vacation chutti—"cooking isn't training," I can just hear him—and he might threaten to send all the Lady Workers back to their villages. But if it's practical help the ladies want, then it's practical help they'll get.

Saroya and I can do that—we'll talk about vitamins and why it is so important to clean the vegetables as everyone is chopping. It's so simple. I learned about this by helping my mother in the kitchen when I was five years old. My mother called it "learning by doing." One thing is certain—the ladies will get more out of the training if they are actually doing it too.

Learning by doing,[6] or active learning, is our training strategy for the TCF teachers in 2010, as well. I watch Taffy captivate her audience as they actively engage with the materials in front of them, and then I duck across the courtyard to talk with Lateefa.

Lateefa surprises me by asking if the other ayahs, Zakia and Noor Banu, can join our conversation. "Of course," I reply. Nasheen Noor, the TCF volunteer coordinator in Karachi, agrees to assist with translation since the ayahs do not speak English or Urdu and my Punjabi is still rusty after so many years of disuse. The five of us find an empty classroom and begin our conversation.

I learn that all three ayahs are from Goth Dhani Bux, and Lateefa and Noor Banu are the two original ayahs for the school. They confirm Seema's description of an ayah's responsibilities.

"When the school first began," Lateefa says, "I went to talk to my neighbors and tell them about the new school and distribute pamphlets door to door. I brought these neighbors and their children to show them the school. Some people also came to me because they know I am working at the school. They say, 'Is it a good school?' And I say yes and take them to the school to show them that it is."

All three ayahs have children: Zakia has two, and Noor Banu and Lateefa each have five. All of their children are enrolled in TCF schools, except that Lateefa has one blind daughter and a blind grandchild who are in a school for the blind. All the other children are in either primary or secondary TCF schools even though their mothers are uneducated.

Lateefa tells me that she went to primary school through the third grade and can write her name; Zakia says she completed primary at level five, and Noor Banu admits that she never attended school and can write only her name. However, when TCF begins an adult literacy class in Goth Dhani Bux, all three ayahs plan to attend.[7]

I ask the ayahs about their work at TCF. They all talk at once, and Nasheen has to scramble to keep up with them.

"We get up in the morning, do our house chores, and get the children off," Nasheen translates. "Then we come to the school and do the cleaning chores: dusting, cleaning of the bathrooms, mopping, sweeping. If the children have any problems or need cleaning, we do that, too. Lateefa and Noor Banu come to school at seven o'clock in the morning and go home at one o'clock. Zakia comes at noon for the afternoon and stays until 5:30."[8]

"Sometimes some children come to school without brushing their hair or with their uniforms not clean," Lateefa says. "I tell them they should come to school neat and clean. Not every day, but when new admissions come in I have to do this. Sometimes the older children don't take care of things, either, and then I have to do it with them, too. When the older kids don't come neat and clean, I tell them to brush their hair, clean their teeth, clean their uniforms, and then come to school. I tell them tomorrow they should pay attention. If they don't listen, I tell them three or four times."

"The children are generally well behaved in the school," Nasheen continues to translate. "The kids who come here don't have any behavior problems. Some of the older boys are different when they are outside in the community, and the girls are generally better behaved than the boys outside. The boys are better behaved in school. But the boys say their salaams to the ayahs on the outside, even if they have graduated, and they treat the ayahs with more respect."

I ask the ayahs what changes they have seen in the community since the TCF schools have come. "One big change," Lateefa replies, "is that at first the family sent only the older boy to school, but now they send all the younger children, even girls, and now all the children in the family are literate. Within the community, also, the people treat each other better, and most of the children in the community are going to school. The children are better behaved in the community and treat each other better in the family."

Lateefa compares her children's school experiences: "TCF children are better off than the children at the blind school. TCF children receive more opportunities and are exposed to more things; the teachers do more for the children. When I look at other children in the community, they are disrespectful, they use bad language, they misbehave. But the children who come to TCF don't use bad words, don't misbehave."

"The TCF mothers say the children imitate the teacher," Zakia adds. "How they sit, how they walk, and what the teachers tell them to do at home. The children say, 'The teachers have asked us to behave this way, and you, Mother, have to behave this way, too.' My daughter gets very annoyed with me when I am working at home and drop something on the floor. My daughter will come to me and say that her teacher has said to her not to litter either at home or at school, so she must pick it up. I must do all the things my daughter tells me. So who is the mother and who is the daughter?" Zakia laughs. "My daughter puts all the household pots in the corner in a row and does her lessons and teaches the pots as though in school."

Noor Banu concludes: "My husband used to work, but is not working now. But my son was a TCF student and is a telephone operator now, and his son is in a TCF school." Even though she does not read or write, Noor Banu can clearly see the value of education for her children.

Our interview ends when the Sanobar Javeed, the principal, asks Lateefa to ring the gong for break period. The gong, a circular metal plate hanging on a tripod of sticks, serves as the school bell.

I thank the ayahs for their conversation and invite them to give me suggestions or other comments about TCF in the next few days while I am at their school.

CHAPTER 11

~

Behind the Citizens Foundation

After lunch, while the first day of teacher training continues at Goth Dhani Bux, I return to the TCF central office for a series of interviews with senior management and training staff.

My first conversation is with a tall, distinguished gentleman with a short silver beard and soft-spoken manner. Asad Ayub Ahmad, the CEO of TCF, tells me he came to TCF from a more lucrative position in private industry, because "by cutting back on my lifestyle, I could begin to contribute more to the development of the country."

I tell him a bit about myself, including the name of the university from which I have recently retired. "My son was accepted at your university," he says, "but when I came to TCF, it became too expensive for him to go there. I did my studies in Austin, Texas, and really liked it. Multicultural experience is very good. I would like my kids to have it, too, but we are happy that our son is attending university in Karachi. I did my undergraduate studies here."

Asad Ayub's office is a glass enclosure on the perimeter of the large, open room of young men and women I met yesterday. When I remark on the office design, he says, "We encourage open communication. There is a lot of open space in the office, and by and large there is a reasonable amount of open communication throughout TCF. Not as much as I would like. You know, we have regional and area managers who are retired military, and they are used to the military style and they have a different way of communicating."

I am surprised to hear that the regional and area managers are recruited from the military and ask Asad Ayub to tell me about it.

"There are two aspects that retired military bring: One is discipline. Their job is tough. They need to be traveling around . . . to visit schools and get things done. Being an ex-army person helps. People will listen. . . . These military people . . . are disciplined. They can deal with the government. When they go to a community, the local miscreants are not going to mess with a colonel. The military can handle the locals.

"The second thing is, former military are retired and already have a pension, a house of their own, and medical benefits. A civilian coming to TCF for the same pay wouldn't be as financially secure or experienced as retired military."

Pakistan has a long history of educating young men for military service, and since 1947 the country has been intermittently governed by the military.[1] Hiring retired military officers as regional and area managers is a unique solution to some of the obstacles in getting things done in Pakistan, though I can understand that having ex-military men as managers in an organization that prides itself on open communication and transparency might create some unexpected challenges. I ask about this.

"Yes, hiring retired military is a pragmatic solution," Asad Ayub agrees. "TCF was developed by businessmen who are very practical. They were practical about the design of the schools. For example, to function with the lowest of costs, vans can only hold eight people, so the school is built for just eight teachers. . . . An all-female staff gets more girls to come to school . . . and makes it possible to get a better quality of teachers for the same pay. . . . That kind of practicality.

"The great part of TCF's success is because we are so practical," he continues. "Our overheads are 10 percent, and we watch our spending like hawks. . . . We have constant consciousness, making sure to keep that practical culture alive. Even in my case, the car I was entitled to—I reduced the value of that car, emphasizing that message. . . . When we train the trainers in Islamabad, we house them upstairs from the office instead of in a hotel and save the organization 400,000 rupees.

"It is sometimes frustrating for me, because I come from an oil industry background and now my family can't afford that lifestyle. . . . But we all have the same focus here."

I ask if TCF has considered asking for financial support from agencies or corporations outside of Pakistan.

"We are looking at outside grants, but not to go out of the country. We have approached the USAID [U.S. Agency for International Development] . . . but we want to work on our own. . . . We don't want strings attached to what we want to do. It's a question of survival of the country.

"Education is the key. We don't want to get into restricting ourselves or overexpanding because of somebody else's agenda. If we can get some extra support from outside agencies, we are all for it. . . . But USAID is interested in some public-private partnership, like having TCF run the government schools, something like that. That won't help the country. We have the most corrupt person in Pakistan as the president. If U.S. gives money to Pakistan through the government, we are a little bit hesitant to take it. We have been approached by those who want to be our subcontractors if we get money from USAID, but we don't want any strings attached. We want to do what we do best: educate poor children.

"I'm hoping, even in the case of USAID, maybe this time around they will look to where they are spending their money. But because we don't do things like hire a lobbyist, we will plead our case and hope people will know that TCF is Pakistan citizens and not the Pakistani government.

"We are very open. But we are low key. We haven't really tried to sell ourselves, so not many people know about us. Our plan for the next couple of years is to support the schools we have, instead of trying to build more schools. We don't want to bite more than we can chew."

I am impressed with Asad Ayub's humility and forthright statements and intrigued with the practicality of hiring retired military men as managers to perform those tasks that were such stumbling blocks for me as a Peace Corps Volunteer. I think hiring former military officers to circumnavigate the Pakistani bureaucracy, procure permits, supervise local school personnel, and arrange for the efficient distribution of materials and supplies is brilliant. But I wonder if the retired military are as knowledgeable about education as they are about distributing materials and obtaining permits. I wonder how they evaluate principals and supervise teachers in the classrooms.

When I ask Asad Ayub to elaborate on this aspect, he refers me back to Shameem Jahangir, the staff person who has been helping us in Goth Dhani Bux for the past few days and whose glassed-in office is next to his.

Smiling and as polite and poised as ever, Shameem has just returned from the training site. As she ushers me into her office, she tells me that the Summer Science Camp teacher training at Goth Dhani Bux is going very well. I apologize for missing the afternoon sessions, but I am eager to talk to her away from the classrooms. As the manager for academics, with responsibility for overseeing curriculum, Shameem is the perfect source for information about evaluation, supervision, and training at TCF.

"The regional managers work directly with the schools," Shameem explains. "If the teachers have any problems with the logistics, they go to their area manager or regional manager. The managers have a certain number of schools under them. The guide lessons that we write go to the regions, and the managers distribute them to the teachers."

"The Education Department is divided into three divisions," she continues. "Training, Evaluation, and Academics. The Evaluation Division mostly visits schools, evaluates teachers and principals, and reviews reports. The Training Division does in-service training in the summer and the preservice for new inductees in the spring.

"My job is in the Academics Division. I work on the guide lessons for English and math and visit schools to find out how the books and lesson plans are working out. I write reports so the training can address any problems in the guides or lessons.

"The Academics Division also reviews textbooks. We look through the new national curriculum and try to make changes that we feel are appropriate. Right now our aim is to change the books we use in English and science. We are reviewing these books . . . and trying to find publishers who will make some changes for us. The books that come from Singapore, India, and the West have a lot of topics our children cannot relate to. We've been able to identify some publishers who will make the changes we request."

Shameem takes me across the office to meet Rahilla Fatima, the training manager for TCF. I am becoming confused talking to so many people with so many titles, and I say so. Rahilla laughs and then describes her responsibilities: "Basically, in the Training Division, we have professional development for the school staff. We have three main training programs: Training of Trainers, Preservice Training, and In-service Training. We will add another training program, a Principals Training, focusing on developing the principal at each school, enhancing her capacity to deal with most of the things that she comes across in school."

"We think that stronger principals will strengthen the school from the inside," Rahilla continues, "with less of outside support from the area managers. We want to have the principals learn how to implement our centralized teaching plans. We are able to cater to specific needs of clusters,[2] but we want to take the principal into the circle and have her take . . . a more prominent role in setting targets for her school and make informed decisions with the maximum amount of information and data.

"We want principals to be in a position to inform us of the issues and concerns and have possible solutions to the problems themselves, instead of just asking us or the regional managers for solutions. This is a need that has been growing. We cannot handle things the same way now that we have more schools."

I tell Rahilla that I have observed the principal at Goth Dhani Bux, Sano-bar Javeed, during the past week as she helped us set up for the teacher training and that I am impressed with her competence and diligence. "Yes, she is very responsible," Rahilla agrees. "We have about 20 percent attrition of principals, but we are confident that we have a reasonable percentage of 80 percent who . . . come up to the challenge of their responsibilities—another reason to train them."

She continues: "I personally conduct Training of Trainers sessions and also visit schools, developing training. It's a mix: visiting schools, meeting teachers, developing and conducting trainings. We also write manuals from the drafts that teachers provide. Each trainer gets a manual; a separate one for in-service and for preservice training.

"We visit the schools mainly to insure or follow up from training, to see if the training is being implemented or what is needed for on-site support. We do some short, on-site support as well. The actual questions happen on-site. We go and have sessions with the teachers, regional teams, and so forth."

This reminds me of my days with Saroya in Sheikhupura, following up our lady workers' training with visits to their village social centers, helping them solve on-site problems, gathering ideas for future trainings, and providing support for their ongoing programs.

December 11, 1963
Sheikhupura
Training Follow-up Visit
Saroya and I went out to Ferozwalla this morning where the Lady Worker was building a smokeless chula.[3] Across the courtyard from her, the women of the house were cooking over their campfire, as usual. Tanveer told us how hard she was working building that chula—and she was working hard—but no one was paying any attention to her.

We helped Tanveer finish the chula, and that night we called some of the village women together, including the chairman's wife, and gave a cooking demonstration on the smokeless chula and talked about the benefits of using it.

The next day Tanveer built another smokeless chula in the chairman's compound. We convinced the chairman's wife to watch and contribute her ideas. The point we tried to get across to Tanveer was that while you are building the smokeless chula, you talk about its design and why that design is important. You get the women to help you build it and then give a demonstration on how to use it. Then you

> follow up and help the women keep using it—and listen to their ideas and help them make theirs work better.
>
> Tanveer didn't know that there was more to the lesson than just building the chula. We'll have to stress this in our next training.

I tell Rahilla about my experiences with lady workers when I was a Peace Corps Volunteer. She recognizes some similarities to today's TCF training practices. "At times, we also go to someone else's training because they want us to see what they are doing," she says. "But today we also have access to cell phones and email."

In my last senior staff interview of the day, I discover that TCF is more than just a pragmatic organization led by successful businessmen and retired military officers. A thread of idealism weaves through the leadership structure, as well.

Riaz Kamlani, the vice president for education, is all energy. He talks fast, moves quickly, thinks in quantum leaps. His path to TCF leadership began during a year of volunteering for several organizations in Karachi while trying to start his own nongovernmental organization.

"I was based in South Africa at age twenty-eight or twenty-nine and had an idea my career had gone pretty well," Riaz recalls, "but when I looked ten or twenty years down the road, I knew what I did *not* want to do with my life.

"I came across a local article in the newspaper that, in the context of apartheid, talked about an institution that took students from the South African slums and put them into a BA program . . . and focused on experiential learning, entrepreneurship, and volunteerism. I decided that this is what I wanted to do in Pakistan. You see, in Pakistan, we don't have apartheid over race, but we have apartheid of social class.

"I wrote a business plan, formed a board of directors, did some fundraising, and brought my family back to Pakistan. For about a year, I was financially unemployed, but I started volunteering in a couple of nonprofit organizations. TCF was one of those organizations. I was also teaching at a government college here, volunteering at an organization there, working with the fishing community. At the same time, I was trying to start my project.

"I worked at TCF part-time, and then in 2008 the board of directors wanted to reorganize. They wanted a note taker, and so I did that job, and they asked me if I would step into the position of director until the organization could be reorganized. At the end of that time, they said, 'Why don't you join us?' And my initial response was 'No, I want to do my project. Thanks, but no thanks.'

"But then over the next two or three months, I began to realize that I believed in this organization, the integrity of the people who were running it. They worked with the same population I wanted to work with, and so why create something new when you can play a small part in something that already exists? So the project I had focused on for three years, I put away for the time being."

Riaz continues, describing his current position. "I came to TCF in July 2008 as a vice president. I am responsible for education, volunteers, human resources, and all things related to the outcomes of the model.

"One has to have a short- and long-term set of priorities. In the short term, there needs to be a system of stabilizing training. In the longer term, the vision is *positive change*. Education has the power to educate people for positive change. Good education, creating the character of a person—by that route, you can change everything.

"In the future, volunteers should do this organization and all the work. The citizens, not any one person, own TCF. Our task is to create projects for volunteers that they can handle on their own. For example, volunteers started the Mentors Program.[4] . . . We have fundraisers and outposts all around the world—U.K., U.S. Yes, the executives are on salary, but our workers are mostly volunteers. In terms of fundraising volunteer hours, we have as many people working as volunteers now as on staff.

"Our biggest challenge right now is quality issues. When you grow fast, you realize that every school in the country must have the same quality. The teacher availability in every area is not the same. There is a strong culture of education in Punjab, especially for women, but in other provinces, not so. We want to make sure that we get a uniform structure right across the board; that every school has the same curriculum, teachers, and quality as the others.

"Our mission is to bring about an enduring *positive change* for communities with greatest need through the power of quality education. We want to enable moral, spiritual, and intellectual enlightenment and create opportunities to improve quality of life.

"Our organization has a deep-rooted culture of passion and empathy. . . . Our vision is to remove the barriers of class and privilege to make the citizens of Pakistan agents of positive change."

There it is again, I think: my old Peace Corps goal to facilitate social change. But in this case, the leaders working toward social change are educated and worldly Pakistanis rather than an idealistic, naive American Peace Corps Volunteer. These are the people I was looking for when I was assigned to Dhamke to help change the patterns of village life so many years ago. Where were they then, I wonder? They were just babies, I think.

During the two generations since my Peace Corps days, pragmatic, idealistic, educated Pakistanis have emerged and are taking leadership positions for positive social change in Pakistan. The people I am meeting at TCF are some of these leaders.

The idea of Pakistani ownership for solving the problems of education and for taking responsibility for advancing social change is the biggest and most stunning change I have seen since I have returned to Pakistan.

CHAPTER 12

~

Training in Karachi, 2009

First thing the next morning, back at Goth Dhani Bux, the ayah Zakia greets me with a big smile and a suggestion. "Ma'am," she says, touching my sleeve and pointing to a five-gallon plastic barrel at the edge of the courtyard, "the children need cold water to drink."

I am embarrassed, because I don't quite know what she is saying. In my confusion, I think she is asking me for some cold water, so I slip off my backpack and hand her a plastic bottle of water and apologize that it is not very cold.

"No, no," she says, pulling me toward the staff bathroom—a small closet next to the staff room, equipped with an Eastern footplate toilet and sink with running water. She turns on the faucet, fills her closed hand with water, and gestures *not* drinking it. I get it. The running water in the school is not potable; hence, only the plastic water barrel in the courtyard can be used for drinking. After sitting in the sun all day, I imagine that the water in the barrel is even warmer than the bottle I handed to her.

But Zakia is not finished. She gestures to the plastic bottle, shakes her head, and again says, "No, no." She pantomimes tossing the water bottle onto the ground and adding more bottles to it.

By now, we have attracted the attention of Sanobar Javeed, the principal. Sanobar explains to me that Zakia means that water in individual plastic bottles is plentiful but expensive, and when the plastic bottles are discarded in the street, they contribute to the mountains of litter clogging the canals, alleys, and pathways. Zakia's solution, says Sanobar, is to do away with the individual plastic bottles *and* the small barrel and to supply cold water to a rooftop cistern that will run, clean and drinkable, through the faucets.

I'm not sure how I can implement Zakia's suggestion, but I am pleased that she has come to me with her idea. It indicates her sense of empowerment as a TCF ayah, I think, and also how well she has internalized the TCF values of social responsibility. When yesterday I asked all of the ayahs to come to me with other ideas about TCF, Zakia had listened—and followed through by alerting me to her suggestion. I think this would not have happened in the 1960s. It is a very hopeful sign of the changes that are taking place in Pakistan.

Later in the morning, I ask Sanobar to tell me about her job as the principal of Goth Dhani Bux secondary school. I can see that her duties are varied and numerous.

"I have a master's in education with a specialty in administration," Sanobar says with her arms open wide, "and this is the perfect job for what I studied. As principal, I am responsible for academics, teacher relations, maintenance overseer, and other nonacademic things.

"When I first came, this was a primary school. Now this is a secondary school with a morning and an afternoon shift of 270 students in morning, 270 students in afternoon, 540 students in all.

"Anything I can do myself, I do, but if I can't do it, then I call someone. I also supervise summer camps and all the other special programs that come under training. I am also a trainer of trainers—TOT—and I make up guide lessons for my teachers. For example, in a chapter from the national curriculum, if the teachers don't know how to deliver the lecture . . . I put guidelines in the lesson for them.

"I like it even more when I am training," Sanobar confides to me. "I am good at it. They like me as a trainer at the head office."

I know that one of the biggest problems in the Pakistani education system is teacher attendance and evaluation. In government schools, teachers cannot be fired, and they are not held accountable for their teaching or for the success of their students. I ask Sanobar about this.

"At TCF," she answers, "there are four evaluations for teachers per year. Once the teachers are evaluated, the principal and another trainer meet at the head office and review the evaluations. If there is something weak or lacking, then we plan a training. If a teacher is not good on her evaluations, we give her another chance and train her again.

"In all the years, I have never seen a teacher get fired for academic performance. But if it is something extreme, outside of academics, they will fire her.

"For example, a teacher was transferred into this school and she was not proper. The kids in her class were out of control, and her lesson plans were not good and she was way behind of all the teachers. I gave her three weeks and checked on her, but she did not improve. I called the area manager, and he saw that she was not teaching. He asked her if she doesn't want to teach. But she decided on her own to leave. The area manager said they would give her another chance, but she said no; she just resigned. But she was not fired.

"TCF has award ceremonies to celebrate the students who pass the matriculation exams. Teachers are also rewarded for 100 percent attendance. I received an end-of-the-year award for above-expectation work. They evaluate ten thousand rupees for excellent work, five thousand rupees for above-expectations work. I received five thousand rupees for above-expectations."

I tell Sanobar about my experiences as a school principal and ask her how she handles discipline of children. "The first week of school after vacation, the children do activities and learn about the rules. If children misbehave, I usually tell the teacher to deal with it herself, but in extreme cases they come to me, the principal," she answers.

"My relationship with the children is very academic, but if a child stops coming to school, I counsel with the parents. For example, if a girl stops coming to school because she gets her period and her parents say it is time for her to get married, I go to counsel with the parents and tell them to let her come to school. There is a lot of emphasis on girls getting married early. Once they have received their matric [matriculation], they have to stay home. But now a lot of girls are being able to study after matric. This is a change.

"Parents come to school to talk to the teacher about their child twice a year," Sanobar explains, "once each term. Usually it is only [for] academic problems, but sometimes other problems as well. Most parents come. If the parents do not agree with the teacher about the child, they can come to the principal.

"When parents have problems with their child, they come to ask me. This is a change from before. Initially, we did not have a good response. The parents would only come if the teacher insisted. In 2005, the teachers called a meeting for parents, but no one came. This was very disappointing. Then the teachers discovered that the parents were on different shifts, so they changed how to schedule the interviews. Parents were encouraged by this change and decided to come.

"The Annual Day at the end of the year—parents come to that. They have refreshments and little games for parents—very good response.

"Students get a lot of encouragement from such programs as these Science Camps . . . so I have encouraged a lot of children to come. For the Summer Science Camps, the teachers get paid, and so do I.

"It is good that you have come here," she concludes, "because you are experienced and our teachers can learn from your experience and also the prestige of you teachers coming here is always positive."

Our conversation ends, and I peek into the classrooms to see what is happening with the Summer Science Camp teacher training. Taffy is walking between tables of teachers and student volunteers, stopping to observe and ask questions as she goes. In her classroom, they are working on electricity, putting together simple series and parallel circuits. The student volunteers are interspersed among the teachers, and everyone is talking quietly, attaching wires to bulbs and batteries trying to make the bulbs light up. Each learner has a lab sheet to complete, as well as the necessary wires, batteries, and bulbs to test.

At one table, a student volunteer-learner stops Taffy and shows her his electrical series circuit. "Is this correct?" he asks.

Taffy doesn't answer directly, but instead asks, "Does it match the diagram on your student lab sheet? Do all the parts match?" When he answers in the negative, Taffy continues, "What else have you tried? What do you think?" Taffy has provided the necessary information and equipment for every learner to construct a series circuit and a parallel circuit. What she has *not* supplied is the correct answer.

Capitalizing on a "teachable moment," Taffy interrupts the work of the others engaged in the lesson and calls attention to the student volunteer's question: "Is this correct?"

"Are we really looking for *correct* answers?" Taffy asks. "Why are we asking you to mess with these wires and fill out these student lab sheets? Why do we have you working in small groups? Why do we encourage you to talk about your work together? Do we really want you to find *correct* answers?"

Taffy's point is that inquiry-based learning does not seek certain specific answers, but rather requires children to work together to solve problems and discover answers for themselves. The learning, Taffy emphasizes, is based on the *questions* the children ask, not on finding the correct answer. The teacher's role is to facilitate children's *questioning* rather than to tell them the answers.

The TCF teachers talk briefly about this strategy and nod in assent. This is something they have heard before in TCF training. But putting it into practice while they are learning new content is another matter. Taffy forges on: "Not only do you teachers need to master the content of new material in this training program," she reminds them, "you also need to become comfortable with and practice the methods of teaching required by inquiry learning."

The student volunteers look puzzled and a little bored. Finding the correct answer has been their modus operandi in mastering curriculum content in their colleges.[1] Inquiry learning as a teaching strategy is an idea that is new to most of them.

Across the courtyard in Karen's classroom, the primary teachers and their student volunteer assistants are busy constructing racers from small wire spools, rubber bands, toothpicks, and small washers. Karen has reminded everyone that there is no right or wrong answer. "A racer will be successful if it can travel at least one meter on its own," she says. "At the end of the morning, the racers will compete against each other to see which racer can go the longest distance in the shortest time."

As with Taffy, Karen is not providing correct answers. Her objective is to have the teachers and volunteers work together to design and test a racer that will meet the given parameters. There are many design possibilities, and she wants the teachers and volunteers to discover their own and share their findings with each other.

The wire spools that were so puzzling to the TCF staff during the procurement phase of the Summer Science Camp project finally make sense and are being put to good use. There is much talk and laughter in Karen's classroom as teachers and volunteers construct their racers, try them out on the floor of the classroom, and take them back to their desks for design modifications.

Taffy and Karen are good models as facilitators for critical thinking and discovery rather than dispensers of "correct" answers. I hope that the area managers and central office staff watching realize how productive the noise and semiconfusion in this kind of classroom is, and that they are impressed by how fully engaged the teachers and volunteers are with the projects.

Nancy and I meet in the supply room to cut patterns for the solar cookers for the final project the teachers will do in the morning. Nancy and I are roommates and have been having a running conversation about the news from the local paper and the changes we see in Pakistan. Nancy has been back to Pakistan twice since our early Peace Corps days in 1962 and has many observations about Pakistan's history and development over the years that I am interested in hearing.

"Partition was an extremely traumatic and deadly event," Nancy says. "In 1947, the borders had not been finalized, and there was almost no organized transition of police or military. The result was one million people dead, whole trainloads beheaded, neighbors killing neighbors, huge confusion and huge losses. And then, thirteen months after independence, the founding leader of Pakistan, Muhammad Ali Jinnah, died, and the country did not have a constitution for years.

"Throughout its relatively brief history as a nation," she continues, "Pakistan continues to harbor an overwhelming fear and suspicion that India is behind every possible sort of problem. The problem of disputed Kashmir is still festering. The guerrilla-type fighting over Kashmir for the last fifty years has been a training ground for many of the jihad and other guerrilla fighters of today.

"With help from India, East Pakistan broke off and became Bangladesh in 1971. We read rumors in the daily news, 'Karzai's Government Is Pro-India' and 'India Supports the Unrest in the North-West Frontier and Waziristan.' In the U.S., it is common to hear that Pakistan helped develop the Taliban as backup in case of a war with India, and Pakistanis fear that the U.S. is currently tilting towards India.

"In 1962 and even today, Pakistan sees every political event through a lens that says, 'India is our enemy and is actively trying to bring us down. We need the guerrillas; we need the nuclear bomb; we need to keep our troops along the Indian border.' And this is magnified by a general perspective that says behind every event there is a conspiracy, and if not led by India, then by Israel or the U.S. working for Israel.

"When we were here in 1962," Nancy recalls, "there was a huge effort in agricultural development: USAID, British and German technical experts, the Ford Foundation, Asia Foundation, Save the Children, CARE, and UNICEF and other nonprofits. It was a very promising time. Basic democracy local government was being introduced. . . . I felt I was among pioneers.

"By 1977, the first time I returned to Pakistan, the population had increased 50 percent, the government was in a civilian phase, and Zulfikar Ali Bhutto introduced socialist-type policies that many said benefited the rich more than the poor. . . . I visited a village near Khanewal[2] where the four sons of the zamindar showed us all of their new equipment and laughingly told us that the four of them had declared themselves the operating committee of the socialist village and had been given all sorts of benefits, including big tractors and other machinery from the government. The poor villagers, of course, probably didn't even know about this."

Nancy is quiet for a minute before continuing. "The mullahs objected to Bhutto's policies, so he gave them some of the things they wanted to make Pakistan into the mullah's vision of an Islamic state. It became a capital crime for a Muslim to be baptized. Many of the Christian schools that served the poor were closed, but some of the English-medium schools in major cities that served the upper class were allowed to continue.

"By 1977, agricultural production had increased enormously with the impact of the Green Revolution, and Pakistan had a surplus of wheat and rice. More young people were being educated in Urdu-medium schools. Community health programs were in place, including family planning programs. I visited the national office of the Girl Guides in Lahore and found an enthusiastic group of girls, all in their green uniform shalwar kameez with small white dupattas over their shoulders. They were packing for a camping trip in the mountains. One of the staff members told us that the girls loved to wear their uniforms to school, because then they did not have to wear the larger dupatta. Overall, things in Pakistan looked good and the standard of living was improving.

"In my last week in Pakistan in 1977," Nancy remembers, "as I was riding a late-night train from Islamabad to Peshawar, my two colleagues and I were rudely awakened by soldiers waving their guns at us. It was the middle of the night and General Zia-ul-Haq had staged a military coup. He was the second military ruler and not interested in leading the country towards a more modern democracy, but rather his version of a more strictly Islamic state. In 1979, he passed the Hudood Ordinance, which implemented changes such that in the courts, women were reduced to being half a person as a witness, and veils and conservative head coverings for women became the norm. There were prison sentences for people seen smoking or eating or drinking anything in the daytime during Ramadan, and other applications of Islamic law. The Federal Sharia Bench declared *rajm*, or stoning, to be un-Islamic; Zia-ul-Haq reconstituted the court, which then declared rajm as Islamic.

"Zia made the Secret Intelligence Service, ISI, into an extremely powerful, secretive, and independent agency that many say was closely involved with developing the Taliban and even today may carry out national policy. Zia-ul-Haq was killed along with the American ambassador in an airplane crash in 1988."

Nancy continues her reminiscences and tells me about her next visit to the country. "The last of the Soviet troops left Afghanistan in 1989, and when I came back to Pakistan in 1991, the country was still reeling from the effects of the war. Peshawar was an armed camp with pickup trucks carrying armed men, and there seemed to be Kalashnikovs [automatic weapons] everywhere. The population had grown so that I hardly recognized old landmarks around where I had lived. The University of Peshawar, dating back over a hundred years with a beautiful campus full of lovely gardens, was unkempt and almost empty. Almost all of the English-language books on the library shelves dated back to the 1960s when there had been U.S. aid for education.

"There were refugee camps holding thousands of people. The bazaars were full of arms and smuggled goods. We had to have a mujahideen guard come with us in our van when we went up to the Afghan border at the Khyber Pass. Along the way, we saw huge walled compounds belonging to different Afghan drug lords. The compounds were twenty or more acres with thirty-foot walls and armed guard towers along the tops. Clearly, these operations were not under any government control.

"The drug trade was having a huge impact on Pakistan, first in increase in drug use, addiction, and crime, and second, much of the profit was going to legitimate investments. It was said that Afghan drug lords controlled a large part of trucking and other industries. It is clearly in the drug lords' interest that the Pakistani national government be weak.

"In 1991, the population had increased another 50 percent, to 118 million, and the general economic conditions did not look as good as in 1977. In 1989, the USA pulled out all aid, citing the fact that Pakistan was developing a nuclear bomb. Bhutto began the bomb project in 1971 after the loss of East Pakistan and suspicion that India was developing a bomb. As long as the U.S. needed Pakistan to fight the Russians in Afghanistan, the USA ignored the bomb issue.

"A friend teaching at Karachi University in 1991 told me that she had hardly been able to teach because the university would be closed down day after day with tough guys flaunting their guns and demanding that this or that should or should not be taught, that women wear hijab, and that classes not be coed."

Nancy recalls revisiting the Girl Guide headquarters as she had in 1977. "There was a troop there getting ready to go on a camping trip in the mountains, but they all had their heads completely covered and they were not wearing their Girl Guide uniforms. Their leader told me that 'it's just the fashion.'

"During the 1990s, the government alternated between Benazir Bhutto and Nawaz Sharif. Both of these governments had corruption problems. In education, the patronage system gave teaching jobs to people who knew they didn't even have to show up at school. The 1990s are called the "lost decade" by the 2009 World Bank report on education in the Punjab. General Musharraf's military takeover in 1999 was welcomed by many."

Now Nancy compares those past visits to her current one. "In 2009, the population in Pakistan is close to 180 million people, 20 million in Karachi alone. There are huge new developments of high-rise apartments and condos, large wealthy homes, and extremely crowded slums.

"Relations with India have been more normalized, and cable TV has Indian networks. Although women on the streets are more covered and modest than at any time since the beginning of the country, people go home to TV shows from outside Pakistan that show scantily clad women in high dramas of love and mayhem."

Nancy and I both remember the plethora of movie houses and their colorful billboards and blaring music of the 1960s. "The number of movie houses has greatly decreased, but the video stores are everywhere. American movies are for rent and purchase, and everyone recommends the film *Charlie Wilson's War*," she concludes with an ironic chuckle.

We decide to keep a list of all the changes we have seen in Pakistan. Nancy, by far, has the most comprehensive catalog.

The next morning, our last at Goth Dhani Bux, we stow our luggage for the midafternoon flight to Lahore and immediately begin to assist the teachers and student volunteers with their end-of-training activities.

One group is running small wooden cars down a four-meter (thirteen-foot) wooden ramp covered with long strips of paper. Each car is equipped with a plastic bottle cap that has a hole in its center to allow colored water to drip onto the paper at equal time intervals as the car rolls down the plank. This is the most exciting portion of an activity whose purpose is for learners to represent the definitions of speed and acceleration in a concrete way and then create bar graphs to illustrate the difference between a car traveling along a flat surface at a constant speed and one accelerating down an inclined surface. Some cars veer off their ramps; others leave big blotches of colored water on their respective papers. But every teacher-learner is actively engaged and is experiencing the same kinds of difficulties and successes her pupils will face during the Summer Science Camps.

The student volunteer-learners seem to be having the most fun of all. One young man tells me that he has never participated in these kinds of activities and, though he knew the definitions of both speed and acceleration, he never fully understood them until now.

"*Shabash!*" I say. "Good show!"

Finally, as our last activity, we help the teachers assemble solar cookers and set them around the courtyard in the sun. The teachers place a small jar of water inside each oven, along with a control jar of water outside, and record the changing temperatures at ten-minute intervals to see which jar of water will boil first.

The teachers are enjoying this activity, and I overhear quiet debates about shadows, angles of the sun's rays, and reasonable times for water to boil. I am reminded, again, of my training days in Sheikhupura, and the lady workers' struggles to build smokeless chulas and make them work.

As I move among the teachers, snapping photos with my digital camera, several teachers reach for their cell phones to take *my* picture. In my Sheikhupura days, I had to coax women to let me photograph them with my thirty-five-millimeter camera, and the women never saw their images. Today, reciprocal instant imaging is another reminder of the modern changes that have come to Pakistan.

During the last hour of the morning, our training team gathers the teachers and volunteers together for some final words about inquiry-based learning, the science activities, and any questions or comments still lingering. Karen reminds everyone: "Science is a way of approaching problems, rather than memorizing facts and figures. The kinds of experiences you have just had with science allowed you to experience the thinking and working process that a scientist or engineer uses when looking for answers to problems. This is the kind of learning that is most valuable to developing critical thinking skills and confidence.

"The key ingredients to success as inquiry-based teachers," Karen concludes, "will be in preparing your classrooms so that students can access materials and actively participate in each lesson. The more care you spend in setup and organization, the smoother the process will be with children. Rather than telling the children what to look for or which answers are *correct*, your job is to facilitate children's *questions*."

As the TCF vans arrive to take us to the airport, the schoolyard volume swells with laughter, hugs, and wishes for a safe journey. Our team is on the way to Lahore to repeat the Summer Science Camp training with teachers and student volunteers there.

The teachers we have just trained in Karachi will reconvene at Goth Dhani Bux and another TCF school the following week when the Summer Science Camps begin. Karen and Sofia will return to Karachi at the end of the Lahore training to assist them. Taffy, Nancy, and I will remain in Lahore to assist the teachers in three Summer Science Camps there. At the end of the summer, our team will meet in Karachi to debrief with the TCF central office training staff and to observe regular TCF classes in the new school term.

But for the moment, I am preoccupied with leave-taking and last-minute travel preparation. I am looking forward to returning to Lahore, the city where I spent so much of my time as a Peace Corps Volunteer, and am eager to visit my village, Dhamke, only a few miles outside the city, and Sheikhupura, the former headquarters of my lady workers' Village Aid project.

I am ever closer to "going home again."

CHAPTER 13

$\sim$

Arrival in Lahore, 2009

In 1962, Allama Iqbal International Airport was brand new and boasted of its ability to handle aircraft as large as the Boeing 747. I remember the airport as a dusty field of parked planes that passengers had to walk around to reach the hall that served as the terminal. The terminal itself always seemed to be crammed with bearers carrying suitcases on their heads or pushing baggage wagons, and crowds of noisy hawkers, beggars, and flower *wallahs* selling garlands of marigolds. I remember the din under the vaulted ceiling, the flies, and the suffocating sweat-filled heat.

All this is changed in 2009. The new Allama Iqbal International Airport, inaugurated in 2003, is the second largest airport in Pakistan. In addition to the old terminal, now used exclusively for the annual hajj passengers, there is a new air-conditioned terminal used for overseas and domestic flights, and an airfield with a brand new runway and parking for thirty-two jets. The new terminal has VIP lounges with wireless Internet for first- and business-class passengers, duty-free shops, restaurants, cafés, ice cream parlors, confectionery shops, book and toy stores, souvenir shops, and flat-screen televisions that show flight times in both Urdu and English.

Complimentary trolleys and uniformed fixed-price porters have replaced the baggage wagons and bearers.[1] The 1962-era dusty walk across the airfield has been replaced by seven air bridges that dock onto the aircraft during departures and arrivals. A new project to expand the immigration and customs hall and the international and domestic arrival and departure halls is under way and will double the number of check-in and immigration counters when it is completed in 2010.

Today's main terminal has two prayer rooms—one for women, the other for men—both appropriately decorated to create the right setting for Muslim prayers, and both with ablution places.[2] I do not remember prayer rooms in Pakistani airports in the 1960s, and in the Lahore of 2009, I begin to feel the difference of the omnipresence of Islamic law. For instance, though we have no liquor or beer to declare, I read that "Import of beer or liquor is not allowed, though non-Muslim foreign tourists can purchase liquor from an authorized vendor against a permit. . . . Hotels having a liquor-vending license can sell beer or liquor to non-Muslim foreign tourists staying in the hotel but drinking in public places is prohibited." In the 1960s, beer and liquor flowed freely in the restaurants and lounges of city hotels and desi country beer was easily obtained in the bazaar.

As at our arrival in Karachi, several TCF drivers in white Suzuki vans meet us at the terminal entrance. Karen and Sofia are met by their relatives and plan to stay with them while they are in Lahore. For the five days of teacher training, Taffy, Nancy, and I will stay at a hotel often used by TCF workers, located at Liberty Market in the heart of Gulberg. After the teacher-training phase of our assignment, the three of us will move to the residential Gymkhana Club in a quieter neighborhood several city blocks from the hotel.

The traffic confusion on Lahore streets is similar to that in Karachi. When we arrive at the Best Westin (yes, Best Westin) Hotel, our driver, Illyas, escorts the three of us into the lobby. We are greeted by a suave young Pakistani desk clerk in a shiny black business suit and highly polished shoes. He answers our questions about restaurants, shopping, and Internet service in superb English, inflected with Punjabi and Urdu cadence and the inevitable Pakistani tag question, "*Why* not?"

I love it!

After the first of many suppers of chapatis and *sagh-gosht*, a spicy dish of spinach and meat, Taffy, Nancy, and I decide to take a sunset stroll through the Liberty Market across the road from our hotel. For me, it is a walk down Memory Lane or, rather, an excursion through the familiar loud, colorful, pungent, smoky, blurred cacophony of Lahore city life at its teeming summer height.

As we leave the hotel's restaurant, a beggar woman with a baby on her hip, a deformed old man, and several wiry young children approach me for baksheesh. I remember their gestures: the woman touches her mouth and the mouth of her child with her dirty dupatta, the old man pleads through rheumy eyes and outstretched hand, the young boys grin and elbow closer asking to carry my bag or lead me to a "very good shopping." I am suddenly awkward and mortified, as discomfited and dismayed now as I ever was as a young Peace Corps Volunteer. I know I cannot possibly give these people what they most need and worry that if I give to these few, I will soon be surrounded and inundated by many others. I give a coin to the woman and old man, shake my head at the boys' requests, and keep moving.

Just as I catch up with Taffy and Nancy, the street is plunged into blackness. Load shedding. Stunning. Disorienting. However, within minutes, a chorus of unmuffled gasoline-powered generators tunes up and fills the air with a staccato drone, dimmer, blurrier lights, and diesel fumes.

The market becomes a backdrop for performance art and street theater. We stop to watch a trained goat and monkey perform tricks of balance and agility on each other's backs. We walk under awnings draped with fabric, cheap toys, gilded and glittering *shadi* wedding decorations, ready-made shalwar kameez, Western shirts for men, T-shirts emblazoned with sports logos for boys, dresses, hats, and tiny sandals for babies. We pause beside wagons loaded with fruit neatly piled in descending-order pyramids and quickly pass stalls laden with radios, CDs, wristwatches, embroidery, costume jewelry, and cheap flip-flop *chapli* sandals. We carefully consider the wares of the two-wheeled-cart wallahs: ice cream, lemonade, and fruit drinks of every color and description. Several young entrepreneurs shoot firecracker-propelled miniature parachutes into the sky, and we watch these drop gracefully to our feet.

The shops are reopening for the evening trade, and it feels like a weekend even though it is really a Wednesday night in the middle of the workweek. The mood of the crowd is jovial, and though there are many more men than women and no other Western women, I feel very comfortable and safe strolling along the marketplace, ducking into shops, and bargaining for a *kurta* shirt for my grandson. The moon is a hazy orange ball overhead, and the night feels like black velvet against my skin. I remember this Lahore.

In the morning, our driver Illyas arrives early for our trip to the TCF secondary school in Phengali II, an impoverished section of Lahore and the teacher-training site for the Lahore Summer Science Camps. But first, we stop at the Lahore TCF head office in Model Town to meet our local TCF support staff and pick up last-minute supplies for the training session that will begin after lunch.

Like the Peace Corps office in 1962, the TCF office is housed in a former residence behind high walls on a tree-lined street. When we pull into the parking lot, I am again transported back in time. Even though small white vans replace the Land Rovers and jeeps of the 1960s, this courtyard is the same: a dusty square of hard-packed dirt under low-hanging tree branches alive with birdcall and laden with flowering vines.

Inside the building, the entry hall is full of activity. Three men sit at a reception desk and shout into cell phones; several other men perch on benches along the walls. The tiled floor is piled with boxes of supplies waiting for transport to the TCF English-Language and Science Camps around Lahore. Several dozen young men and women, student volunteers for these camps, mill about, waiting patiently for similar transport. I overhear the students making dates for evening activities, much as we did as young Peace Corps Volunteers when we met at our office to collect mail and catch up with each other before returning to our assignments. Now, as then, the energy is contagious.

Sanober Adeel, the assistant manager of volunteers and the woman responsible for procuring and organizing all the supplies for our Lahore Science Camps, invites Taffy, Nancy, and me into a suite of interior rooms. I am impressed with her calm manner and efficiency. She knows the exact content of each cardboard box in the hallway, where it came from, and when it will be delivered to its respective school site. I am amazed at Sanober's success in finding all the supplies for the Science Camps and doubly amazed that these supplies are boxed and ready to be transported so that the teachers will have them to use when the camps begin. This kind of efficiency and ease of transportation, this sense of responsibility and commitment to the job, would have been a miracle in the 1960s, I think. It would have made a real difference to the success and sustainability of my lady workers' training programs in Sheikhupura, I am sure. I see this efficiency as a big change in Pakistan.

We continue our tour of the TCF offices. The main room is lined with desks and computers, all facing each other, arranged as the central office at TCF headquarters in Karachi is arranged, though on a much smaller scale. Several women dressed in shalwar kameez come forward to greet us. One of the women is Neelam Ernest, the regional manager for education and our liaison with the Lahore TCF office for the next two weeks. Neelam is very polite and eager to be helpful. She tells me that she knows I want to visit Sheikhupura and my village, Dhamke, while we are in Lahore and that she will be delighted to accompany me. I am delighted, as well.

Behind the large space of the main office, a former drawing room houses the office of Col. Muhammad Anwar Awan, the regional manager of Lahore North. Upstairs in a former bedroom is the shared office of the two area managers for the Lahore Region, Maj. Ali Sher and Maj. Naeem Ullah Khan. I ask Neelam if she can arrange interviews with these managers in the next few days, and she tells me that they can meet with me after the teacher-training session this afternoon.

I am astonished to get an appointment so quickly. My Peace Corps experience of making appointments that happened only after days of waiting, cajoling, or baksheesh—if they happened at all—make me doubtful. However, my experiences thus far with TCF management lead me to expect commitment. Times have changed. This time, I suspect, the appointments will be honored.

Taffy, Nancy, Sanober, and I leave for the Science Camp teacher-training site at Phengali II, on the outskirts of Lahore. At first, the highway is tree lined and divided by a grassy esplanade, but as we go farther and farther from the center of the city, the road widens and becomes a rather barren four-lane highway.[3]

The flat farmland and canal system that I remember from my Peace Corps days is gradually being turned into high-rise neighborhoods and multiple-story apartment buildings and shopping areas. Old men on bicycles ride on the side of the road and there are a few animal-drawn wagons, but by and large, motorcycles, buses, small vans, and private cars are the predominant form of transportation. I still have not seen a tonga, the major transport of my earlier Peace Corps days.

As in Karachi, I sit in the front seat of the TCF car to take advantage of the seatbelt, the only one provided to someone besides the driver. Our car travels fast along the highway, and I close my eyes every time we approach another vehicle. Oncoming traffic heads straight toward us, at or above our own speed, until the last second when one of the drivers pulls away. It is nerve-wracking to watch Illyas zigzag between the slender markers placed in the roadway to reduce speed. To me, the markers seem more of a challenge than a cautionary reminder. Illyas is a good driver, however, and he avoids them and vehicular disasters with the skill and enthusiasm of a racecar driver.

We speed on past fields green and lush with corn and wheat. The Punjab is the breadbasket of the country, and the new concrete neighborhoods abut the old fields in stark contrast.

Some things have only partly changed outside Lahore, I notice. Small boys still jump into the canals along the roadways—though these days the boys wear shorts—and cows are still driven through the side streets in herds. Old men still sit at the side of the road on their charpoys, though present-day charpoys are webbed with brightly colored plastic strips instead of old-fashioned lumpy rope.

The TCF secondary school in Phengali II is a sanctuary. The doors open onto a small yard for vans and, up a few steps, to an open quadrangle of green grass, flowering shrubs, and small trees surrounded by two levels of airy classrooms. At the far end of the quadrangle, an outdoor stage serves as a gathering area for children and teachers. There is a small canteen, a library, and several rooms designated for science labs and computers. Though similar in design to the school in Goth Dhani Bux, this school, built in 2004, is larger and feels more spacious and open to the fields and trees outside its walls.

The classrooms are equipped with double desks and a chair for every student. Blackboards and a teacher's desk are in the front of each classroom, and overhead fans and fluorescent lights adorn the ceilings. Every classroom has a wall of windows on the outside and on the inner courtyard side. Luckily, the windows open for cross-ventilation, because just as we arrive, load shedding claims the electric power for the overhead fans. The heat in the classrooms, in spite of the cross-ventilation, becomes intense.

Fakhra Khan, principal of the Phengali II school, greets us. Her shalwar kameez is freshly pressed and fashionably coordinated. I am aware of my wet and wilted appearance. My shalwar kameez, donned fresh only hours earlier, sticks to my back and chest like a second wrinkled skin.

We spend the morning setting up the classroom for the first meeting of the Lahore teachers and student volunteers. As at the first day of training in Karachi, Taffy and Karen will team-teach this first session, and Nancy and I will observe, assist, and retrieve supplies from the library-turned-supply-room across the courtyard.

Before the training day begins, however, the sky darkens to leaden gray and a breeze quickens to gust and whoosh through the open windows, covering the floors first with dust. Then, suddenly, horizontal sheets of water race through the windows. The parking lot becomes a pool, pelted faster and faster by drops of rain. But soon the intensity of the rain begins to ebb, and the pool is reduced to puddles of brown water and thick oozing mud. Within twenty minutes, the rain is gone and the sun is once again solidly overhead, bright and hot as ever. The rainy respite from the heat reminds me, once again, of Dhamke.

June 29, 1963
Dhamke
There was a fierce storm last night. It wrecked the wires we had just strung up for Rana's electricity—again. It started out as a dust storm but ended up thundering and lightning and raining! We cowered under our dupattas until the dust quit, but then Saroya and I pulled our charpoys onto the roof. We got soaked in the rain but the wind was wonderful and I was almost cold. It felt great! We slept on the roof

all night. In the morning my courtyard was full of mud and the alley
in front of the house a mucky, slimy, slippery mess of gunk. Who
cares??? The rains have begun. It's finally cool!!![4]

Just past noon in the 2009 rain-soaked courtyard, the TCF vans begin to
arrive, bringing fifteen teachers, two principals, and twenty-seven student
volunteers to the first session of Science Camp training. As in Karachi,
the classroom, designed for thirty students, is overflowing. Teachers and
student volunteers cluster at desks pulled to the center of the room to form
tables. The Lahore training managers watch from chairs set around the edge
of the room.

Karen begins the session by discussing the goals of the training. She explains the teaching strategies of inquiry learning and the ways to set up the
classrooms for optimal exploration and participation of every learner.

The teachers are polite and attentive. The student volunteers, like their
counterparts in Karachi on the first day of training, seem a little bored and
above it all. At the break, I am amused to hear one of the young male volunteers ask for permission to wear denim blue jeans to the Summer Science
Camps. The student volunteers have been instructed to wear loose-fitting
Punjabi clothing as appropriate to the season and their status as teaching
assistants. But this college student laments that his blue jeans are more comfortable and allow him to be "more relaxed."

I can't think of anything hotter in this temperature than long, heavy
denim jeans but refrain from expressing my uncool opinion. Fashion trumps
comfort when you are young, I remember, and these Pakistani students are
no different than the students who wanted to practice-teach in flip-flops and
tank tops in freezing February temperatures at my university. My students
were willing to be cold to be hot. The Pakistani students are willing to be
hot to be cool. They all make me laugh.

At the end of the training afternoon, I return to the TCF office in Lahore to
talk with Colonel Muhammad Anwar Awan, the Lahore Region manager,
and the two Lahore area managers, Major Naeem and Major Ali Sher. Taffy
and Nancy go back to the hotel to refresh.

Colonel Anwar is gracious and affable and begins our interview by describing TCF's regional system to me. "TCF is divided into four regions,"
he says. "Two are in Karachi: one in the city and surrounding areas, and
the other is in Sindh. Lahore Region covers most of the western Punjab
Province: to Gujrat and the Jhlum River, Sheikhupura, Faisalabad, and all of
Lahore. The fourth region is in Islamabad. Another regional manager looks

after the northwest portion of Punjab, including Islamabad, the Frontier, and a portion of Azad Kashmir."

The colonel describes himself as "one of those lucky people that is an original member of TCF." He goes on: "We started with three schools in the Punjab in 1996. There is no looking back. Now I have 156 schools to look after. In our system, all schools start with primary. Matter of fact, when we have two or three primary schools, and the kids are about to graduate out of class five, we start to look around for a place for a secondary school so that all these kids from the primary cluster can go on.

"In Lahore Region, we now have 17 secondary, 3 higher secondary, and 136 primary schools. . . . We are trying to go to the new areas in the southern Punjab like the Khanewal area and explore areas where people have less education. More than 21,000 children are coming to our schools in Lahore region."

In the middle of our interview, another dust storm suddenly gathers momentum outside the building. Tree branches struggle against the wind, and leaves are pried loose and whip against the windows. Thunder, lightning, and rain follow in quick succession, and again the parking lot outside turns to a sea of mud. Inside the building, all work has halted, computers are down, and it is dark. No one seems to mind, however, although the storm diverts the colonel's attention and stops my interview.

I climb the stairs looking for the two majors and find them in their joint office space, waiting for the storm to subside. I introduce myself and tell them a little about my experience as a Peace Corps Volunteer in the Punjab in the 1960s. I am accustomed to most of the people I interview being at least twenty years younger than I am and therefore being unable to relate to the Pakistan of the early 1960s. These two are both in this age category. In addition, they share the office space, sit side by side at adjacent desks, and take turns answering me. I decide to interview them together.

I ask them about themselves and their responsibilities at TCF.

"I came straight to TCF Lahore from the military in 2007, because my family is in Lahore and I did not want to go to Karachi," says Major Naeem. "I served in military for several years, and I came to TCF because my military training was helpful. They were trying to set up the area, and I wanted to do something positive with my life and have a change. When I came here, there was one lady in charge of the entire area. One of the schools was too far away, and she could not reach it very often. Our military training helps us to go to faraway places; we can travel and can get to places not possible for the others. And we can convince people to do things that ordinary people cannot."

Major Ali Sher then provides his background. "In military, I was an educationist and taught in that department. After retiring, at first I taught in Peshawar, then came to Lahore after five or six years and then joined TCF. I came to TCF in 2006, first to Khanewal District for one and a half years before being posted to Lahore. I came to the job because I saw an advertisement and had helpful military contacts."

Remembering my conversation with Asad Ayub Ahmad, the CEO in Karachi, I ask the majors if there is ever any misunderstanding between military-trained managers and others at TCF. "No, there is no problem," they insist. "It is a marriage, and we serve different aspects of TCF. We work as a team." One adds, "We work under regional managers and do not have much to do with head office in Karachi."

Naeem and Ali describe their responsibilities as area managers in a team-like way, helping each other to present a clear description. "We visit each school once a month, and when we visit a school, we have several procedures of what we do: check their accounts, see their registration, check their attendance. And then we are partly responsible for the education also. If I go to a school and ask the principal, 'What is your problem?' and she comes up with a problem such as 'I have no textbook,' . . . my job is to get her a textbook through the TCF Education Department."

Naeem continues: "I tell the regional manager, so I keep track of what each principal has asked for and help her to get it. I check the building, whether it is being maintained, check the bathrooms that they are clean, check the classrooms, and make sure the teacher is teaching according to the program, the lesson plan. One time, the principal reported some theft, so I went to the police and tried to solve the problem."

"And we have to see that teachers are on time and that the vehicles are one time. I look after the vehicles that are for my schools," Ali Sher adds.

I ask a how they evaluate teachers.

"We are responsible that the teachers teach according to the lesson plan and teach in such a manner that it is easy for students to follow," Naeem answers. "We sit in the classroom and observe, and then we ask the principal also for her feedback on how to sort them out. If a principal is having some problems with a teacher, I counsel the teacher. If I have a complaint about a teacher from a principal, then I interview them separately and then I will advise her and monitor her.

"Has the teacher improved? Has she followed my advice? Or is she still persisting in her ways? If I am not satisfied, then I will give the teacher an advisory note and things like that, and if that doesn't work, then I will inform the regional manager and write a report that I have advised her and guided her but she is not responding."

Are teachers ever fired or transferred?

"Actually, firing is not an option," says Ali Sher, "because we spend so much time and effort and money in training them, and if a teacher has put in two or three years . . . firing is not a preferred option. Firing would be done only when all other things have failed. We don't like to fire teachers. But it happens. There are good and bad people out there. Sometimes we have to keep on visiting, but we prefer not to fire because we then have to train a new person."

When I ask what happens if a teacher is rough with a child, I get a very agitated response from both men. "There is no chance for that to happen!" they answer at the same time. "It is against TCF policy. Beating is totally forbidden. There is no slapping, either. They don't dare. The policy is very clear. There is no second chance. If a teacher hits a child, then she goes home."

My next question is about how new teachers learn TCF policies.

"There are rules written in Urdu and also in English. The principals have a manual, but not the teachers. The area managers have no manual, but a job description. We are training principals for two days. The principal is our partner. Principals sometimes have a university degree, but they are usually a teacher who has been there for the last ten or twelve years. Mostly they teach the teachers and show them how to dress and how to act."

I ask what the majors see as the future of education in Pakistan and whether TCF will ever take the place of government schools. Their response is interesting.

"No! TCF will never take over for the government schools," answers Naeem. "The government schools have been here for the last sixty years, and there are many thousands of government schools. TCF has only six hundred schools.

"TCF schools go to areas where there is no other school, to poor areas neglected by the government. They are far away from the city and are for poor people. The standard of education is very satisfactory in TCF schools—equal to Beacon or Lahore Grammar School.[5] Not so in government schools.

"Our teachers are trained teachers, and people know that it is a good facility and we guide the children, and parents come to the school for parent-teacher meetings and . . . to ask progress of their children. Parents know children get more education at TCF and they mend their ways and change their habits."

"Education has come a long way," adds Ali Sher. "Now people are aware that they should want to progress, and they know that to have progress in everything, they have to get education. This is a change.

"For example, one girl was very brilliant, so her parents said she can go to tenth grade and no more. So the principal went to her father, and he said, OK, I'll send her for one more year, and he sent her for a third year and again she has got good marks, so she convinced her father to give her one more year and he did. She graduated third in Lahore and received several prizes and then her father was very proud. The family got much attention from Karachi and I think the girl is going to a college now.

"There are so many good stories about TCF," he concludes.

What has influenced people to send their daughters to school? I ask.

"Parents will send their daughters to TCF schools but not to any other schools because there are female teachers, the schools are close to their homes, and the girls do not have to go so far away. If there is no TCF school available, they don't send them," Naeem answers.

"It is more word of mouth," observes Ali. "Once families send their daughters to school, they see that she is a better person now and she is taking some changes in the house and better hygiene. . . . They see children growing up better, so they make an investment. Education is having an impact; the school has brought up the children.

"TCF has educated eighty thousand students, the ones who have been neglected. We don't refuse anybody even if they don't have money to pay. We have scholarships. Now there are students who are coming back and getting jobs at TCF, and some 10 percent are going to college and to other things. The children feel that they can now achieve some other possibility."

"We are very happy to have joined TCF," both men agree in conclusion. "At TCF, it is a very safe feeling, and mentally we are satisfied."

"At the end of my day, I am happy," adds Naeem. "I have done something more with my life than only a job."

I leave the majors and the TCF office and return to the Best Westin eager to change clothes and get some exercise. However, the hotel is situated on a busy street of broken sidewalks and harrowing traffic. There is no exercise room, and my usual run of five or six miles is impossible. Instead, Taffy and I decide to take a walk and try to regain a sense of the city we once knew so well.

Crossing the street without being run over by a motorcycle, car, bus, or truck or causing them to collide into each other is a major accomplishment in today's Lahore, we discover. When the traffic lights change, everyone surges forward. Vehicles in the turn lanes turn—or go straight ahead; vehicles in the main traffic lanes go straight ahead, or turn one way or the other. The system seems capricious and, for the two of us trying to navigate it, terrifying.

Taffy and I wait at the curb through several traffic light changes. Finally a rickshaw driver on the side of the street shouts, "*Chal-lo!*"—Get going! We clutch each other's arm and make a dash for it, reaching the concrete buffer in the middle of the street. Cars, scooters, motor rickshaws, taxis, and buses all whiz by. We wait a long time for a break in the flow, stranded on the median strip.

At the next quasi-opportunity, we grab hands again and sprint to the far side of the boulevard. Breathless, we shout with exhilaration at our success—and narrowly miss being hit by a motor scooter that has decided to take its chances on the sidewalk.

We continue on and soon hear loud chanting perforated by cheers. A crowd of young men emerges from a park across the road from us. They are marching to protest load shedding and are shouting in unison and raising their fists in the air. As their numbers grow, we notice cars begin to turn around and vacate the street. The boulevard empties, and we are better able to see the action. The danger of the whizzing traffic is replaced by the potential danger of protesters becoming an unruly mob. There are no other pedestrians on our side of the street and no women at all.

Several young men set fire to a pile of rubber tires. The stench is distinctive, and the smoke blackens the already heavy air. Taffy wants to cross the road to get a closer look, but I am chicken. I do not feel threatened, but I am aware of our very American faces and our gender, and I do not want to make myself any more visible or provoke any kind of incident. I am content to walk less conspicuously, I hope, on the other side of the street.

The crowd grows larger as we walk, and by the time we reach the Best Westin, a rally has spontaneously taken over the intersection in front of our hotel. We now have ringside seats to more tire burning and louder chanting, but our venue is more secure. Uniformed police also watch from the sidelines, but emotions do not escalate and eventually the crowd evaporates into the coffeehouses and tea stalls on the side streets.

It has been a day of reentry, reminiscing, and revelation. I love being back in Lahore. But I am ready to rest.

Children at Dhamke social center, 1962

Children in TCF kindergarten class, 2009

Dhamke from canal, 1962

Dhamke from canal, 2009

Dhamke bus stop, 1962

Dhamke bus stop, 2009

In Leslie's house and lane, 1962

In Leslie's house and lane, 2009

Jerry, Bivi-gee, and Envir, 1962

Leslie, Jerry, and Jerry's wife, 2009

Rana's nephew, 1962

Rana's nephew, 2009

Leslie in Eid finery, 1962

Leslie in the doorway to her Dhamke social center, 2009

Leslie and village children, 1962

Dhamke children, 2009

Leslie and some children she worked with, 1962

TCF Summer Science Camp students and teacher, 2009

Women at Dhamke social center, 1962

Leslie interviewing TCF ayahs, 2009

CHAPTER 14

~

Training in Lahore, 2009

Our first full day of teacher training in Lahore begins with an unexpected fizzle, at least for the primary teachers. They and their student volunteers gather in one classroom so that Karen can demonstrate a dramatic introductory activity for "States of Matter," their first lesson. Nancy and I distribute the carefully prepared lesson plans and student lab sheets to each teacher and student volunteer.

"First, be sure you have done the activity at least a day before you do it with the students and are familiar with the equipment," Karen begins. "Think about the procedures that might be difficult for the students, and think of ways you can help them through things that are difficult. It is important to be in your classroom early enough to have all the equipment arranged for easy student access."

As in Karachi, the classroom is set up with desks pushed together and all the materials needed for the lesson in the center of the desks. Karen explains that all the supplies for the summer camps will be available in a central storage area in each school and emphasizes that all materials should be organized and easy to find so that classrooms can be set up before class begins.

She continues: "Today we are going to do some interesting experiments that will help us understand more about the natural world. First I will do a demonstration for you that you must watch very carefully. You will then work independently making measurements and observations with your group."

The teachers and student volunteers break into small groups to explore the materials on each table for the first activity: some baking soda, unflavored gelatin, vinegar, small measuring spoons, a clear plastic cup. When they have finished touching, smelling, and looking closely at each item, Karen holds up each and asks: "What state of matter is this?" She helps them describe and identify whether each is a solid, liquid, or gas.

Next, Karen puts a half teaspoon each of alum, baking soda, and unflavored gelatin into a clear plastic cup. Everyone agrees that the cup is holding solids. Karen measures the height of the materials in the cup and records the number.

Karen now adds two tablespoons of vinegar and swirls the cup gently. She holds it up so that everyone can see the expected reaction—foam rising to the top of the cup to show that the solid has changed to a gas after the liquid was added—but nothing much happens.

When Karen did this demonstration for the Karachi teachers and students, the foam spilled out of the cup and all over the table. The Karachi teachers and students had similar results with their own experiments.

Not so in Lahore. Enough foam forms in Karen's cup so that she can make a measurement and the lesson can continue. But the drama is lost, and Karen is clearly baffled. The student volunteers, particularly the males, seem unimpressed.

At the midmorning break, I notice that the student volunteers have banded together and separated themselves from the teachers. As in Karachi, the young men are majoring in physics, chemistry, or engineering, and the young women are studying economics or business. All of them are about the age I was when I first came to Pakistan, and they seem to have the same veneer of bravado I remember about myself. I am curious about why they are volunteering their time in such hot conditions when they could be enjoying their summer vacation elsewhere, so I ask them about it.

"We are encouraged to do volunteer work by our college program," one young man tells me. "But for me, it is the first time I am in a school such as this. I think it will be interesting to show the children about science."

I discover that for most of the volunteers, it is their first experience in a slum school, and most are a little anxious about working with disadvantaged children. I tell the volunteers that I admire their spirit of adventure. I also admire TCF for giving them the opportunity to view another side of Pakistan and to participate in its change.

We trainers have other things on our minds, however. We wonder, along with Karen, why her first States of Matter demonstration fizzled, or rather, fizzled so little. When Karen instructed the teachers and students to observe by touching, smelling, and looking at the powders, she deliberately disallowed tasting as another way to observe. Had Karen tasted the raw materials, she would have discovered that instead of ordering baking *soda*, Sanober Adeel had ordered baking *powder* as one of the solids to be changed by adding the liquid, vinegar.

Both baking soda and baking powder are white and chalky-looking, but their chemical properties are slightly different. Baking soda is sodium bicarbonate, an alkaline salt used as a leavening agent in effervescent drinks and fire extinguishers; baking powder is a mixture of starch, acid, and only a trace of sodium bicarbonate and is used to make cakes and dough rise. The small amount of sodium bicarbonate in baking powder caused Karen's foam to rise in the plastic cup, but only by a fraction, making her demonstration far less dramatic than she had anticipated.

After the break, when training resumes, everyone is more relaxed. The primary teachers and student volunteers continue with a lesson to identify clay and aluminum shapes that will float in water. I stroll among the teachers and students volunteers, observing their efforts to determine the characteristics of objects that float and those that sink and to determine the amount of cargo that can be carried on floating containers of different materials and shapes. Karen's classroom hums with activity and exclamations of dismay when a clay boat sinks or surprise when one is able to support a cargo load of three hundred paper clips.

Across the courtyard, Taffy is conducting a lesson called "Mystery Powders" with the secondary teachers and their student volunteers. Taffy has paired the student volunteers with TCF teachers and deliberately desegregated all-male and all-female groups.

In Punjab Province, after the primary level, boys and girls are separated into same-gender schools. Most of the young men volunteers are accustomed to taking the lead in mixed-gender situations, even when they are the younger, less-experienced members of the group. By pairing young male volunteers with more experienced TCF female teachers, Taffy hopes to establish that the female teachers are the leaders and their male volunteers are the assistants.

In Taffy's classroom, the teacher-student pairs begin testing the physical and chemical properties of baking soda, cornstarch, salt, sugar, and plaster of paris. They will use the data they collect during these tests to identify an unknown substance, a mixture of two of the known substances. For these secondary teachers, baking soda is not an issue, and Taffy is able to proceed with her lesson as planned.

As Taffy circulates around the room answering procedural questions, she emphasizes that teachers should not tell their students what answer they are supposed to find. "When one of your children gets a result that you know is incorrect, have her explain exactly what she did. Chances are, she made a procedural error. Tell her to redo the test and make a suggestion about the procedure that will allow her to get the desired result. But, do *not* tell her what she *should* see."

Again, as she did in Karachi, Taffy is articulating the teaching strategies for inquiry learning. And again, the teachers nod in assent and recognition of a TCF teaching strategy they have heard before. Taffy's classroom is alive with talk and productive questioning. I notice that the female teachers are quietly leading their student volunteers.

At the end of the day, despite the earlier baking soda issue, we are greatly encouraged by the determination and goodwill of the teachers and student volunteers in Lahore. We look forward to the final training day in the morning and then will have the weekend to refresh ourselves before the Summer Science Camps begin.

That evening, Taffy and I walk through narrow streets congested with pedestrians, cars, and motorcycles and into a dark building set back from the street. We climb three flights of stairs to a shadowy hallway leading to the office of one of the local distributors of science materials with whom Sanober had contracted. Load shedding has disrupted the flow of electricity in this part of the city, and the air is stifling. I am instantly drenched in perspiration.

Rafique Ayub, the patriarch of the science supply company, is expecting us. His eldest son leads us to his office through a passageway of desks piled with ledgers, papers, and well-thumbed catalogues. Ayub greets us effusively and offers bottled water, juice, tea, and biscuits and insists that we accept. He is dressed in traditional Punjabi shalwar and kurta and looks comfortable and relaxed. I can see that, under his desk, his feet are bare and, hot as I am, I feel at home in his surroundings. I sit back to appreciate the familiar ambiance of conversation and hospitality.

Taffy asks about the availability of inexpensive pan balances for the TCF children to use in their classrooms. Rafique assures her that he has sent someone to fetch such a balance from his storeroom in the old bazaar of Anarkali and it is "just now coming."

While we wait, Rafique entertains us by pointing out the finer points of a flimsy hanging balance that he just happens to have on hand, hoping to dissuade Taffy from the balance she has requested. After Taffy rejects the hanging balance, Rafique extols the superiority of an expensive, totally inappropriate precision balance in a glass case. Taffy rejects that as well.

Eventually, Taffy brings the conversation around to baking soda. "The baking soda that Sanober ordered for the primary classes did not arrive," she says. "Baking *powder* was delivered instead. We must have baking *soda*, sodium bicarbonate, so that our experiments in the primary classes will be successful."

Rafique smiles and nods in seeming assent. "But," he counters, "primary teachers do not use baking *soda* in their classrooms. Primary teachers use baking *powder*—which is for cooking. Only secondary teachers use sodium bicarbonate for science."

Taffy and I look at each other and try not to laugh. Rafique sent baking powder on purpose. As a supplier of scientific equipment, he "knows" that primary children only cook; they do not do science.

For me, Rafique's sense of indisputable authority rings in my memory. I experienced it so many times in Dhamke and Sheikhupura when Rana Sahib and Ikram Mohyddin made gestures of cooperation and assent without really supporting my request or accepting its legitimacy. Here again, in Rafique's hot, stuffy office so many years later, I recognize the same attitude of dismissal.

Monday, February 24, 1964
Sheikhupura
Lady Workers Training
I left the Lady Workers in Saroya's good hands and went to see Mohyddin. . . . [I] waited an hour for him to spare me a minute—and finally he appeared. I asked him to come speak to the Lady Workers the next day, the last class day of training.

Mohyddin assured me that absolutely he would be there. Not only would he be there, but he would give us the jeep to get the Lady Workers out to the village on Wednesday for their meeting with village women.

He never came, never sent word that he would not be there, never sent the promised jeep to transport the Lady Workers to the village.

Early Friday morning, I cycled to Mohyddin's office to make sure he would at least come for the final graduation inspection. He was not there. So I waited . . . but finally gave the final inspection myself.

In an overall way, I am pleased with the training program . . . and the Lady Workers . . . have more enthusiasm and respect for their work. But how can they respect their work when Mohyddin, has so little respect for it he doesn't even come to their last day to congratulate them. . . . Because we are women, I guess, our ideas and accomplishments are easy to dismiss.

On the last day of the TCF training of 2009 in Lahore, however, the capriciousness of Rafique Ayub and my days in Dhamke and Sheikhupura seem like ancient history.

Not only do the two TCF Lahore area managers, Ali Sher and Naeem, attend the teacher-training classes, but midmorning, several additional TCF personnel and a group of USAID representatives from Islamabad stop by to watch.

USAID is involved with the dispersal of the U.S. dollars recently allocated to Pakistan in the Kerry-Lugar Bill,[1] and during the morning break, Taffy, Nancy, and I enthusiastically tell the USAID personnel about TCF and the Summer Science Camps. They are interested in our point of view as former Peace Corps Volunteers and seem as impressed with TCF as are we. We hope their visit to this TCF training site will be a positive influence on the dispersal of some of the Kerry-Lugar money.

The training day finally ends. We help the teachers and student volunteers pack up the supplies for the two other Lahore Summer Science Camp venues: the TCF schools in nearby Roranwala and Ledher. When the camps begin on Monday, Taffy will assist the teachers at Roranwala, and Nancy at Ledher. I will return to assist the teachers at the school at Phengali II.

While Taffy and Nancy and their teachers take the supplies to their school sites, I meet with the five teachers and principal of Phengali II to help them reorganize their storeroom and decide which supplies they will need for their classes on Monday morning. When everything is tidy, we retreat to the principal's office to await my transportation back to the city.

We are a merry group. The teachers remind me so much of my lady workers in Sheikhupura. I am comfortable chatting with them in my rusty Punjabi, and they are not shy about trying their English with me. There is a lot of excited chatter, laughter, and "high five" slapping of hands in our conversation. By the time Taffy, Nancy, and Illyas arrive in the car, I feel I am saying good-bye to good friends. I am looking forward to working with these women for the next two weeks.

The next day, Sunday, finds Nancy, Taffy, Illyas, and me traversing the fiery concrete and brick walkways of Shalimar Gardens, under the blistering midday sun. In 1962, as the guest of several teachers from a village near Dhamke, I visited Shalimar Gardens for the first time. I remember a lush green haven of flowering trees and hedges, brickwork avenues and waterways, arched doorways of painted tiles and graceful Persian lettering, fountains spraying cool mist into shallow pools of clear water, and a gardener with a goatskin bag over his shoulder watering pots of geraniums and marigolds. Mostly I remember the order and peace of walled acres filled with serenity.

The intervening years have not been kind to Shalimar Gardens. I walk along the brick pathways trying to gain a sense of recognition. Instead of a cloistered sanctuary of green, the lawns are now bare patches of dirt and dust. Crumbled tile and brick are scattered indiscriminately or piled next to the once elaborate archways. Rubble is everywhere. The reflecting pools are repositories for trash, and the fountains no longer spray refreshingly.

In 1962, the gardens seemed vast, and I saw few people whenever I visited. This Sunday in 2009, even under the midday sun, the park is full of teenage boys and young men hanging about, eager to engage in conversation. Not wishing to be disturbed, I try to ignore them, but several persist and intrude by standing in my path to have me take their photo. I am irritated by their intrusion.

I look up to see Illyas carefully watching these interlopers and am grateful for his assumed protection, though I do not feel endangered or threatened in any way. I am dismayed, however, by the changes time, overpopulation, and lack of infrastructure support have brought to this once beautiful sanctuary. And I am hot!

With the refrain of a tune about mad dogs and Englishmen running through my head, I catch up to Nancy and Taffy, undone by the blazing glare of the midday sun. The three of us make our way back to the entrance gate and sink gratefully into the safe haven of our air-conditioned car.

Weaving through the late afternoon haze of traffic and street theater, we stop to buy ice cream. It is our last evening in Liberty Market. In the morning, we will move to the Gymkhana Club, where we will stay during the next two weeks of Summer Science Camps.

CHAPTER 15

~

Summer Science Camps, Lahore

Half an hour before classes are to begin on Monday morning, the outer courtyard of Phengali II school is filled with fifty young boys, all dressed in the TCF school uniform for boys: khaki shirt and trousers, black shoes and belt. The boys are excited and jostle each other good-naturedly for school-yard space. Several are talking with the male student volunteers who have also just arrived. A few of the bolder boys step up to greet me with a smile and handshake as I make my way up the steps into the building.

I walk toward the classrooms, expecting to see the teachers bustling about, pushing desks together, and setting up the materials for the boys to use in their first activities. But the classrooms are empty except for the tables and chairs randomly placed around the rooms, and none of the materials for the first lessons are set out. I wonder where the teachers are and am a little disappointed that nothing seems to be ready. The time for classes to begin is quickly approaching.

I find all five teachers and the principal, Fakhra Khan, sitting around the table in the teacher's room, joking and laughing together. We greet each other, and I ask how I can be helpful setting up the five classrooms.

"But Ma'am," says Dilshad, one of the teachers, "we need to set up only *two* classrooms. Only fifty boys are very easy for us in two classrooms. We are accustomed to thirty boys in each classroom."

"But we have enough teachers and classrooms so that we can have *five* classes," I counter. "Only ten students in each classroom will be better for the children to use the materials. Five classrooms will give each of you an opportunity to practice the lessons you learned in training. Today each of you can teach the lesson you planned during our meeting on Saturday. And each of you will have a student volunteer to help you. Five classrooms. *Why* not?"

Why not, indeed. In my haste to get everyone organized and the classrooms set up, it never occurs to me that the teachers might want to team-teach their lessons today and need only two classrooms. I have assumed that in two classrooms, only two teachers will take the opportunity to teach and the other three teachers will just watch.

I have also assumed that because the teachers have not set up the classrooms in advance, they do not understand inquiry learning strategies. Later I discover that two of the Phengali II teachers are science teachers, while two are English teachers and one, the youngest, is a computer teacher. They are accustomed to having the children help with classroom setup and are not worried about having everything ready when the boys enter.

The Phengali teachers and I have different ideas about *timing*, I later realize, not about setting up the classroom for inquiry-based learning strategies. Having two or three teachers for each class of twenty-five students would have been an appropriate student/teacher ratio. But I think of this much later.

At the moment, the Phengali teachers, unfailingly polite, cheerfully agree to my organizational plan. I help the teachers set up all five classrooms: one each for the States of Matter, Clay Boats, Seeds, Spool Racers, and Newspaper Towers lessons. Fakrah, the principal, prepares a schedule so that over the course of the week each teacher will have an opportunity to teach all five lessons to the ten boys assigned to her classroom. We are ready to begin.

The student volunteers lead the boys into their respective classrooms, and I begin my rounds, checking that each teacher has the supplies she needs, helping several teachers understand what they need to do first. From my experience with teachers in many different classroom settings, I quickly discern which teachers are confident and which need more support.

Dilshad, an English teacher, is expanding the lesson on seeds by having her boys observe and draw the root and stem systems of some of the plants in the school courtyard. Sakina Bivi, the other English teacher, is assisting her boys with their spool racers and participates whole-heartedly in their project. I notice that, appropriately, she is *not* answering the children's questions of "Is this correct?" but instead redirects the boys to discover whether their racer *works* and if not, why not.

Both Dilshad and Sakina have an effortless rapport with the boys in their classes, and both use English and Urdu interchangeably and effectively.

Dilshad easily finds time to talk with each boy about the plant he is drawing, and Sakina is so enthusiastic about her boys' designs for the spool racers that she draws a crowd from Dilshad's classroom. I am impressed with these well-organized, experienced, and energetic teachers.

Their student volunteers, Maaz and Abuzar, are equally impressive. Both are majoring in science at the prestigious Lahore Upper Management School and, though they have never worked with slum children, their interactions with the boys are natural and unstrained. Maaz and Abuzar treat the boys like younger brothers.

I cross to the other side of the courtyard. The two science teachers are also busy in their classrooms. Their delivery, I notice, is more traditional and direct than that of Dilshad and Sakina. The first teacher, Sarah, draws a diagram of a plant on the chalkboard and has her boys copy it on their lab sheets. She labels the stem, root, and leaf in English but gives her instruction in Urdu.

After I watch for a few minutes, I tell Sarah about the real plants in the courtyard that Dilshad's boys are drawing and suggest she might want to have her boys draw real plants rather than merely copy the diagram on the chalkboard. If Dilshad and Sarah had been teaching together, I realize later, Dilshad might have suggested and modeled this for Sarah. Perhaps I should not have interfered with their initial team-teaching plan.

I step into the other science teacher's classroom. Nazia is conducting a lesson on the states of matter by dictating words for her boys to write on their lab sheets. She tells me that the boys must first write the procedures and then do the experiments. I am not sure Nazia understands that the purpose of the lab sheet is to record the results of the experiment rather than to be a prescription for it. However, I decide to watch in silence.

I begin to see the point of Nazia's method. Once the boys have finished writing on their lab sheets, she and her volunteer, Hamza, go around to each table to help the boys identify various substances and describe its state of matter: solid, liquid, or gas. Together, Nazia and Hamza demonstrate the baking-soda-and-vinegar procedure and show the boys how to measure the foam to determine the changed state of matter, gas. Then Nazia and Hamza leave the boys on their own to work at their tables in pairs, measuring, mixing, and testing the powders and other substances in front of them. Finally, Nazia and Hamza help the boys record the results of their observations and experiments on their lab sheets.

Nazia's method is more prescriptive than inquiry, and her teaching is more traditional. However, she does give each of her boys an opportunity to handle the materials and do some experiments. Each boy is required to record his work on a lab sheet, and even though every lab sheet is the same, each boy is actively engaged in the lesson and the outcome of his experiment. Nazia sort of gets it, I think.

In the fifth classroom, I am surprised to find Fizzah, the youngest teacher, sitting at her desk watching Zohaib, her student volunteer, conduct the lesson on spool racers. Fizzah's teaching experience is with computers, and she is happy to turn the lesson over to her student volunteer, thinking he knows more than she does about science.

I chide myself, again, for interfering with the teachers' initial team-teaching plan and step in to help Fizzah become more fully engaged with her class. Once she begins, Fizzah is full of energy and is really quite helpful, working with each boy one-on-one. However, she continues to allow Zohaib to lead the class, and he seems comfortable with the responsibility.

For me, a teacher educator, it is clear these Phengali II teachers are experienced and committed to their tasks. I love going from class to class, watching and asking questions of the teachers and children and feeling useful, even though the language and some of the teaching methods are different. I hope my presence is helpful and not distracting.

At the end of the day, the Phengali II team and I have lunch together, and I ask the teachers about themselves and their experiences as learners. All of them, they tell me, had been students in government schools. They are eager to tell me about their experiences as students and how those experiences shaped them to be different kinds of teachers.

Dilshad begins: "First, I want to say that over the years in government schools, there is no education going on and the students are free to do each and every thing. There is no one to care for them. The teaching is lecture mode only, the teachers have been trained this way."

Sakina concurs. "In government schools, the teachers were not interested to come in class to teach us. When they come, they say, 'Open your books to page ten.' You have to write to page twenty, and that's your whole class. You can run, you can jump, and the teacher goes with the rest of the staff to make 'gop-shop,' gossip.

"The government teachers never want to do anything," Sakina continues. "They just think teaching is a kind of very easy job. They don't think that they are responsible for the next generation. They are not building their country, reshaping their students. Teaching is a most difficult job if you are going to reshape someone's mind, body. . . . It is too difficult.

"The majority of government institutions are full of irresponsible persons. They just sit. Their teaching is not directed towards the kids. It's OK if sixty or seventy out of eighty kids do not pass the examination. There is no one there to ask why these students have failed. The teacher just says, 'What I can do?' They have maybe eighty kids in a class. . . . I even saw two hundred per class with no division. They are not responsible. They don't care."

Fakhra agrees. "I worked for one month in a government school, Government High School for Girls, in 2006. In the government schools, it is not so good. There is no one to take charge, and the teachers do not care for the children. They are sometimes lazy and do their own work while the children are running around in the classroom. Not in all government schools, but most of them. In the government school where I worked, it was like this.

"In Pakistan, two professions, teaching and nursing, are not very much respected by people. Because people think if a person is not so dependable and not so dedicated . . . they can go and teach. They think that anybody can be a teacher."

Dilshad interrupts. "While most of our teachers were careless and irresponsible, . . . I also want to tell about one of my teachers who was really good and took great care of us. One day, I went to her, but she was teaching a class. When I went to the door, she came to me and said, 'What's the problem, my child?'

"I said, 'Ma'am, I was absent due to illness. I have lost some of my chapters and I can't afford any tuition. Please guide me.'

"She said, 'My child, I haven't any spare period, but you must come to me in break time daily. I will teach you.' And she really guided me until I understood all my lost chapters.

"From there, I decided that . . . now I want to be a good and responsible person for all, like my teacher was for me. I am a very energetic person. I want to do all work. I never like to sit idle. I like TCF just to do my own work.

"At TCF schools it is different," Dilshad concludes. "There are so many activities. The teachers consider the students . . . their quality, their mind, their liking of things. We learn what they need, how they learn, what they want according to the authority, according to the inspection."

Fakhra sums the differences between government schools and TCF schools from her experience. "We are careful of the children, but in government schools, there is less care. In government schools, all subjects are different, the books are very easy," she says. "For example, they begin English ABC in sixth class. So, when these students come to TCF schools, they do not know the alphabet, so it is very difficult for the teachers. The teachers have to work very hard to teach them, because we do not refuse entrance to them. It is up to the teacher, but she has to work hard with these children.

"In government schools, there are male teachers in boys' schools and female teachers in girls' schools. In girls' schools, there can be a male clerk, or in boys' schools, a female English teacher, but that is all. In my experience, I think it is better for children in grades four, five, and six to have female teachers. A female teacher can understand the psyche of the children and know how to teach them with love. Male teachers might be too hard on the children."

Fakhra explains that the teaching policy at TCF schools "is to teach with love, and we are not allowed to beat the children. In government schools, children can be beaten with a stick. . . . The policy is to not beat them, but they beat them anyway. Because they cannot be fired in government schools, they feel they do not have to answer for beating the children.

"But at TCF, we have to answer for all activities day by day. On a daily basis, there is a checking system. The assistant education manager, area manager, and principal visit teachers in their classrooms often and are responsible for what is going on. Area manager, assistant education manager, etc. . . . all will ask the principal what is going on in her school.

"In government schools, the teachers have more pay and other things, but it is not so good as at TCF," she concludes.

I tell the teachers that I am impressed with their teaching and congratulate them on using their student volunteers effectively. We go over the lessons that each teacher will present in the morning, according to the schedule Fakhra has drawn up, and then settle into some good natured gop-shop.

The teachers describe themselves as a family: Fakhra, Dilshad, Sakina, Nazia, Sarah, and Fizzah. I can see that they interact as sisters who really care about each other. They travel to and from school in a TCF van and spend most of their time together.

When Illyas arrives with Taffy and Nancy to take me back to the city, I leave the camaraderie of my new friends in a flurry of dust, hand waves, and shouts of laughter. I feel welcome and at home in their sisterhood.

Taffy and Nancy's morning has been as interesting as mine, and we trade stories as we drive through the village, dodging lorries and donkey-pulled carts in our path. Taffy is excited about how well the girls at Roranwala participated in the day's activities.

"They were totally engrossed in what they were doing," Taffy says. "When they used the pan balance and added paper clips to the buckets to find out how much the various objects weighed, they cooperated with each other beautifully. It was so rewarding to watch them. . . . One girl stands out. During the activity to build a tower using newspaper, she made a series of cones decreasing in size—it was huge. And she was so proud of her structure—taller than any of the others."

"In my school," Nancy adds, "the teachers were very businesslike in following the lesson plans. As far as I could tell, they may have lectured a little more than you would like, Taffy, but they basically had the children doing the experiments and allowed the kids to actively interact with each other. The classroom atmosphere was happy and good humored. The college student volunteers were very involved, interacted well with the students, and really worked quite hard at the teaching. They were so impressed and surprised that 'these kids' were so bright and able to learn so much. I hope this realization stays with them for the rest of their lives."

We lapse into silence, lost in our own thoughts, until Illyas pulls into the driveway for the Gymkhana Club, our home for the next few weeks.

CHAPTER 16

~

The Gymkhana Club, 2009

I visited the Gymkhana Club in 1962 and remember the country-club feel of its vast green lawns, sweeping driveways, and imposing edifice. At the time, I was particularly impressed with the attentiveness of the serving staff and the formality of their dress. Each bearer wore a stiff plumed turban, starched white shalwar and high-necked jacket, and a long red sash around his waist. Only missing was the Rajput scabbard and blade. My every wish was their command.

The Gymkhana Club of 2009 is different. When our car arrives at the Upper Mall gate, we are greeted by uniformed police bearing arms. They inspect the trunk of Illyas's car and peer at us suspiciously through the windows. We pass this first inspection only to undergo another one at another gate around the corner. The armed guards at this gate inspect our car and, reluctantly it seems to me, wave us through.

We disembark and walk to a modern, two-story brick building with accommodations for overnight guests. Three more sentries dressed in olive-drab uniforms, each holding a rifle across his chest, guard this building.

We ascend tiled steps and I struggle, unassisted, to open the large glass double doors leading inside. Gone are the turbaned doormen. In their place, two clerks stand behind a shoulder-high reception counter.

The clerks eventually notice us and greet us with unenthusiastic courtesy. One explains the exit/entry and laundry systems and gives us two oversized keys for our rooms. "The keys should never leave the building but always be deposited at the reception desk whenever you exit your rooms. No exceptions," he declares emphatically.

"In a separate building, you will find a formal dining room with attached sitting room for cigars, coffee, and dessert," he continues. "A buffet dinner is served there or outside on the lawn in the back garden after 8:30 every evening. Breakfast is delivered to your rooms. You can buy snacks at an informal café or in a small grocery cum sweet shop near the pro shop of the golf course. If you would like to swim, the club pool is open for ladies between four o'clock and six o'clock in the afternoon."

Somewhat abashed, Taffy, Nancy, and I carry our oversized keys, luggage, and various bags of teaching supplies up the open winding stairway to our rooms on the upper floor. The electricity is off, but a generator provides backup air conditioning, and the lights, though on low, illuminate a dark hallway.

After we unpack, Nancy, and I go swimming in the pool with the ladies of the club. Most of the women are dressed in gauzy shalwar kameez and sit on lounge chairs beside the pool. Those who are in the water wear long-sleeved Lycra wetsuits as swimming costumes. Nancy and I are the only women in briefer attire: Nancy in a modest one-piece bathing suit, I in running shorts, jogging bra, and T-shirt.

The pool is crowded with small children, but Nancy and I manage to swim laps in two designated lanes on the far side of the pool. There is not much difference between the warm silky water under us and the muggy dense air above, but it feels good to me to exercise and stretch my arms and legs freely.

At the end of my laps, a woman sitting poolside supervising several children in the water tells me that I am very "sporty" and swim very well. She envies me, she says, and wishes she knew how to swim. Uneasily, I look for the children she is supervising and hope they are self-sufficient in the water, before I thank her for the compliment.

Nancy and I towel dry in the ladies' dressing area and walk back to our rooms along the lush green golf course, built originally in the nineteenth century by and for its British members. The course has been redesigned many times since then. The residence hotel, the informal café, and the outdoor dining area are Pakistani additions to this former British club. I look out at the parklike setting of the grounds and hope to be able to run around them in the morning before leaving for my school assignment.

That evening, at 8:30, Taffy, Nancy, and I dine alone in the formal dining room of the club. The food is a delicious buffet of cold salads, spicy curries, rice, lentils, chicken, chapatis, and a smorgasbord of tempting desserts. At the end of our meal, I ask for some coffee and am told it would be served in the adjoining sitting room. Puzzled, I tell the waiter that I would prefer to have my coffee and dessert at our table, but I am told, firmly, "Madame, it is not allowed." No coffee in the dining room. No exceptions.

We leave the dining room just as the first wave of Pakistani diners is seated. A party of a dozen or so young women in stylish silk and cotton shalwar kameez arrive to celebrate. The room begins to buzz with late-evening chatter and laughter, but we are ready to end our long day. We trudge wearily across the dark lawn to our rooms, absorbing the heat, conundrums, and contrasts of Pakistan that have been part of our day.

So begins our stay at the posh Gymkhana Club. It seems far away from the Badshai Mosque, the old fort, the Anarkali Bazaar, and the haunts of my former days in Lahore. The city is bigger, noisier, hotter, and more congested than I remember it, but I love being back in the middle of its exotic confusion. Tiring as it is, I am happy to be here.

Early the next morning, dressed in gauzy white shalwar kameez and running shoes, I slip out of my room, deposit the oversized key at the unattended reception desk, and quietly pull open the glass doors leading outside. I am hoping to run on the Gymkhana grounds before the early morning golfers arrive and the heat of the day descends.

The outside air is heavy with humidity, but the dawn is rosy fingered. "Red sky in the morning, sailors take warning," I chant. Perhaps we will have rain by midday to clear the oppressive air.

I weave around to the pro shop to begin my run of the golf course and discover a crowd of Pakistani men, all waiting for their tee time. I try to go around them, but my way is blocked by golf carts and a sign that says No Entry. Remembering the "Madame, it is not allowed" of the previous evening, I am not quite brave enough to trespass.

I reluctantly change direction and jog to the gate to run on the tree-lined sidewalk. Even though it is still very early, cars, motorcycles, and buses crowd the roadway; it is the beginning of the workday. I remember that, in summer, offices open in the early morning and late afternoon but are closed during the heat of the midday sun.

I feel very visible and foolish in my makeshift running outfit, which, by now is clinging to my back and chest like soggy tissue. I look up to see faces plastered to bus windows, heads turned my way, motorcycles aiming straight at me. Everyone seems to be staring at me, through me—much as I remember them staring in 1962.

I duck into a nearby park where runners in most cities can run unnoticed. For the first time since my return to Pakistan, I feel the restrictions placed on women by their clothing and by the expectations for suitable physical activity they must accept. I feel very out of step.

I return to the Gymkhana Club for a shower and breakfast, bothered and hot. I am homesick for the comfort of running clothes that wick perspiration away from modestly exposed skin and for the freedom, as a woman, to run.

Later that morning, the second day of Summer Science Camp, Illyas drops me off last, after Taffy and Nancy. This gives me a chance to look at their TCF schools, Roranwala and Ledher.

Roranwala, Taffy's school, is just for girls and is the most beautiful TCF school I have yet seen. The inner courtyard is alive with flowering bougain-villea that cascades from the second-story railings to the lush green lawns below. At one side of the compound, a small playground with metal swings, a slide, and a climbing gym is nestled in a small garden. The girls, dressed in school uniforms of khaki shalwar kameez and white dupattas draped over their shoulders, are waiting for classes to begin. The girls are well groomed, bright eyed, and excited.

Ledher, Nancy's school, is equally compelling and beautiful. I stay only a few minutes, but have a chance to look at the posters along the hallway and stairs leading to the second floor. Displayed on the walls are child-drawn ren-derings of different professions and career choices: doctor, teacher, postman, fireman, greengrocer, tailor, policeman, blacksmith, barber, potter, cobbler. The doctor and teacher posters portray women in those roles.

It strikes me that everywhere I look in a TCF school, there are reminders that life can be different from the way it is outside the school walls. Inside are order, beauty, opportunity, and a work ethic that challenges each member of the community to work hard and be attentive. The children smile, help each other, and are polite. They stand when an adult enters the room and do not interrupt when a teacher is speaking. It is refreshing to observe the respect children and teachers have for each other.

When I arrive at my school, later this morning than I was the day before, the teachers are again waiting in the teacher's room for classes to begin. No one is bustling about setting up her classroom. Again nothing is ready for the children.

I discover that Fizzah is absent and that Zohaib, her student volunteer, has no idea which lesson he should present today in her stead. Nazia offers to team-teach Clay Boats with him and combine their classes. Then Dilshad and Sakina decide to teach States of Matter together, and Sarah switches her planned lesson to teach Seeds and Newspaper Towers.

I note with rueful humor that the teachers will be team-teaching as they had originally planned after all, and it occurs to me that these kinds of unexpected changes happened often with my lady workers in Sheikhupura so many years ago. They mystified me then.

Now, as then, the women step in and help each other when an aunt dies, an unforeseen visit must be made to a relative in a distant village, or for some reason one of them must be absent. In Sheikhupura, I saw these unexpected changes as a cover for irresponsibility and lack of commitment to the work.

Today, the reason for Fizzah's absence is the death of a relative. Nazia's offer to change her teaching plans and work with Zohaib is an acceptable solution. I decide not to interfere and trust that the teachers know what they are doing and are committed to their work.

While the teachers set up their classrooms, I ask Fakhra to tell me about one of the boys I noticed yesterday. He looked older than the other boys in his class and was completely engrossed in the lesson on seeds. At one point, I heard him ask his teacher for permission to help several of his younger classmates find nodules on the root system of the plant they were observing. He explained to his classmates how the nodules absorb water and gave detailed directions about how to replant each plant in the courtyard.

"Usman began in class one after a few years at government school," Fakhra tells me. "He began in TCF primary level one, and he is just now beginning level five. He is fifteen and most of his classmates are four or five years younger. His teachers need to work harder with him so that he can catch up.[1]

"Would you like to talk to him?" she asks.

"In fact," I reply, "I would like to talk to *several* students and their parents. Girls and boys. Is this possible?"

"Yes, of course," Fakhra says. She agrees to ask Usman and several other Phengali students for interviews with them and their parents. Part of her responsibility as principal, she reminds me, "is to make home visits to families to determine if they qualify for TCF scholarships," among other things. "I am happy," she says, "to arrange several visits to TCF families near the school and to ask Tahira, the principal at Taffy's school, to arrange visits to families of girls in her school."

In the middle of the morning, Fakhra and I set out for Usman's home in the village. I am surprised when Usman greets us at the gate to his family compound but then realize that his presence probably makes our visit less intimidating for his mother and sisters.

Usman's home is much more affluent than I expect. His family owns a small marble factory and chicken hatchery in the village. We are ushered into the bridal bedroom of Usman's older brother. This room has a marble doorstep, polished wood door frame, concrete floor, and ornate bedroom suite embossed with mosaic mirrors and mauve and gold garlands. The double-sized charpoy is covered with a woven tapestry of deep maroon, navy, and purple, and similarly colored pillows abut the head- and footboard. In the corner of the room, another tapestry covers a portable TV. The room is spacious, clean, and orderly. I am hesitant to sit on the bed, but it is the seat of honor, so reluctantly I accept.

Usman's mother and three young women serve us, offering a cool soft drink and biscuits from the bazaar. I am reminded of my home visits in Dhamke, though never have I seen a village home with such a lavish bedroom. I expect the furniture is part of the new bride's dowry, but think it impolite to ask. The women are proud to show the furniture off, however, and I must admit, it is breathtaking.

Usman's mother is very gracious. Dressed in an orange shalwar kameez and enveloping black dupatta, she answers my questions with poise and dignity.

"I have four sons," she tells me. "Usman is next to the youngest. . . . The oldest son runs the marble factory, next son is in first-year college in government school and has done matriculation and will be married. Then comes Usman, who is fifteen and a student in fifth class at Phengali II. Usman is the first for TCF, but there are two others in TCF schools: one daughter in Phengali I class five; one other son, Sohaid, at Phengali II."

"I send my children to TCF," she says, "because in government schools, they were not learning. They were just passed and not making improvements, so I learned about TCF and changed the children to them. . . . After matriculation, Usman will be learning more education. After college, he wants to join police."

Usman's mother asks me if I would like to see the marble factory and the chicken farm. She straddles the back of a motorcycle, which Usman drives, and I follow in the TCF van to her family business.

At the marble factory, two workers are cutting stone with loud saws. The chickens are housed at the back of the compound in a large coop—hundreds of them pecking and clucking about on the floor of the building. Usman's father has gone to Karachi to buy more marble, I am told, but I meet his older brother and inspect the chickens. I remember Dick's dozen chickens in Dhamke. What a difference!

Fakhra and I return to Phengali for dismissal. All is well, and everyone is enthusiastic about how well the morning projects succeeded. I overhear two of the student volunteers, Hamza and Zohaib, talking about one of the boys they worked with in their combined "Clay Boats" class.

"He is so intelligent," Hamza remarks. "It is hard to believe."

"Yes," agrees Zohaib. "He is so quick, before any of the other boys, and always has the answer and another question, before I have time to ask it. I am amazed at his attentiveness."

The two see me eavesdropping and include me in the conversation. They are surprised, they tell me, that these boys are so smart, so eager to learn, and so quick to understand. I am delighted with their observations and tell them how important they are to these children and what good role models they are.

Today, these student volunteers have learned an important lesson about Pakistani children from the other side of the village wall. The TCF founders are wise, I think, to enlist the help of all Pakistanis to bring social change to their country. I expect that these young volunteers will never again look at a street child and judge him hopeless and stupid. Their experiences as assistant teachers in the Summer Science Camps are part of the larger solution to the problem of street children and education in Pakistan.

Is this the unfinished business I came to Pakistan to resolve? I wonder.

The next afternoon, Tahira, the principal at Roranwala, has arranged visits to the homes of two of her students. She keeps up a running commentary on the neighborhood as Taffy, Nancy, and I follow her through its winding alleys of bricks and bits of rubble. Unattended children and a small burro run behind us through the maze of sagging electric wires and one lone tree.

We enter the small courtyard of Mehsoor Salim's family and again are ushered into the best room of the house. In this case, the best room is the *only* room and is a marked contrast to the village home I visited the day before. The room is crowded with two charpoys, a portable sewing machine, a large tin trunk, several straight-back wooden chairs, an electric pedestal fan, four small children, and several women—it is home to two families, seven people, and not much different from my village home in Dhamke. Mehsoor's mother looks about twenty-five and has the saddest expression I've seen in a long time. Her eleven-year-old daughter Mehsoor, however, has a face full of life and energy. Mehsoor's short brown hair is cinched on top with two small ponytails, and her brown eyes sparkle with curiosity.

I ask Mehsoor what she likes best about her school. "I like the teachers very much," she tells me. "Especially my kindergarten teacher and English teacher. . . . They make us feel good. I want to be a teacher, a science teacher."

Mehsoor's mother did not attend school and has "only a little literacy," meaning that she can write her name and read a few Urdu letters. She tells me that she "goes to school meetings to find out about problems of her children." She is eager to have her children go to school because she lives very near to the school. Her neighbor told her about TCF and she decided that, as soon as her child was old enough, she would enroll her. If there is a TCF school for adults someday, she says she will join. Then she will have a better chance to educate her girls, to guide them.

I ask Mehsoor's mother why she wants to educate her girls.

"The same as I've just told you . . . to live a better life, not the same life I have or the suffering I have. A better life. A better understanding. . . . To make them earn some money to be independent. Being a girl with an education, she has a better opportunity to decide about her life. Women don't have any authority in their homes or decide what to wear, but once a girl has an education, she has the power to make a better life."

Mehsoor's mother goes to the sewing machine to show me a small shalwar kameez she is making to sell in the bazaar. She tells me that she learned to sew at a sewing center and that she is teaching her children to sew. Her husband works a little bit as a laborer on intervals, whatever he can find. This house is her mother-in-law's house, but her in-laws have died, so only her husband, his brother, and their four children live here. She tells me she is very happy to have me visit her in her house.

"I am satisfied for the time being that Mehsoor is able to read and write better than me and knows about washing her teeth, using soap—these good habits," she says. "Many children go to TCF from this village, and I am happy to have my children in TCF."

My next interview is down a sun-baked lane, around the corner, in another courtyard full of children, several young women, a grandmother, an uncle, and a few chickens. A mud wall and the unblinking stares from several sets of brown-eyed women on nearby roofs surround the courtyard. I am reminded once more of my goldfish-bowl days in Dhamke.

As we enter the courtyard, a woman making chapatis in a mud-baked oven on the side of the courtyard greets us with a smile. Several other women, sitting on a charpoy under a tree, rise to greet us. Soon Taffy, Nancy, Tahira, and I are seated on the charpoy, under the tree, surrounded by curious women and children.

Shazir Aabad, the TCF student we have come to see, has two brothers and two sisters. Her father is dead, and her older sister will be married soon. Both of her brothers study at TCF, one at the Phengali secondary school, the other at Phengali primary school. Shazir joined TCF in the kindergarten class and is now in class five. She is twelve or thirteen years old.

"The best thing about school," Shazir says, "is the teachers and the playground. The teachers are very nice, and there are so many things at school that we don't have at our home. I want to become a doctor," she adds. "We have studied about different professions at school. My cousin who also attends TCF wants to become a lady police. Four of her uncles are policemen. She watches the traffic police from her grandmother's house in the city."

I ask Shazir if her mother has gone to school.

"No, she is illiterate. . . . She has not gone to school. There is no time. She makes jewelry and sells beaded jewelry in the bazaar or in the village to make a little money. She learns how to make these just with personal interest, no special instruction. Some other women do this, but not all."

I ask Shazir's mother and aunt why they want to send their girls to school. "To live a better life and also the demand of others for marriage for a better wife," they answer.

Is she happy that her children are in school?

"Yes, I am satisfied and happy to have them in TCF. I want my youngest girl to go, but there is not enough space always. Principal says she needs more space in her school for more children."

I have heard this lament before—that there is not enough space in the TCF school for all the children who want to attend. TCF responds by building more schools in a cluster so that several TCF primary schools will feed the TCF secondary school in the area. It is difficult for the supply to meet the demand for space, however, and some children must wait until space opens or a new school unit is established in an existing TCF building.[2]

At the end of the afternoon, we say good-bye to Tahira and return to the Gymkhana Club for a siesta and late evening dinner. My visits to Usman's, Mehsoor's, and Shazir's homes make me impatient to visit my old village of Dhamke and the town of Sheikhupura where I trained the lady workers for women's Village Aid social centers in the 1960s. Nancy is eager to return to the villages near Khanewal, the site of her Peace Corps community development project, as well. We are looking forward to these visits at the end of the week, our third week back in Pakistan.

Visiting in the villages this afternoon, sitting on charpoys surrounded by women, flies, children, and heat, I feel that I have never left Pakistan. But, my conversations with the women and young girls about their hopes and dreams for an education remind me that many things have changed since my last village visit in 1964. I am eager to see what these changes are in Sheikhupura and Dhamke.

CHAPTER 17

~

Sheikhupura and Dhamke, 2009

The two-lane asphalt road connecting Lahore and Sheikhupura, the small town where Saroya and I lived during the second year of my Peace Corps assignment, is unrecognizable to me in 2009. Through the shimmering haze of noonday sun, I look in vain for the once-familiar sight of the bus station, Bedami Bagh, with its buses, trucks, and teeming humanity honking and shouting their way through its crowded entrance. I see instead the access to a six-lane superhighway that now links Lahore to Islamabad by way of Sheikhupura.[1]

I give up trying to recognize anything and silently take in the green fields and distant smokestacks as we whiz by, outside the city limits. The sun is blinding.

Eventually, Illyas pulls off the highway on the outskirts of Sheikhupura. I am expecting to drive into a bustling town of shops and neighborhoods centered by a quadrangle of redbrick government buildings in a garden of overhanging shade trees and flowers.

In the 1960s, the population of Sheikhupura was about 25,000 and lush green fields stretching to the horizon surrounded the small urban city center. During Moghul times, Sheikhupura was the royal hunting ground of Jahangir, and I remember Jahangir's park of Hiran Minar on the outskirts of the city as a cool, refreshing respite. I cycled to Hiran Minar whenever I needed a break from my neighbors and the din of living in a town. In fact, I could ride my bicycle or walk wherever I needed to go in Sheikhupura in 1963 and could circle the entire metropolis within an hour.

I am stunned by the Sheikhupura of today.

With a population above three million, the sidewalks and streets spill into each other, congested by motorized traffic, people, animals, shops, noise, confusion, and, on this day, unending oppressive sun and haze. The city is now surrounded by large-scale industrial development stretching beyond the horizon, dwarfing the mud-walled villages at their feet and scarring the once lush fields of rice, grain, and wheat with belching smokestacks.

I can identify nothing on our cacophonous dizzying tour. Not the bus station, bazaar, civil line government buildings, railway station, basic democracies offices, or neighborhood where I once shared a double flat with Saroya, Bill, and several other Peace Corps Volunteers. I might as well be in Karachi or one of the suburbs of Lahore. Nothing looks familiar, and I am dazed.

I finally abandon the quest to find my old neighborhood and ask Illyas to take us to a TCF school. We have six to choose from in Sheikhupura, including one near the remote village of one of my lady workers.

The TCF primary school in Nurpur Virkan was built in 2007 with funds donated by Dawood Hercules Chemicals, the largest ammonia/urea fertilizer industry in Pakistan. The chemical plant hovers above the mud walls of the village and sprawls over 228 acres of once fertile farmland to produce 1,350 metric tons of urea and 815 metric tons of ammonia per day for fertilizer.

The TCF primary school sits on two of the village's formerly farmed acres and enrolls 240 children. On this hot summer afternoon, the children are nowhere to be seen, but inside the school gates, the classrooms are ready for their return in just a few weeks. The inner courtyard of the school is bordered by potted flowering plants and small decorative trees. Everything is bright, airy, and well ordered.

As we stroll through the school building, I notice signs posted outside the principal's office delineating the duties for teachers and ayahs. The teachers' duties are in English, the ayahs' in Urdu. Other signs are posted outside each classroom. The weekly schedule for classes posted outside a fourth-grade doorway lists, in English: Mathematics, Science, Urdu, English, Social Studies, Games, Art, Library, and Islamic Studies. This array of subjects is an enormous change from the primary school days of the 1960s, and I am sure that the children no longer chant their lessons in unison or use wooden slates for paper and charcoal nibs for pencils as they did in the 1960s.

The changes in schooling, and indeed the very presence of such a beautiful school in this once remote village, are staggering and, of course, welcome. But I feel a twinge of wistfulness for the once undisturbed rice fields stretching beyond my sight, and the dusty dirt roads leading to mud-brick compounds even farther away. I am quite sure that the fertilizer plant that has provided this TCF school also employs many local, landless farmers and that its presence is healthy for the country's, and Sheikhupura's, economy. But I am homesick for the past and heartsick at the destruction of the idyllic agrarian environment I remember with such nostalgia.

We push on toward Dhamke, my first village home.

Dhamke, I tell Illyas, is behind a bus stop on the edge of the Jaranwala Road. I remember that to get there from Sheikhupura, one must turn right onto the Jaranwala Road and head northwest toward Lyallpur, now called Faisalabad. I trade seats with Neelum and try to direct Illyas to this road.

Unbelievably, in all this confusion of superhighway traffic and signage, we find an exit for Jaranwala, turn right onto a dusty wide road that is under construction to become even wider, and join a long line of cars and motor-bikes bumping along to Jaranwala. Roadside shops and fuel stations have replaced the trees that lined the once narrow blacktop road. I try to see past them, across the still verdant fields to the villages I suspect are on the other side of the vista.

The lively scenes before me contrast sharply with the faded sepia snap-shots tucked into a manila envelope resting on my lap. I have brought a few old photographs of Dhamke and my friends who lived there in 1962 and hope these will help identify me.

Illyas drives as fast as conditions of road construction will allow, and I desperately search for something that looks familiar. I ask Illyas to drive a little more slowly because I almost remember where I am—and then I spot a landmark.

We have arrived at the bus stop for Dhamke. Only now, it is not a bus stop but a thriving crossroads of shops and fuel stations. We pull over in front of a vintage blue bus, decorated with swirls of colorful flowers and Arabic letters. The passenger section of the bus has open windows and bench seats—just like the bus I rode when I arrived in Dhamke the first time. In fact, judging from its dilapidated condition and exposed motor, this could be the same bus.

In front of the bus, under a web of drooping electric wires, a donkey hitched to a cart with one wheel in a mud puddle, watches us. Two bicycles are parked beside a tower of red Coca-Cola crates under an awning of cor-rugated tin held in place by slender poles. Next to the bicycles, an open counter supports three burners and three metal cooking pots. Several mini-vans, two small cars, and a tractor are parked on either side of the road, and a sign, in English and Urdu, points east, across the road, just where I think the village should be.

It is not the sleepy bus stop of the past with its few shops and dhoti-clad farmers lounging about, pulling on hookahs. But it definitely is the bus stop leading, as a sign by the side of the road says, to *Dhamke, 0.75 km.*

I tell Illyas to pull onto the lane leading to the village and stop. He wants to drive in, and Neelum, anticipating a long dusty walk in the heat of the day, urges him to continue. But this time I insist. I know if I can walk from the road I will find my way. At least, I think I can.

Taffy, Nancy, Neelum, and I open our doors and step out into a furnace blast of hot summer air. Reflexively, I pull my dupatta over my head. It helps to shield the sun, and it also seems to be the right thing to do.

The lane is much broader and more treeless than I remember. As we approach the village, I notice a small car parked beside a straight brick wall under a thatched roof. The parking area is wide and swept clean except for a pile of discarded bricks and construction bags and a mound of dried cow patties. I am amused at the juxtaposition of a car parked next to cow patties and suspect that cars have replaced bullocks as the villagers' mode of transportation.

My friends follow me as I twist around the village lanes, noting that most of the houses, once mud, are now of brick or cement. The lanes are now paved with brick as well, as are the open drains along their edges. The lanes seem narrower and more crowded, and the buildings on both sides appear taller and darker. I am surprised at the number of small shops, open for business selling soft drinks, biscuits, soap powder, and sweets. In 1962, there were no such shops.

Up a small rise in the middle of the village, I stop at the double gate to a compound at the end of the lane. A young man comes up behind me and I ask, rather casually, if he knows where I can find Rana Sahib.

"Ah, Rana Sahib," he says, and promptly disappears.

Unfazed, I open the gate and walk into a once familiar courtyard, now completely enclosed by brick paving, leading to open doorways and separate rooms. At one end of the courtyard, I see a portable electric washing machine, about the size of the metal drum I used in 1962 for its prototype.

I look up the stairs to see if the woman of the house is at home. Of course she is. I introduce myself and ascend the stairs as though I have been here only yesterday. It feels very natural. I am home, because it feels like home, though nothing looks quite the same.

The young man from outside the gate reappears and asks me to follow him to the front room of the house. This room has been added since 1962 and is furnished with an upholstered couch, two glass-topped coffee tables, a mantle, a dining room table, and several straight-back dining chairs. Over the mantle, traditionally the storing place for pots, plates, and treasures, hangs a large faded photograph of a man, circa 1945.

Pointing to the photo, the young man asks, "Is that the Rana Sahib you are wanting? I'm sorry, but he is no longer with us." The likeness is not of anyone I remember as Rana, the zamindar and Union Council chairman.

A young woman and her two children come into the room, followed by another man I do not recognize. They offer us cold drinks, and one of the children is dispatched to the bazaar to fetch some.

I pull out my manila envelope of old photographs and show the pictures of me, Bill, Dick, Carol, and several village women, children, and babies. We chat amiably, but it is clear to me that these people do not know the people in the photos.

Taffy, Nancy, and Neelum sit on the sofa, snapping digital photos and watching me try to communicate in Punjabi and remember names. For me, everything is *almost* familiar, but not quite. Rana did have a parlor of sorts, but I do not remember it being so fancy.

I look up from the photos on my lap when a dark-haired man in a khaki-colored shalwar and kurta comes into the room. From the chin up, he is Rana Sahib! I want to throw my arms around him in a big bear hug, but of course I do not.

It turns out that this is Rana's son, born in 1966, two years after I left Pakistan. He tells me that his mother and Rana married in 1964; she was his second wife. I instantly remember Rana's proposal to me in 1963—to be that second wife—and realize, aghast, that if I had accepted his proposal, this middle-aged man could be my son.

Rana's son looks exactly like the man who protected me as one of his family and helped me so long ago. Now I am sure I am in the right house, talking to the right people—or at least, to their relatives.

And then a tall, silver-haired man arrives and comes up to shake my hand.

"I am Rana's nephew, Mubashar Mahmood," he tells me. "I was in secondary school when you lived in this village and I visited my uncle from time to time. I am the son of Rana's sister, and I remember you very well."

I show him my photographs from 1962.

"This young girl is my wife, before we married," he says. "And this is Bill and Dick who lived in the rest house outside the village," pointing to my photo of Bill and Dick. "And these are Dick's chickens. But you lived in the small stable nearby and wore shalwar kameez but no burqah. There was a young shopkeeper that befriended you. Do you remember him?"

"Yes," I answer. "Ata Mohammed. We nicknamed him 'Jerry' because he was so lively. Does he still live in Dhamke?"

"He still lives here, but he has been very sick. Perhaps it will not be possible for you to visit him," Mubashar replies.

The woman with the two young children interrupts. "Ah, yes, I remember. You came to the weddings of Envir and Ata Mohammed."

Several more women and children crowd into the room to look at my photos and listen to the conversation. The more we talk, the more we all begin to remember.

"Please come to visit my mother, Rana's second wife," Rana's son says. He escorts me to the bottom of the stairs leading to the second floor, the women's portion of the house. I climb up the stairs and step into the past.

Looking over the carved railing on the roof onto neighboring courtyards and distant fields, I see a familiar view. There are more houses now, and some of the fields have turned into dusty flat squares of crumbling brick. But the canal is still at the edge of the village and the towpath beside it has become a dirt lane. Beyond the canal is the rest house where Bill and Dick stayed and where I ate my evening meals and sometimes fell asleep on a charpoy under the trees in the heat of the Punjab summer.

The second story of Rana's house is still the purdah section, though more rooms have been added since the last time I was here. I note a Western-style bathroom and a sink with running water in the corner.

Rana's second wife is waiting for me, sitting on a charpoy, smiling and nodding in welcome. She does not know me, nor I her, but we share a memory of Rana Sahib. He died, she tells me, in 1994 and would have been happy to see me. Rana told her many things about me, she says . . . how I lived in a mud house, wore village clothes, helped village women with sewing and literacy. I am surprised and touched by her words.

After a few minutes, I am called downstairs. Rana Sahib's first wife is waiting for me in her house down the lane. A flock of women and children accompany me to her house. She is sitting cross-legged on a charpoy in a room that is a bit more elegant and a bit cleaner than the house we have just left, her former home during my Peace Corps days.

Rana's first wife is old, thin, and small, but her eyes are bright and her speech clear. She tells me that she remembers me taking her mother-in-law to the hospital in Lahore and asks if I still eat sagh-gosht and chapatis. I am flabbergasted! I had forgotten about that trip to the hospital, though I had written about it at length in my 1962 journal. And I did, indeed, request spinach and spicy meat with my chapatis whenever invited to share a meal with her. This gives Nancy and Taffy a chuckle, as well. I order sagh-gosht and chapatis every time we sit down in a Pakistani restaurant for a meal. It is still my favorite Pakistani meal—and not easy to find in upscale restaurants.

Rana's wife laughs with us and takes my hand into her bony fingers. Her eyes are moist and her smile radiant as she gives me her blessing when I say good-bye. I do remember visiting her in her upstairs purdah quarters, but, as she was a woman in strictest purdah, she was never allowed to visit my social center or me in 1962. I am amazed at how much she recalls from that time.

Our next stop is my former home, the stable that I transformed, with Bill and Dick's help, into two rooms—one for me to sleep, eat, and wash in, the other for women to gather in and use as a social center. At the time, a small courtyard that held a latrine, tree, washing machine, and ladder to the roof for summer sleeping separated the rooms.

I recognize my house by its location, nothing more. Instead of stepping into my courtyard from the street, we step into the front room of a two-story private residence. My old bed/sitting/washing/eating room is now a bed/sitting room, of sorts. The room across the courtyard, the former social center, is another bedroom/storeroom. The courtyard is an enclosed, low-ceilinged dark room with a staircase in the back, where my ladder used to be. Upstairs are three more rooms—all dark and small. There is no roof for outdoor sleeping, and I wonder how anyone is able to rest during a Punjab summer, especially on this closed-in second floor.

This two-story domicile is nothing like the home I remember—except that the rooms are still very dark. I learn that Union Council secretary Younas and his family lived in the house after I left it and that Younas now lives in Lahore.

Mubashar points to a spot behind the new front door. "This is where you built your latrine," he says. "And right above it, there was a tree. The tree grew very big over that latrine," he laughs. "It was the first latrine in Dhamke until my uncle, Rana, built one for himself."

I don't remember that Rana built a latrine, but I am pleased that his nephew remembers ours. Perhaps we made a bigger impression on the "patterns of village life" than I realized at the time.

As we step out the door, a young man in sweatpants, T-shirt, baseball cap, and flip-flops approaches me. "My grandmother lived next door when you were here," he says. "Please come visit her."

He motions me toward a splendid pair of double doors under a marble entranceway in the next lane. I know those doors and entryway are new additions to Dhamke and am curious to meet this young man's grandmother. I expect she is one of the pair of eyes that watched my every move in 1962 and wonder if she ever stole underwear I hung to dry in my courtyard.

But before I can follow the young man inside his grandmother's doors, a rotund, beaming woman with a dupatta covering her smile interrupts my stride. She is Jerry's wife, transformed from the slight, shy fourteen-year-old bride whose wedding I attended, into a look-alike of Bivi-gee, Jerry's mother. She has the same insistent, assertive, good-natured manner as Bivi-gee and greets me warmly.

"Please come to Ata Mohammed," she says. "He is very sick but he will want to meet with you."

I follow her to Bivi-gee's old home, where we attended Envir's wedding festivities and Jerry's wedding. Again, everything is the same and everything is different. Inside the main room of the house, instead of just one mantle holding cups and plates, there are *five* mantles, all covered with woven Pakistani cotton and a large collection of fancy dinner plates with scalloped edges and old-fashioned Moghul designs. Over the main mantle is a large photograph of a well-muscled, bare-chested Jerry in his prime. This is the Jerry of those bygone days in Dhamke. It is obvious that the family is proud of him and that they have prospered over the years. I am happy for their success.

Jerry's wife leads me into another room and beckons me to Jerry's charpoy. On the bed is a bent, shrunken old man with a short white beard and balding head. His eyes are rheumy, and he is unable to speak. With his wife's help, he is prodded upright on the bed. I think he has probably suffered a stroke, but no one elaborates on his sickness, so I just forge ahead. He reminds me of my father, unable to speak after his stroke, but alert and aware behind his garbled tongue.

I sit close to Jerry and begin talking to him in my halting Punjabi. I tell him who I am and about the time I was in Dhamke. Jerry looks at me piercingly and makes a sound, but I am unable to understand what he is trying to say. I do not know if he remembers me, but he seems engaged in our conversation, so I keep talking about some of the things we used to do in Dhamke. I wish I had brought the photos of his wedding with me and can only show him photos of Bill, Dick, Carol, and me in our wedding finery.

Fearing that we are overtiring him, I stand up to leave. Jerry tries to move forward on his charpoy but falls back. There are cries and murmurs from the women in the room; I know it is time for me to go.

I am so sad to see the once robust young man with the engaging grin and unstoppable energy in such a sorry state. More than anything else, Jerry's ill health marks the end of that era for me. It is time to put the past behind me and concentrate on the present and future in Pakistan.

But I want to take one final look back at the rest house where Bill and Dick stayed when we all lived in Dhamke.

Just as they did then, the women and young girls who joined us on our tour within the village disappear as soon as we step outside the village walls.

A crowd of young boys, Rana's son, Rana's nephew Mubashar, and a school-master replaces the girls. As we walk out to the rest house, the schoolmaster tells me that Dhamke now has two government primary schools, one for 214 boys, the other for some girls, and five private schools. He adds that he has passed his matriculation and is the schoolmaster of one of these private schools.

This certainly is a change from the 1960s, when there was one boys' primary school down the road from the village and the only school for girls was in a room off Rana's courtyard, with lessons led sporadically by Rana's older sister—and me, at my struggling social center.

When we reach the rest house, I am pleased to see that it is still standing. In fact, except that it is now abandoned and its walls are abused by graffiti, the rest house is remarkably the same. The village has moved closer over the years, however, and the rest house is no longer the retreat of shaded privacy, away from the prying eyes of village women and children, it once was for me.

But it is unquestionably the rest house that Rana said was marring Saroya's reputation, the rest house where I was almost billeted with unexpected bureaucrats from the Tehsil. It is the rest house of beautiful sunsets, dark clear skies, brilliant stars, and long walks back to the village with Bill and Dick, each carrying a big stick to ward off the pack of snarling dogs always ready to pounce. I remember those dogs and the twenty-four rabies shots in the stomach that Bill and I had to endure after one of the dogs attacked us.

The huge trees—home to crows and vultures that fell, sunstruck, from their branches—still shade the rest house, but the once green fields around the buildings have been trampled to barren brown. With some care and scrubbing, these buildings could, I think, again become habitable, but I doubt that they will. The modern motorways, small cars and vans, motorbikes, and cell phones have put the days of overnight visits to outlying villages aside.

As we turn from the rest house to walk back to the village, I look up to see a village silhouette I do not recognize. Towering over the two-story village houses and brick lanes is the tall minaret of a new village mosque. Behind the minaret is an even taller tower dedicated to the religion of cell phones.

Back in the village, we say good-bye to Rana's family, descendents of my former friends, and new acquaintances. Rana's courtyard is crowded with children and teenagers holding cell phones, each wanting a photo of him or herself with me. It is clear we are firmly in the twenty-first century.

The rest of the day is anticlimactic for me. I apologize to Taffy and Nancy for dragging them down Memory Lane to Dhamke, but they assure me that they have been happy with the day. In fact, they congratulate me on my successful return and tell me they are in awe of my Peace Corps experience. They are astonished that the villagers and their descendents have remembered my time with them in such detail.

I suppose it is extraordinary, now, to think that at age twenty-one I could be dropped among these people and expected to find something productive to do. Nancy and Taffy tell me that they probably would not have survived.

July 2009
Gymkhana Club, Lahore
For the past forty-five years I have regretted that I was not more successful and productive during my year in Dhamke. And yet, my second year in Sheikhupura was very successful and could not have happened without the lessons I learned that first year in Dhamke. In Dhamke I learned how to use my resources and sense of humor, how to apply my intelligence, how to persevere when things were rough, how to live by my wits outdoors, how to teach.

The people in Dhamke remember my Peace Corps days. They remember me. They remember that America is not always the bad guy. As I was leaving today, the schoolmaster said, in a mish-mash of English, Urdu, and Punjabi that he and all the village were happy that I had come back because it shows that not all Americans view Pakistan as a dangerous place where everyone is a terrorist.

Maybe this is the accomplishment of this trip. Today, as a result of my visit to Dhamke, I feel that my time here may not have been wasted after all. Perhaps I did contribute something, even as a young know-it-all/know-nothing idealistic American female.

CHAPTER 18

~

Khanewal and Harappa, 2009

On our final day of the primary Science Camps in Lahore, I rise early to jog before the golfers and commuters are awake. At this hour, the heat is not too oppressive, but the golf course is wet and soggy. I decide to run along the Mall Road instead, past the Pearl Continental Hotel where Taffy, Nancy, and I, hoping for a glass of wine, had dined a few nights ago.

That evening we had walked to the hotel at dusk, entering through a chain of cement barriers and armed security guards blocking the compound. Once inside, we were the only Western women in the dimly lit restaurant, and except for two wealthy-looking Pakistani families and a sprinkling of Pakistani and European businessmen, the only diners.

After dinner, we had planned to take a taxi back to the Gymkhana Club, but the concierge would not allow us to call one. "Taxis are no longer allowed on the hotel grounds," he said. He sent us back to the Gymkhana Club in a private hotel car, instead.

The Pearl Continental chain of hotels, I learned later, is considered a prime target for suicide bombers and other terrorist activities. Its sister hotels in Mumbai and Peshawar had both been attacked in the past nine months.

I reflect on these terrorist precautions as I run past the Pearl Continental on this early morning and then reverse my steps back to the Gymkhana Club. Well, I thought I had reversed my steps. Somewhere I had taken a wrong turn and I now find myself back at the Pearl Continental. My watch tells me it is 7:50, and I have to leave for school at 8:30 sharp. I will be late getting back to the Gymkhana Club, and worse, because it is so late, I will once again be the object of disbelieving stares from commuters on their way to work. My mood darkens as sweat drenches my cobbled-together shalwar kameez running outfit.

When I finally reach the Gymkhana Club, I discover a worried roommate, Nancy, anxiously waiting for me and watching breaking news on CNN: "At 7:50 a.m. local time . . . on 17 July 2009, the J. W. Marriott and Ritz-Carlton hotels in Jakarta, Indonesia, were hit by separate bombings five minutes apart. . . . Three of the seven victims killed are Australians, two are from the Netherlands, and one each is from New Zealand and Indonesia. More than fifty people were injured in the blasts. . . . Both blasts were caused by suicide bombers, who checked into the hotels as paying guests several days earlier."

The Lahore Pearl Continental, the hotel I have just passed twice, *could* have been on this list of suicide bombings. It dawns on me that my morning jogs might be a really bad idea; they make me too conspicuous and possibly too provocative. My running days in Lahore come to an abrupt end.

Later in the morning, at my school, Major Noeem, one of the Lahore area managers comes for a visit. I proudly show him around the different classrooms, all of them full of boys, teachers, and volunteers actively engaged in various projects. He is impressed, but I agree with Nancy's observation of few days ago about the teachers' inquiry-based learning practices: that even though the teachers are structuring their lessons for active participation and are allowing the children to talk and conduct experiments together, the method of instruction is still too direct.

I know from my years as a teacher educator that changing from a method of direct instruction to a method of inquiry—from didactic to experiential teaching—takes practice, many experiences teaching this way, knowledge about how children learn best, a firm grounding in the subject matter, and time, time, and more time. In this brief week and a half of training and practice, we cannot expect a complete change in the teachers' delivery. And perhaps, I reflect, their method of didactic instruction with a good balance of hands-on experiences and memorization is the answer for Pakistan, at least for the present.

When Illyas arrives to pick me up after school, I share my thoughts about the week with Nancy and Taffy. Overall, we agree that it has been a good week. Taffy is particularly exuberant about the final day of the coed primary camp at Roranwala.

"Since the teachers went through the lessons faster than they were designed," she says, "I suggested to Tahira that we have a competition on the last day. I'm not sure how the teachers selected who would compete from each class. At the appointed time, everyone came to the stage area and the competitors went up on the stage. The rest of the students stood in straight class lines, clutching their lab sheets while they watched the competitions. After about twenty minutes, Tahira let them sit down. It was an amazing display of good behavior. Can you imagine American children behaving this well at a school assembly?

"For each event," Taffy continued, "the competitors went center stage and built their clay boats or newspaper towers. The winners got a little prize. And guess who won the newspaper tower contest? The girl who built the tower of graduated cones earlier in the week—she competed against all the boys, and her tower was the tallest by far. I have a picture of her standing by her tower and one of her next to all the towers. It was a great activity and so cool to see. I was so proud of the girl who built the tower."

We are satisfied with the teaching and learning that we have seen in the past two weeks and look forward to the Science Camps that will begin Monday morning for the secondary students. These camps will be an opportunity for the teachers to practice inquiry teaching with learners who are a bit older and more experienced than the primary TCF children. Our hopes are high for the educational changes that are beginning to emerge in Pakistan.

In the morning, we leave the Gymkhana Club early for a weekend jaunt to Khanewal to visit Nancy's Peace Corps community development site and meet some TCF teachers and their area manager. We plan to spend Saturday night in Khanewal and return by way of Harappa on Sunday. Harappa, along with Moen-jo-Daro, is one of the most important archeological sites of Indus Valley civilization in Pakistan, contemporaneous with Babylon, Ur, and the Egyptian pyramids. I've never been there and am eager to see it.

Saturday morning, speeding down the new four-lane highway to Khanewal, we pass service plazas that offer fuel,[1] fast food, a place to pray, and clean modern restrooms. Nancy tells us that in 1965 this road was a one-lane stretch of blacktop that forced approaching vehicles to yield to the sandy shoulder to pass. There were no restroom or gasoline facilities then.

We whiz by trees and planted fields under a blazing sun. Nancy says the trees are the product of a tree-planting scheme of the 1960s. The summer crop of rice stretching green and wide in the former desert of uncultivable fields is made possible by an irrigation system that is the most extensive in the world. The animals we see look healthy, as well. The bullock, the primary beast of burden in the 1960s, seems to have been replaced by trucks and tractors.

The traffic in Khanewal is confusing for me, but Nancy is able to tell our driver exactly where to find her old home and the office of her Peace Corps assignment, the Colony Cooperative Farming Union (CCFU). The building is still there. We are greeted by the current general manager of the project, Muhammad Jamil Gathwala, and ushered into his dark, pleasantly cool office. He is eager to bring us up to date on the cooperative farming union.[2]

"The purchase of tractors and supply of modern agricultural implements brought out a revolution in the agrarian economy," he tells us. "These development activities . . . provided great incentive to the members and to the common farmers also. This institution is proud of its existence as a pioneer of mechanized farming in the country. It is significant that the members of the cooperative farming societies installed their own tube wells and purchased their own tractors after receiving an impact of the working of the union. The members were given credit facilities for the purchase of tractors and implements. As a result, the number of tube wells working in the project has increased to 1,305 and that of tractors has gone up to 838.

"However," the general manager continues, "the CCFU Khanewal is facing financial crisis these days, and monthly recoveries are hardly able to meet monthly expenditures, and due to this shortage of funds, the union has no business at present. . . . There is complete silence at the end of government regarding provision of funds and the institution is going to sink into financial crises. . . . The union is waiting for some miracle which can save their jobs and future of their children, but it seems that the government has no interest in the affairs of the institution."

Nancy circumspectly remarks, "It seems that now almost all of the farmers own their own land, most have their own tractors or hire a neighbor's tractor, and many have bought their neighbor's land and have larger farms. Some former members have sold their land at good profit to expanding towns and highway construction, and the government of Pakistan now buys the major agricultural products at set prices, so perhaps the co-op marketing program is no longer needed. Perhaps the goal of reclaiming the barren land by resettling refugees as tenant farmers and teaching them about scientific agriculture and developing irrigation systems to produce quite modern farms has been achieved."

The general manager nods with polite assent and asks us to accompany him to one of the villages outside of Khanewal to meet with CCFU members. We agree, but first we adjourn to the office of the TCF area manager for Khanewal and join him and a group of TCF teachers for a Pakistani lunch of biryani, spicy chicken, yogurt, fresh onions, lemon slices, and chapatis hot from the oven.

After lunch, we set out for a village about two and a half miles outside of Khanewal. The road into the village is deserted, and the village reminds me of Dhamke as I knew it in 1962 with its sun-baked houses, dirt lanes, and open green fields beyond the village walls. Stray dogs, goats, and open drains complete my nostalgic windswept picture.

Our little group is escorted to a small office near the village mosque and invited to join a gathering of co-op members assembled on charpoys in the courtyard. Many of the men are dressed in traditional long white cotton shirts and dhotis and wear white turbans tied loosely around their heads, the typical farmer's attire in the 1960s. Several of the TCF teachers have accompanied us, so our group is a mix of women and men.

Sitting on one of the chairs at the front of the group waiting for the meeting to begin, I experience an intense déjà vu. I do not quite understand the dialect of the men's conversation and am aware that something is expected of us that I cannot meet. I begin to feel the sun beating on my head, the dust swirling in my face, the hot wind tickling my nose and throat. Waiting for someone to bring the cold drinks that have been offered, straining to make sense of the polite gesticulated words of the village elders, I feel twenty-one again, powerless and desperate to both understand and to flee.

I get up to snap some photos and wander away from the crowd to an adjoining compound. Inside are a group of women, sitting on charpoys, their small, well-nourished children playing at their feet. A baby is sleeping in a dupatta tied like a hammock under one of the charpoys. The women are gossiping and sewing. One woman is sitting cross-legged, stitching a bright pink kameez on a hand-cranked sewing machine, similar to the one I had in Dhamke.

The women look like the women from my social center in Dhamke and are eager to talk to me. I sit down to admire their sewing. One woman grabs my hand and pulls me toward the main room of her house. Along one wall is a tier of shelves lined with plates, cups, and cooking pots above and three large tin trunks below, all covered with cotton cloth of dazzling colors and intricate patterns. Khanewal is in a cotton-producing region of the country and is a long-time supplier to Pakistan's textile industry. This room is a crazy quilt of colors and patterns against the buff beige walls of mud brick. And on the far wall, a full-size refrigerator stands next to a bicycle. No one in Dhamke of 1962 could have afforded such opulence. I jolt awake and realize that I am in the Pakistan of 2009. My feeling of déjà vu panic disappears.

When I return to the courtyard where the men are still meeting, Nancy, Taffy, and the teachers are talking together, separately. We women decide to poke around the village and see if we can find the government school. I am curious to see what the school looks like, even though it is closed for the summer holidays.

The government school is a walled campus of small one-story, flat-roofed buildings arranged around a courtyard. Several brick walkways crisscross the dirt-hardened courtyard leading to the classrooms, the administrative office, and a small bathroom building of footplate toilets, side by side and unpartitioned. My guess is that no girls attend this school.

Inside each classroom, double desks and benches are lined in front of a teacher's desk and blackboard. The walls are bare plaster and the windows have bars over their glass. Scraggly trees and bushes dot the courtyard, and the campus feels sterile. I wonder how many students are enrolled and how actively engaged the teachers are with their students. Several of the men join our group, but no one is able to answer my questions.

Down the lane, I peek over the wall of a mosque and discover an area on the far side of the courtyard devoted to a madrassa. Beneath an overhanging roof are a half dozen knee-high rectangular desks, long enough to accommodate two or three students sitting side by side. Although there are no students at the moment, I can picture them in their prayer hats and long white shalwar kurta, sitting cross-legged on their prayer rugs and rocking back and forth reciting sections of the Quran in Arabic. That image, so disturbing to many in the West, seems mild and harmless to me. When I ask about the madrassa, I am told that it is only for the religious education of village boys who attend the government school that we have just seen.

On our way back to Khanewal to visit Nancy's former home, we stop at the co-op office to say good-bye to Muhammad Jamil Gathwala, our host. He presents each of us with a book of poetry, which he has written and published in Urdu. I know the importance to many Pakistanis of reading, reciting, and writing poetry and am touched by our host's gesture of friendship. It is a beautiful book, and I promise to renew my efforts to continue learning to read Urdu. As a Peace Corps Volunteer, I learned the oral dialect of Punjabi, and my skills reading the Arabic alphabet in which Urdu and now Punjabi are written are still developing.

Nancy's former residence, when we reach it, is on a busy street of small, open-fronted shops and neighborhood traffic. Inside its walls, a chowkidar allows us to look around the tree-shaded garden and the servants' quarters behind Nancy's former bungalow. I tease Nancy that her servants' housing was better than anything I had in Dhamke, and she admits that, as director of the Peace Corps project in Khanewal, she had not only servants but also use of a jeep and a steady supply of Murree beer, her favorite refreshing beverage.

To be fair, her house also included the local Peace Corps office and, for the forty-seven Peace Corps Volunteers in her project, a hostel and necessary respite from their village lives without electricity or running water.

"The CCFU did provide local coworkers for the Khanewal volunteers, however," Nancy comments, "so the Peace Corps Volunteers were able to achieve a great deal in this pioneering project. Unfortunately, the project was cut short by the India-Pakistan war of 1965."

We continue down the road to the residence of the Catholic priest of Nancy's former church. He invites us to attend Mass in a village church in the morning, and we readily accept.

At dusk, Zil-e-hu-huna, the director of TCF cluster education in Khanewal, invites us to browse with her in the old bazaar in Khanewal. I am looking for *makai*, corn on the cob roasted in hot coals and displayed on tall treelike poles attached to open wagons. But I can't find my corn. The old bazaar is too crowded with other vendors and stalls of fabric, clothing, sewing supplies, shoes, electrical appliances, toys, cheap jewelry, and plastic chairs and tables. The streets are jammed with motorcycles, rickshaws, bicycles, and pedestrians. And it is growing dark.

Taffy and I are also looking for modern black burqahs. Our hostess thinks it is funny that we are shopping for burqahs, but she knows just where to take us. We enter a small shop laden floor to ceiling with bolts of fabric in every color, pattern, and palette. An older man and his young son wait on us. In the back of the narrow shop behind a partition of fabric are stacks of cellophane-wrapped, ready-to-wear black burqahs.

Taffy agrees to be our mannequin, and we drape her in a midnight-colored shoulder-to-toe silky robe and long black hijab. Across her nose, just under her eyes, we strap another piece of black fabric. She is covered, head to ankle, in flowing inky grace.

An older man sitting behind us in the shop taps Nancy on the shoulder. Nodding toward Taffy, he says solemnly, "She is much more beautiful this way."

Taffy is undecided on how to take this comment. Is it a compliment? We add it to our store of teaseable moments and snap her photo. She is unrecognizable.

When we leave the shop, the daylight has disappeared, and so have all the women shoppers. The night is black velvet, soft shop lights, and sharp auto headlights. Down one crowded narrow street, up another, I am still looking for makai. At last, we come to an intersection of corner tables, chairs, and street food vendors. A makai wallah holds center stage in front of a samosa stand.

While Nancy orders samosas, I watch the makai wallah swirl husked cobs of corn around a kettle of sand and ash over the belly of a metal drum filled with fire. When the cobs are finished, he brushes the kernels with lemon juice and ground chili peppers, reattaches the husks, and hands me my treasure. It is hot gold. Between bites of peppery makai, roasted chicken, and spicy potato samosa, washed down with 7-Up infused with fresh lemon, I am in heaven.

Finally, we retire to the upstairs quarters of the TCF area manager's office, where three charpoys are ready for our tired bodies. But it is still intensely hot, and I take my charpoy outside on the roof under the stars. After this long, sweltering, interesting day, I am asleep in minutes.

In the morning, we rise early to be ready for Mass in a nearby Christian village. We are early for the service and sit on a bench, barefoot, in the back of the one-room sanctuary facing the altar. The parishioners sit on the floor in front of us, men on one side, women and children on the other. I am struck by the bright colors worn by the women. Their shalwar kameez and contrasting dupattas are richly hued in purple, pink, red, orange, yellow, blue, ivory, aqua, and green. Their outfits sparkle with glass beads in floral patterns; no two are alike.

The men are clean-shaven and wear freshly starched shirts and khaki pants, or blue jeans and T-shirts. The children are in shorts and Western-style dresses. Everyone is washed, combed, pressed, and immaculate. The overflow crowd spills into the courtyard.

The priest, attended by two young girls in white veils and long white kameez and a boy, also in white, dons a green robe over his white Punjabi kurta, and the service begins. I am not able to follow most of the priest's exhortations but enjoy the parishioner's responses punctuated by drummers and atonal singing. Nancy is invited to give a brief message, which she delivers to welcoming smiles and nods, even though she is speaking English and most of those in the audience cannot understand her. At the end of the service, we are surrounded by warm hugs, wishes for our good health, and as in houses of worship worldwide, hope for peace.

After church, we visit the home of one of the parishioners for a cool drink before beginning our trip back to Lahore. The woman of the house, when told that we had been in Pakistan in the 1960s, proudly pulls out a large photograph of herself taken back then. A slim, dark-haired, beautiful young woman at that time, her appearance today reflects the hard life of Christian village women since.

In my village in the 1960s, the Christians were the lowest class, sweepers and cleaners. They also served as midwives and laborers and lived apart from their Muslim neighbors. Christians were often included in Muslim households as family servants, and although their lives were hard and tasks physically demanding and demeaning, they were not persecuted. In Dhamke, both the Christian and Muslim women befriended me. I never detected animosity between the two groups. However, the Christian women knew their place and worked silently when they were in a Muslim courtyard.

I wonder about the lives of Christians in modern Pakistan. Knowing that TCF does not discriminate nor promote a religious or political agenda, I am curious about the number of Christian families that are served by TCF schools. The ayahs and chowkidars, traditionally the Christians in a neighborhood, are important members of the TCF family and, indeed, do much of the initial recruiting for students when a TCF school is built in a community. I make a mental note to find out how many Christian students are enrolled in TCF schools and to learn more about the connection between TCF and the Christians in their respective communities.

After our refreshing interval, we bid our Khanewal hosts good-bye and begin the long drive back to Lahore. Our driver is happy, he says, to stop at Harappa, just off the highway near his village. This is his home territory, and he is eager to show us one of Pakistan's most famous attractions.

Several miles later, we stop at the gate of the Harappa Museum, inaugurated, its sign reads, on March 26, 1967. Inside the gate is a long brick footpath bordered by flowering shrubs and trees leading to a modern-looking cement building. We approach the building under a bower of leafy branches, the cool shade briefly disguising the sun beating mercilessly overhead. Inside the low white building, we are quite comfortable and spend a few minutes browsing among the exhibits.

The museum guide tells us that "Harappa was a city in the ancient Indus civilization, between 3300 BC and 1500 BC, and, though discovered in the early 1800s, it was not excavated until the 1920s. The archeological site includes an area of about 250 acres, and the artifacts discovered here answer many questions about the Indus people who created its highly complex culture."

The guide invites us to walk through the site and promises that we will see structural remains of a neighborhood, a granary, and a very large house. But he admits that "the mud adobe bricks were robbed in antiquity, so the bricks you will see on the sites are not the original."

We reluctantly leave the cool interior of the museum for the sandy path leading to the outdoor excavation site. The sun has not given up. I pull my dupatta over my head and hide behind my sunglasses, to no avail. I am trapped in antiquity for three hours of blistering, dazzling sun.

Nevertheless, the discomfort is worth it. The original Harappa neighborhoods can be seen in foot-high square brick walls lining several excavation areas. A sign, written in English and Urdu, explains:

This area has a series of fourteen houses all built on the same basic plan . . . as is seen today in housing development schemes. . . . These large houses are probably the houses and shops of wealthy merchants. . . . To the west is a large kiln for melting metal or firing pottery. . . . One home is thought to be that of a goldsmith as it contained a hoarde [sic] of gold and agate jewelry.

A little farther along the path, I discover:

This Mound is a result of continuous building by the inhabitants of the city during the final phase of the city around 2200 to 1900 BC. In the lower level there is a large well and bathing and washing platforms that belong to an even earlier period. Unlike Moen-jo-Daro where there were wells in each neighborhood, in Harappa there have been only eight wells discovered. Some of them were private, some public. . . . Much of the top structures were robbed by the contractors who built the Lahore, Multan railway track during British rule. The lower structures were destroyed by the Harrappan inhabitants to reconstruct their houses. The archeological excavations were conducted here . . . 1921 to 1924 AD and 1926 to 1934 AD.

We walk on to another sandy excavation and read:

This Area is from the middle Harappa period around 2450–2200 BC. . . . In the lower level is the largest building of the Indus Valley civilization. This structure was built on a massive foundation of mud brick. . . . Two rows of six rooms are arranged along a passageway that is about seven meters [23 feet] wide and paved with baked bricks. Each room is 15.2 by 6.1 meters [50 feet by 20 feet] and has three sleeper walls with air space between them. A wooden superstructure supported in some places by very large columns may have been built on top of the brick foundations with stairs leading up to form the central passage area. Small triangular openings may have served as air ducts to allow the flow of fresh air beneath the hollow floors.

I have always been intrigued by the ingenuity of ancient architecture, particularly irrigation and cooling systems. I wonder if it was as hot in 2200 BC as it is on this baking afternoon.

It is impressive, I think, that Pakistan is home to two ancient urban civilizations, Moen-jo-Daro and Harappa. Since Partition, the responsibility for excavating and maintaining these sites belongs to Pakistan. Although we are the only visitors on this scorching Sunday afternoon, I think that developing Harappa as a worthwhile tourist attraction is a smart idea and am happy to see that the site is well maintained and accessible to English- and Urdu-speaking visitors.

On our way back to our car, I notice some women in the distance, crossing an acre of sand mounds and scrubby trees. Their gait is slow and rhythmical; they create a ribbon of color across the drab canvas of undulating plain. Our driver tells us that these women are nomads, and the bundles they are carrying on their heads are bales of just-picked cotton.

As we climb into our air-conditioned car and speed along the N5 road back to the twenty-first century and comforts of the Gymkhana Club, I think that of all the contrasts this weekend has presented, those women swaying across the open scrubland in the hottest part of the day are the most arresting.

I settle into the passenger seat, close my eyes, and fall into a dreamy doze. Back in Pakistan. I am back in a country of ancient civilizations, divergent cultural and religious traditions, and baffling modern problems.

CHAPTER 19

~

Leaving Lahore, 2009

Our last week in Lahore, the first week of the secondary Science Camps, we add another activity to one of our teaching days. "We each need to present a lesson on solar cookers this week," Taffy tells us when we return to the Gymkhana Club Sunday evening.

Nancy and I look at each other, nod, and accept the assignment. We begin to gather the materials we will need and try to remember the patterns we had cut out and given to the Karachi teachers to use for their cookers.

It occurs to me that inventing the patterns requires solving a problem. I decide to teach the lesson by posing the construction of the solar cooker as a problem to be solved—the model for inquiry-based learning—and withhold the precut patterns.

Monday morning at my school, forty boys show up for the beginning of Science Camp. Fakhra, the principal, divides the group into four classes of ten students each and tells the teachers that one of them will have a day off from teaching during the week but must stay on campus on her day off. I am pleased that Fakhra has divided the classes this way and wonder if she would have thought of it if we had not divided the primary camp sessions of the past week into five classes of ten pupils each. I also wonder if the "nonteaching" teacher will choose to team-teach with one of her colleagues on her day off.

I tell Fakhra that one day, early in the week, the teachers will need to stay after school for a short lesson on solar cookers. We agree that this day will be tomorrow.

At the end of classes on Tuesday, the teachers gather around me for the explanation of solar cookers. I explain the concept of harnessing the sun's energy to cook food and purify water and note that there are a number of ways to do this. With the materials we have before us—aluminum foil, cardboard cartons, scissors, tape, thermometers, small jars—and any other materials they might think important to use, I ask the teachers to come up with several solar cooker designs that can bring water in a small jar to the boiling point. I tell them that they should consider the parameters of efficiency, reliability, and cost of materials in their designs, and ask the teachers to work together in pairs to design their cooker according to these parameters. I deliberately do not give any predrawn patterns or models.

Even though they have spent the first half of the day teaching their own students, the teachers begin this after-school task with enthusiasm. Dilshad and Sakina, Nazia and Fizzah, and Sarah and Fakhra team together and begin cutting, taping, assembling, discarding, and reworking cardboard boxes to create various solar cooker designs.

Each team creates a different model. Two teams build three-sided cookers—one lined with aluminum foil on the inside and a layer of folded newspapers on its floor; the second with aluminum foil taped to every cardboard surface, inside and out. The third cooker has four sides and is also lined with aluminum foil on the bottom of the box. However, this team has placed their cooker diagonally across another box, to face the sun at a forty-five-degree angle.

The teachers put small jars of water in their cookers and place the cookers in the sun to test for efficiency, speed, and reliability.

I study Dilshad and Sakina's design and ask Dilshad why she has used so much tape. "So that no heat can possibly escape through the cracks where we joined the sides to the bottom of our cooker," she replies.

I ask if it would be cheaper just to bend her cardboard rather than to cut it and then use tape to fasten it back together. She thinks a minute, then puts the question to the others. "Yes," they all agree. "Folding the box would be cheaper than using a lot of tape. But it is *faster* to cut the cardboard and tape it together, because this way will use less labor and be cheapest to produce on a large scale."

When the first small jar of water begins to boil in Dilshad and Sakina's cooker, everyone applauds and high-fives them with congratulations. There is laughter and a feeling of goodwill and accomplishment. We talk about the design of this cooker and why it is more efficient than the others.

As we return to the classroom to clean up the mess we have made, I reiterate my teaching strategy and method with the teachers. "At the beginning of the class, I introduced the concept of using the sun's energy to cook quickly and cheaply," I remind them. "Then I posed the problem to be solved, had materials on hand to solve it, and asked you to work together to come up with your own designs to solve the problem. I asked you questions as you were working, but I did not give you any 'correct' answers.

"This is the method of inquiry that we hope you will take with you and use in your teaching for the remaining days of the Science Camps and in your teaching when regular classes resume in just a few weeks."

I ask how it felt to be an inquiry learner.

"Confusing at first," Dilshad admits. "But it is interesting to try new ways, not trying to do the most correct way."

"It is very good that we had the boxes and tape and equipment ready," adds Sakina.

"Do you think this kind of learning is easier to supervise if you have fewer students in your classroom and the students are allowed to work together in pairs or small groups and share their ideas as they experiment?" I ask.

They all nod in agreement and continue to talk about the solar cookers and how they will challenge their students to make different designs when they teach this lesson.

At the end of the hour, I feel that I have made my point about inquiry teaching, small classes, and the importance of students working and talking together as they solve problems. Our afternoon ends with hugs, laughter, and more hand-slapping compliments. I think we have all accomplished something today. It feels right.

When Taffy and Nancy arrive to pick me up, they are equally energized. I tell them about my experiment with the solar cookers, and Taffy tells us about her observation of a group of girls working on speed and acceleration.

"Once the concept was explained," she says, "the girls worked independently to set up the ramp, place the adding machine tape down its surface, and allow their cars to roll. They took turns with the ramp, helped each other with their cars, and talked about how to correct minor drip problems. I could see that they loved doing things with their hands and manipulating the equipment. Afterwards, one of the girls told me that she loves doing lessons like this. She asked if all their classes could be taught this way."

We three look at each other and say, in unison, "*Why* not?"

We ask Illyas to drive us to Anarkali Bazaar in the old walled city of Lahore. Taffy is still looking for a supplier for balance scales and has been given the name of a shop in the Science Bazaar.

In the middle of a hot summer afternoon, the bazaar is almost empty and many shops are shuttered. At first we think this is because of the heat, but then we learn that the shopkeepers are on strike to protest that persistent pest, load shedding. We wind our way into a deserted back street and discover one shopkeeper still in his lair. He invites us in for a cool drink, and we gratefully accept.

Inside, his narrow shop is crammed floor to ceiling with dusty boxes of every imaginable kind of science equipment. While Taffy talks with him about the best kind of balance scale to provide to primary and secondary science students, the shopkeeper tells of a superior model made in China that is cheaper and more reliable than anything produced in the West. Taffy and our host seem to be talking past each other, and as their conversation drones on, I struggle to keep my eyes open.

Eventually the shopkeeper invites us to look at his supplies in another building. We follow him to his storeroom up some winding stairs, across a passageway, down more winding stairs into a moldy overfilled basement storeroom. I try to follow his conversation as I follow his footsteps, but he gains the lead and disappears behind a huge set of shelves at the back of the basement. Taffy and I look at each other bewildered and are just about to leave when he reappears with a flimsy box of scales and small weights.

"These scales," he says, "are one-eighth the price of European scales that look just the same. These scales are from China, and I can get them very fast. The European scales are much more expensive, and they take many weeks to arrive, if they arrive at all. You must purchase your scales from China."

We see the influence of Chinese entrepreneurs everywhere, from the lettering on vans and trucks to goods of every description in the stores and bazaars. I remember that China is just on the other side of the northern border of Pakistan at the terminus of the Karakoram Highway, and I am reminded how many products in everyday life are now produced in China. I am also surprised that none of the items housed in this storeroom have been produced in the United States.

By the time we are ready to leave Anarkali, the bazaar has come to life. Nancy is looking for glass bangles for her nieces, and we are directed to the jewelry section of the bazaar. It is bustling with women in burqahs and children running about eating ice cream while their mothers and aunts shop.

The choices at the bangle stalls are inexhaustible—row upon row of thin round bracelets in clusters of five or six or a dozen. Every color, every material—glass, plastic, metal, gold, silver, copper, embroidered and woven thread—and every size, to fit the smallest infant wrist or the largest Western woman with arthritic knuckles and joints. With such variety, Nancy takes a long time to make her purchases.

I remember how my hands were squeezed, squished, rubbed, oiled, and kneaded in the 1960s when my lady workers tried to fit glass bangles over my fingers, past my knuckles, and onto my wrists. Every bangle, it seemed, was designed for metacarpals made of bendable rubber instead of bone. It is just too embarrassing to splinter a glass bangle while you are trying it on—and worse to have it pass over your knuckles to remain permanently, removable only by being broken and wrenched across bleeding skin, disgraced. I still have a collection of bangles from my Peace Corps days—a collection of colorful glass shards and large misshapen circles of nonbreakable metal.

On this, our last night in Lahore, we return to the Old City to dine in a restaurant housed in the former home of a *nautch* girl of Lahore.[1] We are the guests of Sanober Adeel, the TCF woman responsible for the procurement of supplies and organization of equipment that made our work at the Lahore camps so effortless. Sanober and her husband are eager to show us the respectable underside of their city.

As we walk through the narrow streets, we are plunged into authentic seventeenth- and eighteenth-century darkness, compliments of load shedding. We enter an old brick building two rooms deep and many rooms high. Our destination is the dining room on the roof, but to reach it, we must climb a narrow spiral staircase cut through tiny rooms and porticos whose ceilings and doors are hung tentlike with tapestries of maroon, midnight blue, purple, gold, and magenta threads.

The walls in many of the rooms are covered with large oil paintings of buxom women in various attitudes and styles, depicting behind-the-scene courtesan life. In one painting, two women are applying makeup and looking into a hand mirror. The Lahore Fort and Badshai Mosque are in the background of the painting, creating a scene that could be occurring right now in this same room, were this the enterprise it was during the British Raj.

I look out a narrow window to what I can see of the Badshai Mosque. It is not illuminated, as it would be if the electricity were on in this part of the city, and the shadows make the mosque an even more imposing structure. The Badshai Mosque and Lahore Fort are nostalgic for me.[2] As a twenty-one-year-old starry-eyed Peace Corps Volunteer, they were touchstones of the passion and mystery of the magnificent Moghul Empire.

Incense and the fragrance of spicy cooking are in the air as we reach the candlelit, semiprivate rooms at the top of the house. Tables are ready for romantic dining, set with gleaming silverware, shining goblets, porcelain plates, and starched napkins. Sculptures of Moghul guards, wild beasts, and torsos of bare-chested men guard our table under three cusped arches. At the other end of the dining room in similar spaces, Pakistani couples and foursomes dine in quiet seclusion. The atmosphere is subdued elegance, secret rendezvous, and exotic seduction. For once, I think, load shedding is positive for its contribution to the mood and legacy of Moghul and British decadence. But there are no dancing girls.

The next day, our last at the Summer Science Camps, my teachers treat me to my favorite lunch: chapatis, sagh-gosht, and Coca-Cola. We take turns posing for photos, and the teachers present me with a neatly wrapped package of metal gold and aqua bangles. Luckily, they fit.

I am a little embarrassed not to have any bangles to give to the teachers, but my affection is genuine and travel tears real. Fakhra begs me to return to work with her staff for at least a month. Dilshad shyly gives me her email address and asks if we can write to each other.

I am sad to leave these teachers. Working with them has been a good experience for me and, I hope, for them. I am less naive than I once was, however, and do not expect that much has been changed by my presence among these teachers and students in the past few weeks. I would like to think that I have helped them understand inquiry methods of teaching and learning. I am pleased with the contributions of the college student volunteers and know they have altered their views of street children by working with them and with the TCF teachers this summer.

The warmhearted reception that both Nancy and I received when we returned to our respective Peace Corps venues reinforces my belief in the value of seemingly small positive efforts, people to people. I am beginning to realize that our Peace Corps presence in Pakistan so many years ago *did* make a difference in some people's lives, a difference that has helped them inch forward with confidence. Perhaps the few ideas I have brought with me to share this summer will make a difference in one of these teachers' or students' or family's lives in the future. I hope so.

At the end of our last school day in Lahore, Taffy, Nancy, and I wave good-bye to our TCF friends and board the Daewoo bus for Islamabad.[3] For the next ten days, we will be on *chutti* in the mountains of Hunza, stretching our hiking legs and breathing the cool, clear air of 14,000-foot altitudes. We will meet Danial, Karen, and Sofia Noorani in Islamabad, travel with them by small commercial plane to Gilgit, and journey north on the Karakoram Highway through the towering peaks of Azad Kashmir. I can't wait.

CHAPTER 20

~

Islamabad: Modern Pakistan

The Daewoo Express is like traveling in a Greyhound bus of the past, with the addition of a polite hostess, cold soft drinks, and overhead commercial TV.

I am curious about Pakistani television, and as we whiz along the highway, I watch the overhead screen, mesmerized by the advertising, which I have trouble separating from the scheduled program. Most of the commercials are for soft drinks or soap powder, but the ads are slick, colorful vignette presentations of middle-class Pakistani consumers enjoying the good life with whatever product is being praised. The message is always "Buy our product and you will have a better life"—not so different from TV ads back home.

I settle into the upholstered reclining seat. There is a luggage rack for my bags and a footrest for my feet. I am prepared for a clean, comfortable, air-conditioned journey to Islamabad.

Outside my window, the plains of the Punjab are green and mud-puddled from a heavy overnight thunderstorm downpour. As we speed north on the divided superhighway, I am reminded again of how much transportation in Pakistan has changed since my last trip to Islamabad. When we stop midway on our three-hour journey, I join a queue of burqah-clad women in the large, well-appointed bathroom and wait my turn to use the Western- or Eastern-style facilities. On my former bus trips to Islamabad, the journey took all day, and the rest stop accommodations were in the nearest field.

Changed also is the way the food and drink vendors ply their wares. No longer do they shove fresh orange slices, 7-Up, or hot kebabs through the open windows of the bus. Today, passengers disembark and buy their refreshment from an outdoor grill, a wall of soft drink dispensers, or an indoor shop of chips, candy, and cheap toys.

Our bus ride ends, and we arrive at our destination by five o'clock prayer time and are greeted, as we have begun to expect, by a TCF driver. We load our baggage, considerably lighter without our teaching supplies, and are driven past several bazaars in Rawalpindi to the TCF headquarters in nearby Islamabad. In 1962, Rawalpindi was the temporary capital of Pakistan while Islamabad was being constructed. I remember looking at the future capital from afar—a heap of white stucco and concrete buildings against a backdrop of mountains in the middle of flat, open nowhere.

Today, of course, Islamabad is the capital of Pakistan and is a thriving community of international embassies, commerce, high-tech industry, tourism, and Islam. Both Quaid-i-Asam University and the Faisal Mosque are located in Islamabad. Rawalpindi is now headquarters for the Pakistan army and, in recent years, has been noted as a place of assassination.[1]

I am struck by the starkness of the streets and the conservative dress of the women in Rawalpindi. In Lahore and Karachi, some women traveled about without hijab or burqah. As I look out of the car windows on our way from the Daewoo station to the TCF headquarters in Rawalpindi, every woman I see is dressed in a black burqah or covered by an oversized dupatta and a hijab around her face.

The men look more conservatively dressed, as well. Many have long beards and wear prayer caps and long white shalwar kurta. In Lahore and Karachi, the men's outfits are khaki or beige colored, and, except for mustaches, men are usually clean shaven. The men in the bazaars and shops I see in the neighborhoods in Rawalpindi look more conservative, less friendly, and more stereotypically Islamic. I wonder if they are.

Our accommodations in Rawalpindi are in rooms above the TCF office. Commodore Tasleem, the Regional Manager Northwest, and Razia Sultana, the Educational Manager Northwest, greet us. They tell us that Karen, Sofia, and Danial will arrive in the morning, and that our travel to Gilgit may have to be delayed a day or two. Karen has unfortunately had a fall and broken her arm; also, the weather in the mountains may postpone our scheduled flight. Our trip will happen in two days, they say—insha'Allah.

Taffy, Nancy, and I squeeze into a bedroom just off the main eating/sitting area of the TCF hostel and settle in. The heat in the main room is suffocating, but our bedroom is overly air-conditioned and freezing. I decide to sleep this night on the roof.

While we are waiting for the Noorani family to arrive the next day, Taffy arranges for us to meet a representative from the Human Development Foundation (HDF). This nongovernmental organization (NGO) was founded by two Pakistani physicians in 1997, according to its website, "to facilitate a non-political movement for positive social change and community empowerment through mass literacy, enhanced quality of education, primary health care and grassroots economic development." The foundation "models the philosophy of distributed leadership and shared responsibility," thereby encouraging volunteers to act as leaders in their own communities.[2] When Taffy tells me the dictum of this NGO is "We help the people to help themselves," my old Peace Corps community development mantra, I am eager to meet with them.

Early the next morning, a young HDF manager, Zulfiqar Ali, picks us up, and we drive out of the city to a small village in the outlying foothills of the Margalla mountain range. The area looks dry and sandy, though there are leafy trees and bushes bisecting the scrubland. The projects we visit remind me of the Peace Corps basic democracy community development projects of the 1960s.

As with those basic democracies projects, the HDF works with local leaders and establishes governing councils to drill wells, raise chickens, and build schools and health clinics. We see several thriving chicken farms of enormous three-story chicken coops, housing thousands of chickens all living in crates. I remember Dick's little coop of a dozen chickens and the trouble he had convincing Rana that chickens could be the staple meat of Pakistan's future. In fact, chicken *has* become that staple and is now widely available and a very popular item on menus throughout Pakistan.

We stop at a well-drilling project and talk to one of the community leaders working with HDF. I am very impressed with his ideas of community development, more so because his ideas seem to be working. The community leader takes us to visit the "lady health worker" in the village clinic and then to an HDF primary school where a teacher-training session is in progress.

Our arrival at the teacher-training site interrupts the PowerPoint presentation of the trainer, but she and her assembled teachers are happy to talk with us. The teachers are all taking notes, and the room is plastered with posters and large newsprint summaries of the training proceedings. Minus the PowerPoint capabilities and newsprint, the scene reminds me of the training sessions I conducted with my lady workers in Sheikhupura. The teachers ask us about education in America, and we chat for a few minutes about teaching, its rewards, and best practices.

At the end of the morning, we meet with Syed Qaiser Abbas, the Islamabad team leader of HDF and a former retired military officer turned social worker. This use of former military expertise seems to be a familiar model for Pakistani NGOs and, I think, a very savvy one.

Syed is a gracious host and tells us more about his organization over Pakistani lunch, served in the modest HDF dining room. I am impressed with the dedication and sophistication of the people I have met and congratulate our host on the HDF program and organization. It is another example, for me, of a Pakistani solution to a Pakistani problem, organized and carried out by educated, caring Pakistanis.

On the way back to our TCF lodgings, we pass the American Embassy and decide, on the spur of the moment, to stop in. This was easier to do in 1963 than it is now. In 1963, the day after John Kennedy was assassinated, a group of us filed into the embassy to record our thoughts and prayers in his memory. We were greeted solemnly by U.S. Marines at the door and ushered inside to pay our respects.

Entering the U.S. Embassy on this hot summer day in 2009 is a very different experience. Our driver drops us at the end of a long barricaded lane leading to one of the embassy gates. Tall fences topped with barbed wire flank both sides of the lane and Pakistani sentries are stationed at various points along the way. We walk down this dusty lane and finally reach a small brick gatehouse at the end.

At the triple-glassed bulletproof window of the gatehouse, we naively ask to be admitted to the embassy grounds to visit the USAID offices. We are told to wait while the Pakistani guards in the air-conditioned structure scrutinize our U.S. passports. Several sleek black official cars drive up to the gate and slip through with a wave from the guards. We continue to stand in the blazing sun.

Finally an American from the USAID office comes to the window of the gatehouse. He seems a little puzzled by our unusual appearance—three older American women dressed in Pakistani clothing, beet red and sweating—but not alarmed that we have arrived without an appointment. He vouches for us to enter the gatehouse.

Inside the gatehouse, we put our purses on an x-ray conveyer belt and walk through an airport-like security booth. Joe Ryan, our American guide, meets us on the other side of the security booth and escorts us to the USAID offices. Even though we do not have an appointment, we are treated with courtesy and friendliness.

At the end of a long narrow corridor, we reach our destination and are introduced to several USAID workers. We have met them before. They are the team that visited our TCF training site in Lahore several weeks ago, and they remember our conversation with clarity. We talk, again, about the work of TCF, which they know well and seem to appreciate. We also tell them about our day with the HDF and reiterate that both NGOs are doing the kind of work that we had tried to do as Peace Corps Volunteers in the 1960s.

The difference, we emphasize, is that back then we were Americans trying to solve Pakistani problems. These two NGOs—TCF and the HDF—are Pakistanis solving Pakistani problems, successfully, and in ways that will be sustained. Because the people in these organizations know their own culture and understand their traditions and foibles better than we, they are far more effective agents of positive social change than we Americans were or ever could be.

We urge our audience of USAID workers, which by now has grown to a small assembly of Pakistanis and Americans, to consider funding transparent private NGOs like TCF and HDF rather than disbursing the funds from the Kerry-Lugar Bill to the inefficient and nontransparent government offices. We are speaking, we assure them, as U.S. citizens with a perspective of working for social change in Pakistan that has deep roots. The USAID team listens attentively to our plea, based on our combined professional experience of eighty-five years and our deeply felt commitment to the people of Pakistan.

Later that afternoon, back at the TCF office, I sit down for a chat with Razia Sultana, the education manager for TCF's Northwest Region. Razia is one of only a few TCF managers I have met who wears a hijab. I am curious about the juxtaposition of that apparel with her job description at TCF. I ask Razia how she became involved with TCF.

"Two years back, I was at Berea Foundation College," she begins. "TCF needed one trainer for computer training, and my colleague contacted me to do it. It was one day training, and I was not willing . . . because I was too busy. I was also working as head examiner at the Open University.

"The head of TCF Education Department met with me and asked me to come to the office and meet with a panel because they were looking for someone to work as education manager," Razia continues. "I came in the evening in the Regional Office and . . . they interviewed me and asked a lot of questions and told me about TCF.

"When they offered me the job, I said, 'I will have to ask my parents. I cannot tell this thing right now.'

"My father said, 'It's up to you.' My brother said, 'What is this? A lot of traveling, 8:30 to 5:30, a lot of work. A full-time job is a tough job for ladies.'

"In the end, after two days, I informed TCF I would come. I was thinking I should do something, but I was not in my mind how I would serve the people. But TCF is the correct way, the right way to serve the people.

"It is a very big change in my life," Razia adds. "I never went out from my home [before]. . . . Now I have to do a lot of travel. In Northwest Region, most of the schools are far apart. When I go, I have to spend five to six days. I go by myself with my driver."

I tell Razia I am curious about her Islamic attire and ask her how that part of her life fits with her new responsibilities and "going alone" outside her house.

"I wear the hijab and *abiyah* now," Razia answers. "Actually I went to Saudi Arabia for *pakrah*,[3] and I feel very comfortable in this dress. I have a little more protection with it on. In summer, it is very hot. My four sisters do not wear hijab. My younger sister wears it when she goes to market. My other sisters don't wear it."

I tell her about my own experiences wearing Pakistani clothing and the rudeness I sometimes experience because I am not also wearing a burqah. I tell her that other Muslim women have told me that when they wear a burqah in public, they feel more protected. "It seems to me," I say, "that when you wear a burqah, or maybe a hijab and abiyah, it tells others— namely, rude young men—that you are not available for their conversation, and that if they intrude on your privacy, they will have to answer to your husband or brother or father."

"Yes, yes," Razia nods in agreement. "I feel relaxed and comfortable in abiyah. When I started wearing this, I never had any problems with it. I feel safer in this . . . and I don't have to worry about the dupatta."

I chuckle at this. Nancy in particular has a running battle with her dupatta. However, we have all discovered the power of the safety pin to keep the dupatta from slipping off our shoulders, and Nancy never leaves our room without it being properly pinned. I, on the other hand, often use my dupatta to cover my head in the bright sun or whenever I feel a situation calls for me to be more modest. My safety pins usually end up lost in the folds of my kameez or sticking into my shoulders as I arrange and rearrange my dupatta many times in the course of a day. As in 1962, I still find the dupatta a necessary nuisance.

"I have only one brother," Razia continues, responding to my idea of male protection. "I love him too much. I always do what he wants. He is one year younger to me, but he behaves just like older. We all sisters love him too much, so he thinks he has the right to order us to do things. He never stops us from things, but if he thinks this job is not good for me or my sisters, I would not do it.

"My brother only wants what is best for us . . . because I am not used to such hard work from 8:30 to 5:30 with so much travel, and before I was not used to this kind of job. That's why he was reluctant. Now his mind is changed. He never minds, but if I go too many weeks he will mind. . . . But, like other men, he will be the same with his daughters," she concludes.

"Speaking of daughters," I ask her, "why do uneducated mothers send their daughters to school now, when only one generation ago they did not?"

Razia quickly responds: "In villages . . . once the mothers see TCF established . . . they get knowledge of TCF and that afterwards their daughters can get a job there. Before TCF, they didn't send their daughters, but their minds are getting changed now. They see that the girls can get jobs back in the schools when they are finished or they can get jobs in their own communities. They see TCF provides for jobs for their daughters in the schools.

"Before TCF, their thinking is, 'School is not important for girls,' but the teachers have meetings with mothers and other people in the village to convince them. TCF is able to use matric-level teachers and then we train them. The training causes a lot of changes in the teachers. Their eyes are looking very bright, and they are feeling a lot better."

As an aside, Razia notes, "Our TCF schools have not been affected by the Taliban issues in Swat. We closed for a few days only. The Taliban have not convinced anyone that girls should not be educated."

As we conclude our interview, Razia remarks, "Before coming to TCF, I did not know about it. It was a sudden change in my life, a turning point in my life. I can say that everyone says of me that I am doing a good job. Everyone is nice. Everyone is working together just like a family. It is very homelike. TCF honors their employees. The people who are attached with TCF do it to serve the people and the country. Every person thinks we have to do something for our country."

If Razia is typical of how education can transform the lives of women in Pakistan, I reflect, the future well-being of Pakistan, when all of its women and girls are given the opportunities of education, is assured.

The next morning, the Nooranis arrive from Lahore. Karen has a black eye, her arm is in a sling, and she has a new shalwar kameez wardrobe—one that she can manage with the use of only one arm. They all settle into the room next to ours. After we catch up on each others' news, Sofia leaves to see a college friend living in Islamabad, Danial checks on our flight to Gilgit, and Karen pays a visit to the local hospital. Nancy, Taffy, and I go exploring.

Our driver takes us to the Margalla Hills, north of Islamabad, so that we can stretch our legs with a short morning hike. The hills, ranging in elevation from 2,055 feet to 4,812 feet, are the foothills of the Himalayas; I am eager to put my boots on their trails.

With some reluctance, our driver drops us in a parking lot atop one of the hills—behind the zoo. Our plan is to hike down to the zoo and meet our driver in an hour or two. The day is young, the air is clear, and except for the soaring temperature, all is well on the trail.

At one point, we meet a young Pakistani couple also hiking down. The young man is eager to engage us in conversation about American politics and Islam. He and the young woman with him (wife? sister? girlfriend?) are friendly, and we chat with them for a few minutes as we hike. Our pace, however, is quicker than theirs, and we soon leave them behind.

The path is littered with trash in some spots, but the views of Islamabad as we descend are breathtaking. From the vantage point of Daman-e-Koh,[4] Islamabad is indeed a well-planned metropolis of broad tree-lined boulevards and coherent traffic patterns. In the distance, the minarets of the Faisal Mosque and a collection of cell phone towers stand upright as modern exclamation points. Islamabad, I reflect, is no longer the middle of nowhere.

We hike to the zoo park, reach it within the appointed time, meet our driver, and continue on to the Faisal Mosque, seen in such splendor from Damen-e-Koh. The Faisal Mosque, I am told, is the largest mosque in Pakistan and South Asia and the fourth largest mosque in the world. Completed in 1986 and subsidized by the Saudis, it is named after the late King Faisal of Saudi Arabia. Unlike the traditional Moghul design of the Badshai Mosque in Lahore, the Faisal Mosque is extremely modern, and looks like an Arab Bedouin's tent. Instead of a dome and minarets, the Faisal has four Turkish pencil-like minarets at each corner and there is no central dome. The floors are highly polished white marble and the walls are decorated with mosaics and calligraphy. The main prayer hall is a huge triangle, large enough to accommodate 100,000 men worshiping at the same time. Women worship in a smaller, adjoining prayer hall. Altogether, in its main hall and adjoining grounds, the mosque can accommodate 300,000 worshipers at one time.

I am enchanted by the symmetry of this modern mosque. Set above street level, it is surrounded by courtyards and white marble pathways aligned in parallel rows along raised beds of struggling flowers. Everything gleams in the sun, and there are many visitors: tourists, worshippers, workmen, burqah-clad women, children. Nancy, Taffy, and I are the only Western women, but in our shalwar kameez and dupattas, we almost blend in with the women we encounter in the washrooms and stairways around the main prayer halls. I am surprised that there is a bookstore and souvenir shop on the grounds. We must pay a few rupees each to hold our sandals before we can enter the mosque.

We take our time walking through the rooms that are open, peering into those that are not. No one seems to notice us, not even to have us take his or her picture. I am reminded that I am in modern Pakistan and realize, perhaps for the first time, that modern Pakistan has very visible ties to wealthy, oil-rich Islamic states. Pakistan, while proud of its Moghul roots in the 1600s when the Badshai Mosque in Lahore was built, is now a modern-day Islamic country, and the Faisal Mosque, sponsored and paid for by Saudi Arabia, is a vivid reminder of that fact.

Later, when we return to our TCF rooms, we shower, change from our sweat-soaked wrinkled clothes, and join the Nooranis at a Pakistani restaurant. I notice many chicken items on the menu, remember the warehoused chickens at the HDF chicken-farming project, and order sagh-gosht and chapatis.

Danial tells us that our tickets to Gilgit are set for nine o'clock in the morning. If it is a good weather day, we will be in the mountains by lunchtime. Insha'Allah.

I am too excited to sleep, even on the roof. I have never been to Azad Kashmir but know the mystery and majesty of K2 and the silk route of the Karakoram Highway from reading and mountaineers' stories. I am eager to see them for myself.

CHAPTER 21

~

Hunza: Another Pakistan

The morning skies are bright blue and cloudless as we fly to Gilgit. Our plane is small, perhaps forty passengers, and the one-hour flight exciting. Outside the windows, beneath us, the view changes from scarred-looking brown mountaintops to spectacular snowcapped peaks of dizzying heights and deep valleys of plunging desolation. If it were not so wonderful, I would be frightened. But our pilot seems to know what he is doing, weaving among the peaks, occasionally banking to the right or left to give everyone a better view. I flit from one side of the plane to the other, snapping photos.

All too soon we land, heart-stoppingly, at the Gilgit airport, on a very short runway at the edge of a slope. We are surrounded on all sides by mountains—very high snowcapped mountains. Our elevation in Gilgit is around 4,800 feet. Some of the mountains around us are over 20,000 feet. It is, for me, a dramatic landing.

The airport terminal is unprepossessing: a small, two-story, rectangular structure with a squat observation tower on top. A lush quadrangle of green lawn and bright flowers between the tarmac and the entryway, however, redeem the chaste impression and make us feel welcome.

The city of Gilgit, on the banks of the Gilgit River, is situated on the ancient trade route that cuts through the Karakoram Mountains from Chinese Turkistan to Afghanistan. During the eighth and ninth centuries, Gilgit was an important trade center of the famous silk route. Today Gilgit is one of the two major hubs for all mountaineering expeditions in the northern areas of Pakistan.

We are in the southwest corner of the Karakoram Mountains, which are part of the Himalayan mountain range.[1] The Karakorams begin where the Hindu Kush stop in the west and stretch north and east to the border of China. The Karakoram Highway is carved through the western edge of these Karakoram Mountains and is the highway we will journey for our week's holiday.

Sher Ali, the guide Danial has engaged for our mountain adventure, and his driver, a man of indeterminate age and appearance, greet us. Both are dressed in the Northwest male attire of white shalwar, kurta, woolen vest, and squashed Pathan wool hat.

We load our baggage into the eight-passenger van, cross a narrow bridge said to be the largest suspension bridge in Asia, and look down at the Gilgit River rushing and roiling with glacier runoff below us. The air is clear, and the sky crystal blue. I hang out my window taking pictures. Everything is so beautiful I feel like I am in a travelogue. The mountains in the distance are breathtaking.

As we climb toward these mountains, the highway becomes breathtaking of a different kind. Our driver yells back at me to close the window, which I do just in time to avoid a throat-full of dust. The tarmac road has disappeared, and we are traveling, full speed when possible, over crushed rock, sand, and loose dirt everywhere. We are heading north along the Hunza River, cut below in deep canyons and rushing wildly to meet the Gilgit and Indus Rivers now south of us.

We reach a checkpoint and are delayed for a few minutes while our driver and Sher Ali argue with the men at the barricade. Sher Ali tells us later that they were just hassling him, but I suspect he had to offer them a bribe for our passage through the highway gate.

We press on, occasionally slowing to accommodate the passing of an oncoming truck or van. The road is narrow, rock strewn, winding, steep, and occasionally terrifying. I hear the crunch of the rocks beneath our tires and can see them slip and roll to the edge of the thousand-foot dropoff on one side and thirty-foot ditch or gully on the other. Either destination for a vehicle, at any speed, would be final. Our driver maintains a steady 40-mph speed around most of the curves, spewing rocks and gravel into the ditches and canyons in a magnificent cloud of dust.

As we climb, the vast expanse of desert and crumbling rock, sparsely populated and bereft of any vegetation, becomes more desolate. Occasionally we see a patch of green on a distant hill, indicating a small farming community that has been able to irrigate its crops by harnessing water from the swift-flowing river and melting snow. But it looks to be a rugged, meager existence.

We stop for lunch at a roadside restaurant in Ghulmat, the first opportunity to rest since beginning our ascent. While we wait for our meal, we browse through the shops at the edge of the tarpaulin overhanging the dining area. Here are the bargains from Azad Kashmir: hand woven wool hats, shirts, shawls, vests, Kashmiri shawls, intricately carved animals, birds and footstools, and sequined purses and jewelry cases. Everything is beautifully made, reasonably priced, and hard to resist. In the distance, in shining glory, Rakaposhi holds court with its majestic snow-covered cape and intimidating height.[2] The weather is perfect.

During lunch, Danial tells us about a school he is helping to build in Murtaz-abad, a village near the town where we will be staying this first night. This school is being funded privately by the mother of a young American woman trekker, Leeza Tschursin, who taught in the small village school for several years in the early 1990s before her untimely death. The new school, Danial says, will be larger than its predecessor with some of the features of a TCF school. Danial, as the CEO of TCF-USA, is lending his expertise and liaison capabilities to the project. He asks if we would be willing to present some of our Summer Science Camp lessons to the students and teachers at this school in the morning. Of course, we agree.

I am curious about foreign-sponsored school-building projects in this northernmost area of Pakistan. I know that Greg Mortenson, a climber turned charitable entrepreneur and coauthor of the book *Three Cups of Tea*, began his Central Asia Institute after helping to build a school near Skardu, in the southeastern part of the Federally Administered Northern Areas.[3] Japanese and other climbers have discovered the villages in these remote northern areas of Pakistan as well and, after trekking through the mountains or in some cases losing a fellow climber to those mountains, want to give back to the villages by building schools. I ask Danial about these schools.

"A problem arises with these schools, however well meant they are," Danial tells me. "When outside sources give money to the local officials, squabbling and corruption often prevent the school from being built, or built well enough to meet the needs of the community. And there is usually no money left, or budgeted for sustainability of the school—money to run it over time. Teachers are not trained, and the school soon falls into disrepair and eventually the village is right back where it began—no school, poor quality of local education, and one or two people well off because they have pocketed the money."

"Even worse," Danial sighs, "because the village has depended on funds as a handout, they do not know how to raise more money or budget what they get. So, they look for another outside source and the cycle continues."

I am sobered by this conversation. It reminds me of the futility I felt as a Peace Corps Volunteer, giving what I thought the village needed rather than understanding that the village best knew its own needs but had to learn how to sustain and support the projects once they were begun.

Danial tells me that TCF does not build schools in these inaccessible northern mountain areas because it would be too difficult to administer them. Hunza is too far from existing TCF school clusters, he says, and the Aga Khan Education Services organization does a good job of providing education in this area. Estimates of Hunza's literacy rate range from 77 percent to over 90 percent, as compared to 54 percent for Pakistan as a whole. TCF does, however, have eighty-two schools in the North-West Frontier Province and in that area of Azad Kashmir that was devastated by the earthquake near Muzaffarabad in 2005, he reminds me. I ask Danial to tell me more about how TCF was involved with the earthquake relief effort in 2005.

"Even though TCF tries very hard to keep its focus on education," Danial says, "all our supporters said, 'You are so well organized and know how to build schools, etc., you have to get involved in earthquake relief.' TCF responded immediately. . . . They were able to use their resources and donors pool to the aid the earthquake survivors.

"TCF went in and set up medical camps with field hospitals. The first baby was born in one of our medical tents. There was an outpouring of donations. We started buying emergency supplies with our own reserves and then funds began to pour in to both TCF-USA and TCF-Pakistan.

"The immediate relief was distributing blankets, food, tents, and setting up medical camps. The next phase was to help the people build shelters, reclaiming some of the material like stones and timber from the houses that had collapsed. The idea was self-help. The people who had lost their homes would provide labor and salvaged material; TCF would provide a design, specifications, tools, and the remaining materials that needed to be purchased.

"First, a three-foot-high wall was built of stones. Then a frame from fallen timber was built over it. Saws were set up in each community to help the people do this for themselves. Then corrugated metal sheets went on the frames for walls and roofs, and fireplaces were built. Winter was not far away. These shelters were first used as homes, and then, when the family was able to build a regular home, they could use the shelters for storage of food, fodder, maybe even the cattle in the wintertime. TCF built 6,300 structures like these.

"TCF also selected certain villages and rebuilt all the homes in those villages. They built four thousand homes from a couple of models designed by TCF architects. The houses had plumbing, sanitation, and used construction techniques and materials recommended by the Earthquake Rehabilitation and Reconstruction Authority. In some villages, TCF built a water system and local mosques—the pillars of the community.

"TCF naturally decided to also build schools where possible. Twenty-one schools were built to help children restore order to their lives. It was TCF's finest moment. TCF got some press from their relief efforts, but mainly it was just recognized in the local areas where the work was done," Danial concludes.

Danial and I continue our conversation in the van after lunch. By late afternoon, we arrive in Karimabad, the capital of Hunza and hub for trekkers from all around the world, and the town where we will stay for a few nights while we explore the nearby villages and mountain trails.

Our hotel is modest, but makes up for its lack of appointments by providing us with a magnificent view overlooking the Hunza River below and the Karakoram peaks above. We are well housed and comfortable. The school Danial is helping to renovate is a short van ride away.

The next morning, on the way to the Murtazabad village school, we stop in the bazaar for some teaching supplies for the science lessons we will present: newspapers, string, and Plasticine. We arrive at the old school in time for a quick look at the classrooms before the children arrive.

The old school sits above a winding road overlooking mountains and green pastureland. It serves 250 students in four small classrooms: secondary level in the morning, primary in the afternoon. Two of the classrooms are equipped with double desks and chairs; the other two have rugs on the floor and wooden chairs, some without slats or backs, along three of the walls. All of the rooms are dark, lit only by small, high windows on the inside wall. The rooms with rugs instead of desks and benches are draped with Urdu and English alphabet letters and colorful posters. I do not see any books, pencils, or paper, but, since it is a Sunday morning in the summer, I assume that they have been put away.

A handful of women teachers and two male administrators greet us and tell us that forty boys and girls, ranging in age from eight to fifteen, will be attending our classes. We decide to assign the children to three groups according to age. The groups will rotate through the classrooms, engaging in the lessons presented in that classroom. We teachers will present our lessons three times, each time to a different group of children.

Karen and I will team-teach "Newton's Laws of Motion" with the few matchbox cars we have salvaged from the Summer Science Camps and will have the children build newspaper towers from the newspapers we gathered from the bazaar. Nancy and Sofia will teach the children how to make spool racers, and Taffy and Sher Ali's twelve-year-old son, Hakim, will teach a lesson on solar electricity.

When we are ready, the children, dressed in their school uniforms—sky blue shirt and pants for boys, sky blue shalwar kameez and white dupatta for girls—assemble in the courtyard to be divided into groups. They look well fed and happy, excited to be at school on a beautiful Sunday morning. I hope they will not be disappointed and think sardonically of American boys and girls of similar age attending school on a gorgeous summer Sunday morning. I expect the American children would not be as well scrubbed or as eager.

In our classroom, Karen is only a little hampered by her arm sling. After our first group of children has tested their matchbox cars to discover one of Newton's laws of motion, Karen joins us on the floor, on our hands and knees, to participate in constructing newspaper towers. The teachers and administrators, watching from their chairs around the perimeter of the classroom, laugh at our antics. The children are delighted and delightfully enthusiastic about the activities.

The second group of children is as energized as the first. Only this time, the teachers watching from the sidelines begin to join in by making suggestions to one group of children, encouraging another group, helping a third.

I take a few minutes to find Taffy's and Nancy's classrooms and observe the same phenomenon: the teachers watching are eager participants in the children's learning, as excited and enthusiastic as the children.

I suggest to Taffy, Karen, and Nancy that since the teachers have all observed our lessons, twice in some cases, we invite them to conduct the third session in each of our classrooms. For me, this has always been the most successful strategy for training undergraduate- and graduate-level teachers. I expect it will work as well in Pakistan, even though it is in a different culture and another language.

Our invitation to the teachers to take over the third session in each classroom is cheerfully accepted. We stay in our classrooms to assist and offer suggestions—but the teachers do not really need us. They know the children and understand what we have been teaching and jump right in.

The morning ends in a flood of creative excitement—tall newspaper towers, forcefully protected from falling matchbox cars, zippy spool racers, sunlight-operated lightbulbs—and satisfies teachers, children, and former Peace Corps Volunteers. For me, this is my most successful teaching day of the summer—accomplished with a minimum of explanation but a maximum of goodwill and understanding on everyone's part. I am proud of us and proud of the teachers who so willingly stepped in and learned from us. I am thrilled at this outstanding coda to our Summer Science Camps.

To cap the day, we are invited to two festive meals: lunch at the home of the village headman, Numberdar, and dinner at the home of Sher Ali. In each venue, we sit on the floor at the edge of a beautiful hand-woven rug in the main room of the house. Other guests, mostly men, sit cross-legged with us and talk quietly to each other, occasionally rising to greet another guest or respond to one of the women who are cooking in the next room.

While we are waiting for lunch, I excuse myself to wash my hands—and poke into the kitchen area to see how the food is being prepared. To my surprise, the large room adjoining the main sitting area is filled with women—all sitting on the floor assembling platters of fresh vegetables, fruits, chicken, rice, potatoes, curry, and large spongy discs of wheat bread. Working together in a tight circle, their vibrantly colored shalwar kameez shimmer in the afternoon sun, and they look like a flock of birds, singing and chattering, enjoying an unexpected gift.

When the food platters are ready, several women come into the room and lay long strips of brightly woven fabric on the rug in front of us, tablecloths without tables. I am surprised and pleased by the women's air of confidence. In the Punjab, I have come to expect women to be more deferential and shy in the presence of men and guests. These women are proud to be serving us and are not afraid to be seen.

Each guest receives a beautiful porcelain plate and a glass tumbler. Then the procession begins. The women file in bearing food. I am reminded of a Moghul tapestry or painting of a sumptuous banquet. I feel like royalty and taste every offering. The food is delicious.

At the conclusion of lunch, the headman of the village gives a little speech of welcome and friendship. Our evening dinner, on the other hand, ends with Sher Ali serving a local cherry brandy that slides smooth as silk down my throat. Both are fitting finales to exotic pleasurable events. I am charmed.

Before sunrise the next morning, I walk through the town of Karimabad before it is awake and bustling with commerce and vehicles. I take a path below the main street of the bazaar and hike along a small canal, built of mountain stone and fed by glacial runoff via narrow stone ditches dug into the mountainside. The only sound is the burble of rushing water and a slight breeze riffling the trees.

At first, I am in a tunnel of apricot trees planted on steep slopes—up on my right, down on my left. A goat wanders into my path, and we amble together for a few hundred yards. The path opens onto a vista of distant snowcapped mountains and verdant undulating fields, divided by stone walls and marked by stone and cement hovels. The hovels, on closer inspection, are houses built into the hillside, and they are not dirty at all. Their small courtyards are swept clean and are organized into sleeping, eating, and washing sections for families, with a separate room and area for animals. The houses look cramped and dark with their shuttered openings for windows and doors—probably a good thing for the long, snow-filled winter months. But in summer, ladders made of slim tree branches lean against one wall in every courtyard. Much of summer living, I guess, takes place on the roof.

As this is the height of cherry and apricot harvest, the trees along the hillsides are laden with bounty. Later, I discover by looking down onto these hillside houses that each roof is a drying place for flat, round baskets filled with apricots. I am told that there are twenty-eight varieties of apricots, ranging in color from pale yellow to green, light orange to vibrant red. Apricots are everywhere in the bazaars, dried and packed in pouches for trekkers, crystallized as candy, dewy and succulent as fresh fruit. I have been told that apricot oil is supposed to make you live longer, and I recall an article in *National Geographic* about the longevity of the people of Hunza, reputedly due to these apricots.

As the sun rises from behind the mountains, the farmyards come to life. I greet an old man walking on the path, a young boy and girl shooing goats, a tired-looking woman hanging clothes on the bushes of her courtyard, and another woman dipping a bucket into the water rushing in front of her house. Several women and girls are already in the fields, gathering straw and carrying it in bundles on their heads to their animals stabled by the side of the path. Everyone greets me with a smile and "Salaam Aleikum." I do the same.

The people are shorter than those in the plains, seem more muscular, and have a distinctly sturdy appearance. In the summer, the women and children are in charge of the fields, while the men hire out as guides to trekking groups and mountaineers. Solo hiking, without a guide, is unheard of in these mountains, and usually the men can make a good living guiding trekkers from all over the world. This year, I am told, the trekking business is not so good because of the international fear of terrorists in Pakistan. On this bucolic morning, though, terrorism seems far away indeed.

Sher Ali has arranged for us to visit the Baltit Fort and his friend's rugmaking factory before we leave Karimabad on our journey north.[4] Sher Ali is proud of both and eager to show them off.

Sher Ali and his son Hakim are magnificent guides. Both speak fluent English and are full of information about Hunza and its people, culture, attractions, and hiking trails. In the winter, Sher Ali is a secondary teacher in Gilgit, and Hakim is in his first year of tuition at his father's school. They are extremely intelligent and knowledgeable, converse easily, and are eager to please us. I enjoy their talk, if intermittently, and am happy to follow their suggestions.

I am particularly pleased to visit the rug factory, where several young women sit in front of a large loom, hand-tying knots of bright wool yarn that has been colored with dyes from local vegetation. I would love to purchase one of their rugs, but my luggage capacity is limited and I must demur. Nancy, on the other hand, has brought an extra suitcase to carry home local rugs and tapestries. I envy her foresight and wish I had done the same. Not only are the rugs beautifully made, the colors exquisite, and the designs of old Moghul complexity or modern simplicity exceptional, but by purchasing one or two, I would boost the income of these women patiently tying each knot. Next visit, I promise myself, I will purchase hand-tied rugs from Hunza. Insha'Allah.

Later in the morning, we continue our journey north along the Karakoram Highway. The highway continues to be heart-stoppingly perilous. I would much prefer to be walking these twisting, rock-strewn, avalanche- and landslide-prone roadways.

From time to time, our vehicle is stopped and redirected around a mound of fallen rocks or a gaping hole. We pass other vehicles trying to maneuver the same narrow ledge. At one point, I look down to see only three of our wheels firmly on the stony path. The fourth, the rear one under my seat, is poised momentarily over a deep gash beside a thousand-foot drop of stone and rushing river below. Our driver races over it, using momentum to keep us from tipping into the crevice.

I close my eyes and vow to get out at the first opportunity. I recall a Peace Corps–era bus trip in the mountains near Murree, standing with the other passengers along the edge of a cliff, holding up my arms to keep the bus from falling as it inched past a similar gap.

When our driver stops to maneuver a particularly wide ditch, Taffy and I disembark. It is only two miles, and two thousand feet up, to our hotel, and I need to stretch my legs to settle my stomach.

Our hike to the Eagles Nest, the mountainside hotel Danial has booked for the night, is peaceful and quiet—if not hot, despite the late afternoon sun scorching the back of our necks. We pass small villages of stone and wide fields of poppies. I wonder whether opium is a staple product of these hills. I am awed by the rugged conditions in which these mountain people live. I imagine what it is like in winter—cold, snowy, and beautiful but bleak—and admire the tenacity of these farmers, herders, and mountain guides. I would not be able to trade places with them and survive.

The Eagles Nest is aptly named: it perches on top of a ridge amid rocky scree and jagged peaks. Behind us are 24,000-foot snowcapped summits, soaring into the sky. Below, the valley where we have spent the past few days is recognizable by its row of cell phone towers and the Hunza River. I have been astonished that, remote as we are in Hunza, first-class cell phone and Internet connections are available 24/7. We are as close to civilization as the briefest click and as far away as the loosest stone on that crumbling highway north or south.

Next morning, early, we leave for Gulmit, a tiny village about seventy-five miles from the Chinese border. It takes most of the day to get there. I have resigned myself to keeping my eyes closed during the most hair-raising feats of our driver. The closer we get to the border, the more numerous are the Chinese construction crews. These workers live in makeshift tents along the roadway, using hand tools and big machinery to pound and shatter boulders into pebbles and repair the many damaged sections of highway. It is a long, tedious process, and I expect the workers will be repairing and rebuilding for the next ten years. I wonder what a wide, asphalt highway would do to this area—bring more tourists and trade and change forever the lives of the people in the distant villages hidden among the rocks, I imagine.

This far north, the air is cooler, the evenings brisker. We arrive at our hotel near the side of the road about five o'clock in the afternoon. The small truck stop down the road from our hotel is loud with truck noise, resplendent with intricately painted and decorated trucks from China en route to Afghanistan. The few shops serving them have a meager supply of goods, mostly from China—dusty secondhand shoes and clothing, flimsy notebooks, cheap toys.

After dinner, we discover the village on the hillside behind the truck stop and walk along grassy pathways to its center, a large dusty square used for polo matches and occupied now by teenage boys playing a pickup game of cricket, using a stuffed sock as a cricket ball. The mosque, flanking the polo field, is a large square building used as a community center. It has no minarets and no call to prayer five times a day.

Along the main street, deserted now, the shops are shuttered. The few villagers I see seem to be on their way home or just out enjoying the evening. The people are friendly and welcoming, and I feel at ease and curious about their lives. I am surprised to see the women walking about freely, dressed in shalwar kameez and dupatta but without a burqah or hijab. Sher Ali explains that the Muslims in this area are of the more liberal Ismaili branch of Shia Islam and find it less necessary to practice strict rituals such as purdah to observe their faith.

It has been refreshing, for me, to feel the more relaxed demeanor of the people and the lack of loudspeakers calling the faithful to prayer in these mountains. It seems we are not constantly reminded of the rules of Islam, here, but rather its simpler beauty and grace. I like this feeling.

The following morning, we rise early for a hike along the Gulmit Glacier to Barut Lake, a day's tramp away. I am eager to be hiking again and enjoy the early morning quiet as we tread uphill, again through the village of Gulmit, and then through a gorge onto the vast rocky slopes of the glacier. Sher Ali tells us that the glacier caused a blockage of the Hunza River in 1992 that completely cut off the valley for over a year. Today it is hard to find the ice that is mingled with black silt underfoot.

The trail to the glacier is difficult in places, with large boulders, an angled rock path, and scary drop-offs on either side. After several hours climbing an increasingly stony and steep path, we encounter water and begin to cross streams spanned by trellised wooden bridges. We pick our way over the boulders in our path. Several young boys appear from behind one of these boulders and offer to lead us to the glacier. We accept and follow their agile steps as best we can, catching up to them at a watering spot of clear, numbingly cold, glacial runoff.

Finally, we reach the glacier face, and it turns out to be a huge black dirt hole at the top of the mountain. I am expecting white, slippery ice, as on the Zugspitze in Germany. Not so here. The ice has mostly melted on the surface, but underneath it is solid and cold. The boys chip off some to crunch. It tastes like dirt to me.

We continue on, across a boulder-strewn moonscape, rock by rock, under a blazing sun that burns but does not seem hot. It is exhilarating to be here without any sign of commercial life or distraction.

We reach our destination, Barut Lake, where we meet Danial and Karen who have chosen to drive into this high mountain respite. An icy Coca-Cola and huge Pakistani meal are waiting for us, welcomed and well deserved. Afterward, with full stomachs, Nancy and I paint watercolors of the lake and surrounding mountains. My rendering shows an aqua body of water trimmed in green, brown, and tan mountains in the foreground, surrounded by purple and white-capped peaks embraced by a brilliant blue sky. The air is clear and fresh. There are no clouds, no bugs, and no beating sun. We paint our way to the perfect ending of a perfect hike.

Back at our hotel, showered and refreshed from the long day, I ask Danial if I can interview him. We settle on the balcony overlooking the sun setting behind the mountains, and I turn on my recorder, eager to hear how, as a

Pakistani living in Chicago, Danial came to be involved with TCF. In the past few weeks, and particularly on our Hunza trip, I have more fully appreciated his talents and have grown fond of him and his family.

Danial tells me he was born in Karachi and educated in the elite private schools of Karachi and Lahore. He earned his master's degree in the United States, where he met Karen. They married with the blessing of his Pakistani and her American parents. As a Pakistani-American family, they are both passionate about Pakistan.

"A bunch of us were interested in education and wanted to do something for education in Pakistan," Danial says. "We were really impressed with the TCF-Pakistan program and decided we wanted to support it because it is so professionally run and transparent . . . so well organized. To do this, we decided to set up TCF-USA.

"We have our own board, own bylaws, and are governed by Illinois and U.S. laws. We are not limited to supporting only TCF-Pakistan, however. If we find another organization, like Bahbud, a Pakistan women's organization that also runs schools, we can support it."

Danial continues: "I've been associated with TCF since the late nineties—first as a supporter. Initially, I approached them with my idea to form TCF-USA but they said someone else was already working on it. . . . But he did not come through and just disappeared—so TCF came back to me and said, go ahead and begin TCF-USA.

"In 2001, we set up a stall at the Association of Pakistani Physicians of North America conference and started getting exposure for TCF. In 2002, we incorporated as TCF-USA."

At this point, Karen joins our conversation. "What Danial has not told you," Karen says, "is about all those hoops he had to jump through to get IRS approval for tax-exempt public charity for TCF-USA. TCF-USA incorporated just after 9/11 happened. A lot of Pakistanis in the U.S. were afraid to lend their name in print to a board of Pakistanis sending funds to Pakistan to build schools. Forms and more forms. It took a long time to complete the process, but without the IRS public charity status, people wouldn't want to donate.

"The IRS kept coming back to us with more and more questions," adds Danial. "We began the process in October of 2002, and many thought we were trying to build madrassas. We answered all the questions, and then more questions. A young lawyer named Suzanne Reisman, a Jewish American from the New York area who had just returned after living in England for many years, was trying to set up her law practice. She had been exposed to TCF in the U.K., and they gave her my name. She called and offered her help. I told her, 'You're the answer to my prayers.'

"Suzanne was the biggest help—drafting letters to the IRS, making me aware of the guidelines for American charities that sent money abroad. These guidelines were only *guidelines* from the Treasury Department. [They] included things like making sure none of the people in the foreign charity were on a State Department list of undesirable people all over the world, and making sure the bylaws of the foreign charity were similar to the bylaws of an American charity, and noting whether they were a public or private charity.

"We wrote to the IRS that not only were we committed to following the guidelines, but we would follow them as though they were the law. We made the guidelines part of our charter," Danial continues. "This took about eight months. Even Pakistanis were scared to donate because they might get a visit from Homeland Security or the IRS or whomever."

"TCF-USA is an independent American charity," he emphasizes. "We have donated funds through Rotary Club in Karachi for rebuilding a village school that was impacted by the earthquake, and we donated textbooks to all of Greg Mortenson's schools in Skardu about three years ago.

"However, more than 90 percent of our work is to support TCF in Pakistan. We have raised close to two million dollars a year from U.S. donors for building and operating TCF schools. Our financial connection to them is that we are donors and they are the donees.

"TCF-USA has support groups all over the country," Danial continues. "We have support groups in six or seven cities and two chapters. Once a support group has a president, vice president, etc., we consider them a chapter of TCF-USA. We have a chapter in the Bay Area of California and in New York/New Jersey/Connecticut—the Northeast region. The chapters support only TCF—no other organization.

"When our support groups started, they were 100 percent Pakistani-Americans, but now other Americans have joined in—like Barbara Janes [Taffy], doing teacher training in Pakistan and raising funds. Another woman from Washington State has also come to Pakistan to do teacher training and give presentations about how she got involved with TCF. Also, there are others who send books and trainers to Pakistan, and they are very well received.

"TCF-Pakistan had never thought of getting this kind of outside help. The first time we proposed it from the U.S., there was some skepticism about it. But the experience has been so great, TCF-Pakistan now welcomes outside trainers. Barbara was a big hit over here, and the way she talks about the staff and they about her is like they have been friends for years. TCF-Pakistan definitely sees the value in it and definitely welcomes it now.

"There are lots of things that are part of my vision for TCF-Pakistan. I have expressed these ideas to the TCF board and management, but I don't know how far they agree with these ideas or if they can do them, given that they have to deal with the day-to-day reality of running a huge network of schools spread over a vast geographical area. I would like to see TCF become a resource for anybody trying to improve education in Pakistan, whether it is providing teacher training and curriculum design to other nonprofits or serving as a model for education reform to the government, so that our impact is multiplied.

"In my crystal ball, I would love to see TCF-Pakistan incorporate human rights and concepts like tolerance into their curriculum. There is an organization in Karachi that publishes books for children and has a peace museum for children. TCF-USA has purchased a lot of those books and given them to TCF-Pakistan, but I have not been able to convince the TCF board to officially make that a part of the curriculum."

I am curious about the harassment of Pakistanis in the United States since 9/11. "Have you been harassed in the U.S. because you are a Pakistani with obvious ties back to Pakistan?" I ask Danial.

"Not myself personally," he answers, "but a lot of people I know have. In that part of the world, a lot of charities have a social side and a political side. If a charity had a political side that was not compatible with U.S. foreign policy, its U.S. operations were forced to close down. Even Hamas has a very active social program of running schools and clinics and so on. When people heard of these politically affiliated charities being closed down, they were afraid to be associated with even purely charitable social welfare organizations like TCF-USA.

"It took a long time for people to get over their fear. It was hard work educating them, telling them about the Treasury Department guidelines, etc. It helped that TCF was the charity we were supporting in Pakistan. From day one, TCF has had a major accounting firm doing their audits. They are so professionally run, they've hired firms to come in and rate them on governance. The schools are open to anyone to see, so anyone can come in and choose the school they want to see—not a handpicked school. All that transparency really has helped."

Are Pakistani-Americans politically involved now? I ask.

"Now they are," Danial confirms. "They were always interested in the politics of Pakistan, but now they are actively learning the ropes of American politics and supporting politicians at the local level, and so forth."

"My impression of Pakistanis has always been that they like to be engaged in talking about politics—but not so much in action," I observe.

"In Pakistan," he explains, "a lot of mistakes were made, right from day one. India had land reforms, but Pakistan did not do meaningful land reforms. We're still not out of the feudal stage, never mind the industrial. A lot of people in politics are still feudal landlords, zamindars, and the tenants farming on their lands have to vote for them.

"The other tragedy is that very early in Pakistan's existence, the army got involved. Democracy was never allowed to take root. Constitutions have been toyed with, distorted. Even the current prime minister doesn't know if we have a parliamentary or presidential system.

"The first election that was fought was the battle in 1964 against self-appointed president and field marshal Ayub Khan by Fatima Jinnah, the sister of Pakistan's founder. Those elections were heavily fixed; there was no way she could have won. People were excited about voting in free and fair elections after Ayub Khan was forced to resign in 1969. In the elections of 1970, the east wing of the country and west wing had different winners. The whole country got into politics, but the sad part was that even though they had won the overall majority in these direct elections, the Bengalis of East Pakistan, who had always felt they had the short end of the stick, were not allowed to form the new government. They wanted to set up a federation where they would have more independence.

"Bhutto and the army felt that what Mujib and the Awami League were proposing was a de facto secession. They said, 'No, you have to put into the constitution what we tell you.' This led to unrest in East Pakistan, a heavy-handed response by the military, and Indian intervention that led to the breakup of the country in 1971.

"Bhutto raised the expectations of the poor with his rhetoric, but he came from a feudal background, one of the largest feudals in Sindh, so no true land reforms happened. He created so many enemies that when General Zia-ul-Haq had a coup against him, no one came to Bhutto's defense. Even though the majority of the population was from Punjab and Sindh where his party had the majority, it was not enough for Bhutto to gain absolute power. Bhutto broke up the provincial governments in Frontier and Baluchistan by putting in strong-armed governors that represented him.

"Bhutto made a promise of socialism—food, shelter, clothing—but didn't deliver. He talked about religious freedom, but when he got into trouble, he pandered to the far-right mullahs. Bhutto did some nationalization, so industrialists were not happy with him, either. Bhutto ended up alienating everybody because of his arrogance. Eventually his handpicked man, Zia, hung him by the neck.

"So, yes, Pakistanis are very much into politics, but because they have been disillusioned so many times, they get apathetic, then come back—as you saw last year in the lawyers' movement when they protested the Supreme Court justices being summarily dismissed."

"With all that being said," I inquire, "what would you like people to know about Pakistan?"

"I would like to dispel the skepticism about Pakistan—that Pakistan is a lost case because corruption and inefficiency are so rampant," Danial replies. "There are exceptions. There are organizations that are doing an excellent job, in a professional manner.

"The Citizens Foundation is probably the largest example. But the Human Development Foundation, whose project you visited in Islamabad, is also doing great work. Others, large nonprofits like Edhi Foundation, the Layton Rahmatulla Benevolent Trust, the Aga Khan Foundation, and countless others are doing good work. Basically . . . Pakistanis are capable of creating something like TCF and running it well.

"We are a religious people," Danial adds. "In their personal lives, the TCF founders are very religious, but don't wear their religion on their sleeves.

"Also, there are a small percentage of people in the country who are finally waking up, realizing they must help—like some of the TCF people who are of the wealthiest class—and this trickles down to the student volunteers, for example. They are beginning to realize that they can't wait for the government to act; they must get in and do it for themselves.

"And finally, I think that instead of imposing foreign models into Pakistan, it would behoove people who want to support Pakistan to look at models created by Pakistanis that have worked and are working. Various arms of the government have recognized TCF. The state bank of Pakistan does an annual report on the status of economy, education, etc., and one of their annual reports had a whole section on TCF. TCF is doing education on a large scale and doing it well. It can be done."

Karen adds, "Change is most effectively done when it is done by people who really understand the culture and want to do something to bring about change. I think it is important for people to be aware that the vast majority of Pakistanis are not terrorists and are not helpless. If given a chance and the right kind of support, they can solve their own problems.

"Pakistan is so many overlapping layers of cultures and social classes," Karen sighs, "not just the rural Pathans like those written about in most recent books about Pakistan. Pakistanis, including Pathans, are all different kinds of people, including people just like you and me."

CHAPTER 22

~

Pakistan: Unfinished Business

On our last day in Hunza, we travel back to Gilgit and arrive safely, if a little road weary, in the late afternoon. It is Taffy's birthday. After we settle into our hotel near the Gilgit airfield, Danial and Karen agree to take Taffy to look at an ancient Buddhist site,[1] so that Nancy, Sofia, and I can set up a proper celebration.

We venture out to the bazaar for some festive decorations and, because it is Friday afternoon, we have the shops mostly to ourselves. We spot a wedding shop and descend like locusts to pick its shelves clean. Pakistani weddings feature elaborate decorations of shiny tissue paper, ribbons, tinsel, and brightly tinted foil to drape the wedding hall, the procession, the bride's carriage, and the bridegroom's horse and head. The shop we scavenge provides us with enough paper crowns, streamers, and strands of glitter for several weddings—and Taffy's birthday party.

We return to our hotel to ornament the garden. The waiters help us move several long tables and chairs to the lawn and happily climb the trellises to string our sparkling treasures. The garden itself lends color: red, orange, purple, pink, and yellow flowers, soft green tree leaves, springy emerald carpet. And no flies. When Danial and Karen return with the Birthday Queen, our Taj Mahal of brilliant riches is ready for her surprise.

Taffy is pleased with our efforts. We adorn her neck with flowers and crown her head with fake jewels. We toast Her Majesty, sing to her, and thank her for her inspired leadership of our Pakistan adventure. She brought us all together and persevered until our journey happened. I would not be here were it not for Taffy.

In addition, we thank Danial for his behind-the-scenes arranging and contacts and Karen for her remarkable organizational skills. Sofia, whom we have all adopted as a surrogate daughter, we thank for just putting up with three senior ladies tripping down Memory Lane in wrinkled shalwar kameez. I cannot imagine myself in her position at her age—my age in 1964—and am in awe of her poise and affability.

We thank Sher Ali for his guidance through Hunza and for his charming family and their gracious hospitality. We raise our glasses of Murree beer and toast Nancy for its unexpected, much appreciated cameo appearance.

And then a cream-filled birthday cake magically arrives under a blanket of blazing candles and we toast the star-lit splendor that embraces our dazzling party. It has been a journey full of gifts.

Taffy's birthday celebration is a fitting close to our Pakistani saga of 2009. But we are not quite finished. Saturday morning, we once again board a small plane to Islamabad and a larger one to Karachi the morning after that.

Early Monday morning, we sit around the conference table at TCF Karachi central office. With us are the women most directly involved with the Summer Science Camp training, procurement of supplies, volunteers, and academic program. We ask them for feedback from the teachers, volunteers, and management staff. Our goal is to address the training, improve it, and perhaps use it as a model for future training programs.

"The Karachi teachers wanted more solar ovens," Naima, one of the volunteer coordinators offers. "One teacher went on the Internet and found other models, but she wanted more examples."

"There are many designs," Taffy responds. "I told the teachers in Lahore that they should ask the children for other ideas. The question to ask is 'What can you try?' Part of the idea is that the children come up with different, better ideas now that they understand the principle."

"Ultimately, we want all of these ideas to spur new ideas so that the children will be thinking," adds Karen.

"One of the most important things is the questioning," Taffy continues. "The follow-up question depends on their answer to the first question. It takes a lot of time to learn this. American teachers also feel they have to rush through lessons. The questioning technique takes a lot of time."

"The children did not understand the concepts behind the activities," Naima says. "The student volunteers just started the experiments, but they did not tell the correct concepts and did not explain how solar energy works, for example."

Taffy is aware of this pitfall. "The problem with some of the student volunteers is that they are focused on how they were taught and what they have memorized," she says. "They understand the concepts on an abstract level but they can't explain them. That's why we are trying to change this way of teaching."

"The same thing happened in my school," notes Nasheen, the volunteer coordinator. "The teachers did not understand the concepts, and the volunteers had to explain it to the teachers. Another volunteer said, Maybe the children should have been briefed about the concepts ahead of time. The volunteers thought that the children should be given the theory and then do the activity."

"No, no. It is the other way around," Karen insists. "The inquiry teaching method is that the children are learning by engaging in the activity and then asking questions. After they have done the lesson plan, there should be discussion about what happened, what questions were most on target. It is important to bring the class back after the activities for a discussion to make sure they understand the concepts.

"This summer, two and a half days for teacher training was not enough. If we had had a week with each group of teachers, we could have shown them how to do this questioning. But, because the time was so short, we did not model the inquiry method enough, but only talked about it in a lecture format. We know some of the training staff want a training video, but we do not want to make a video that reinforces the lecture method.

"When we were in Hunza," Karen continues, "the teachers watched us teach and the students rotated to different classrooms. After watching us teach twice, we asked the teachers to teach, and they did. The teachers were very successful. With more time, we could do this same kind of model teaching in the training programs and then help the teachers practice it with children.

"It is remarkable what the Summer Science teachers *did* learn in the two and a half days before the camps began. We are really impressed. We dumped a lot of stuff on the teachers, and they really didn't have time to digest it all. A better training program would be a three-week session, first with just the trainers to go through all the steps of the lessons and the questioning techniques. The following two weeks, the trainers could spend one week training teachers in Karachi and one week in Lahore. They could have five full days training each group."

"It's a different way of teaching altogether," Naima points out in conclusion. "But the children really enjoyed it."

When we visit the teachers at Goth Dhani Bux later in the morning, we hear a similar story. The teachers also want more specific directions for each activity and ask that the activities for each grade level be tied to the curriculum of that grade. "You should only have activities for grade five at level five, grade eight at level eight, etc.," suggested one teacher. "The activity should match the curriculum we have to teach at each level in the regular school year."

"The good thing about learning something more advanced out of sequence is that, when children get to a later grade, they will understand the equations when they meet the laws," Taffy explains. "Rather than memorizing the formulas, the activities made a picture in the children's brain about what is speed and acceleration. Those little pieces of paper that got splashed with ink from their cars will remind them about speed and acceleration.

"These children will remember the activity they did this summer. . . . We want the children to try things in a different way to see what works. . . . Use those new ideas along with the ideas in the curriculum. Let the children experiment . . . and also bring in the curriculum ideas as well."

Later, when Taffy, Nancy, Karen, and I talk about the ideas that surfaced during these meetings with TCF staff and teachers, we realize that our work with the inquiry method of teaching is not quite finished. Perhaps we will be invited to return for the next professional development training so that we can continue what we started this summer.

Our talk ends when the children file into their classrooms, boys on one side, girls on the other. The genders are not segregated in Karachi secondary schools as they are in the Punjab, and boys and girls share the same classrooms. We are delighted to see so many girls in attendance. In every TCF school cluster, we are told, girls make up 50 percent of the enrollment—a staggering achievement in Pakistan.

This morning, all the children are scrubbed clean and dressed carefully in the khaki TCF school uniform. Every classroom is full but not overcrowded; every child has a seat, a desk, a pencil or pen, and paper. A teacher is at the head of every class, and the air begins to hum with the resonance of learning. The new school term has begun—a testament to another remarkable accomplishment in Pakistan.

Tuesday morning, our last full day in Pakistan, we travel to Keti Bandar in southern Sindh and stop in, unannounced, at two TCF schools. We encounter the same hum of productive activity, the same eager young learners and dedicated teachers. The classrooms are clean and bright and hung with posters and colorful banners. Teaching and learning are going on, full speed.

At one of the TCF schools, I am surprised to see kindergarteners sitting at desks in straight rows, raising their hands to answer questions posed by the teacher. There are no restless five-year-olds here. All are attentive and well behaved. Second graders are reading from paperback storybooks, and fourth graders are working out long-division problems. I watch the first graders for a long time. They are learning the Urdu and English script for different kinds of vegetables. Their Urdu is better than mine, and I find myself swept up by the teacher's enthusiasm and the children's eagerness to please her.

In contrast, when we stop at a government school in a nearby neighborhood, the scene is quite different. I peek into dark classrooms crammed with benches, desks, and children—but no teachers. In one classroom, a girl from a fifth-grade class presides over an assembly of younger children, presumably to keep order.

The principal tells us that none of the teachers have come to work yet this term because they have not been paid. The children, on the other hand, have been promised a gallon of cooking oil for their attendance, and many are milling about the small campus waiting for their cooking oil—and for their teachers. The scene is disheartening, but typical of government schools, and I am reminded again of all the challenges facing Pakistan in its struggle to educate its citizens.

For the past month, I've lived in the past and the present, trying to absorb as much of Pakistan as I could and help its teachers prepare for the future. It has been a rewarding task. We have been met with courtesy and gracious hospitality everywhere we have traveled, always escorted wherever we needed to go with prompt attention and no excuses. I have been able to do all the things I set out to do.

Visiting Dhamke was a highlight for me. Looking back on my time there as a Peace Corps Volunteer, I realize now that the task I had assumed for myself in 1962 was too idealistic, unrealistic, and naive. I now know I did the best I could with the tools of understanding that I had at the time. Those tools, appropriate then, are outdated now.

The problems in Pakistan are still enormous. But Pakistan has its own history, its own culture, and its own ways of moving forward. There are plenty of very talented Pakistanis capable of solving the problems I set out to solve then—and they are succeeding now.

For example, I think about Razia, the TCF education manager in Islamabad. She dresses conservatively and still lives with her parents and obeys her father and brother's wishes as her own. But Razia is also modern: she travels without escort; she is fluent in English, Urdu, and Punjabi; and it is her choice to wear the hijab and abiyah as an expression of her religious observance.

Razia took a big step into the future when she joined the TCF team. It took courage to decide to move from a comfortable family-sanctioned part-time position as a teacher and examination reader to a full-time, out-in-the-open employee in a modern organization. Razia believes in the mission of TCF—to educate the children of Pakistan who have been forgotten—and this propels her.

I can only glimpse at the surface of Razia's move. But I think it represents the Pakistan of the future.

There is still a sharp division of labor in Pakistan, according to social class, caste, tribe, tradition, education, and so on. It is changing, but is doing so amorphously—like a many-legged Chinese dragon swaying first this way, then that, amusing itself, tiring itself, but not always moving forward—each leg just following along, doing its bit to keep moving but not taking responsibility of leadership. Just moving.

The traffic on Pakistani streets is horrendous. Small vehicles, large trucks and buses, people squashed onto motorcycles unprotected, everyone weaving in and out, using his horn to make passage. It all is friendly enough, but the expectation seems to be to surge forward, dodging animals, potholes, and each other, rather than to proceed more judiciously within a unified system that honors all.

Modern Pakistan is confusing—but less so, for me, than the Pakistan of the early 1960s. I see dramatic changes in this modern Pakistan.

For me, the most hopeful change in Pakistan is the unapologetic recognition by the upper class that their privileges are a responsibility rather than an entitlement, that their privileges come with the duty to give back to their country.

TCF is a good example of the privileged people who have figured out a way to give back. They use their own resources of opportunities and connections, their managerial experience in business, their country's resources of retired military who are disciplined and action oriented, and their knowledge of the culture, all to accomplish their goal: educating the poorest children so that ultimately the country will lift itself out of seventeenth-century ideas of feudal rights and dependence on others to become self-sustaining and secure.

TCF gives me hope, because it is focused on educating poor children. But the foundation is doing more than building self-sustaining schools for these children. The men and women at TCF are modeling responsible citizenry as they build. Their leadership is strong, undivided, and idealistic. Their way is rooted in Pakistani culture, religion, and tradition, but their methods are guided by the ways of the Western world. These modern Pakistanis are a hopeful blend of East and West.

This is my story. It is the fulfillment of a lifelong dream to be back in Pakistan, to recognize Pakistanis for their hard work, patience, and generosity, and to wholeheartedly accept them for their differences. I still feel helpless when beggars ask me for baksheesh. They want food, clothing, money. I want to give them a better life and know that my temporary contributions are not near enough. So I greet them with a few words of Punjabi, drop a few coins into their outstretched hands, and hope that by acknowledging their humanity I give them something more than a temporary solution.

But I know there is much more that I can do. In the end, being back in Pakistan has convinced me that we really are all responsible for each other, and that when one person suffers, all are affected. There is hope for us, I think, because Pakistanis know this, too.

Notes

Chapter 1: Arrival in Pakistan, 1962

1. In 1962, a new constitution established a system of individual administrative units called "basic democracies," intended to initiate and educate a largely illiterate population in the working of government by giving them limited representation and associating them with decision making at a level commensurate with their ability. Basic democracies were concerned with local government and rural development and were meant to provide a two-way channel of communication between the Mohammed Ayub Khan regime and the common people and to allow social change to move slowly.

Chapter 2: Work Assignment, 1962

1. *Izzet* is the most prized possession of the Punjabi Muslim man and is, in some sense, dependent on the women of his household. To maintain izzet and position in the community, a man's womenfolk must exhibit their chastity by observing purdah as directed by a passage in the Quran: "Tell thy wives and daughters and the women of the believers to draw their cloaks close around them. That will be better, so that they will be recognized and not annoyed." Carol Holtzman Cespedes, "Purdah Observance in a Pakistani Village," M.A. thesis, University of Hawaii, 1966, 28.

2. The Union Council was the lowest, but most important, of the five tiers of institutions in the basic democracies system. Each Union Council was composed of ten directly elected and five appointed members form the cluster of villages in its constituency. The council was responsible for local agricultural and community development, for maintenance of rural law and order, and for imposing taxes for local projects.

197

3. The Tehsil (subdistrict) is one tier above the Union Council and performs coordination functions between the union councils of the district. Dhamke was the seat of the Union Council of Shadara Tehsil in the District of Sheikhupura.

4. Principal landowner.

Chapter 3: The Vision, 1962

1. Lyallpur is now known as Faisalabad.

2. The United States Information Agency (USIA) provided a trunk full of paperback books in English to Peace Corps Volunteers serving abroad. These books ranged from American literature to contemporary U.S. politics and culture and were intended to be distributed to locals.

Chapter 6: Arrival in Pakistan, 2009

1. Terminal 2 at Quaid-e-Azam International Airport is used exclusively for those passengers making the pilgrimage to Mecca.

2. Defense housing societies were developed in major cities by the Defence Housing Authority of the Pakistani army for its current and retired personnel. The army personnel later resold their plots or homes to civilians. The vast majority of the residents of these neighborhoods are now upper- and upper-middle-class civilians.

3. A semi-sheer cotton fabric used for clothing and household items, preferred by Pakistani women for summer wear.

Chapter 7: Work Assignment, 2009

1. Load shedding is the process by which an electric utility cuts power to some customers in response to a shortage of available electricity. In Karachi and Lahore during the summer of 2009, load shedding was an intentionally engineered rolling blackout to different parts of the city at specified times during the day and night. When power outages occurred, many customers resorted to private generators, thus contributing to the discomfort, noise, and air pollution of the environment. The inconvenience and perceived unfairness of load shedding practices made it a contentious political issue in 2009.

2. Biryani is a South Asian dish of spicy colored rice mixed with meat, fish, or vegetables.

Chapter 8: A Clearer Vision, 2009

1. Islamic guerrillas based in Iran and Pakistan who fought a holy war or jihad against the Soviet forces occupying Afghanistan in the late 1970s and the 1980s.

2. In particular, in 1993–1994 Pakistan launched a Social Action Program (SAP) "to address a number of Pakistanis' basic needs that were not being met. In particular, primary education, basic health care, population welfare and rural water supply and sanitation." The program's funding was to come 80 percent from the government and 20 percent from international sources such as the World Bank, the Asian Development Bank, and the Dutch and British governments. The results of the program are mixed and the failures are attributed to "the absence of community ownership in SAP's projects," the lack of grassroots participation, "poor supervision, political interference in the hiring and transfer of teachers, not enough trained and well-qualified teachers and the lack of relevance of the school curriculum to local needs." "Pakistan's Social Action Program: A Success or Failure?" *YesPakistan.com*, June 18, 2002, www.yespakistan.com/people/sap.asp.

Chapter 9: An Introduction to the Citizens Foundation

1. Dropout rates, particularly after primary school and among girls, continue to be high in Pakistani schools. In the 1970s and 1980s, primary school dropout rates were 50 percent for boys and 60 percent for girls. Today, that rate has improved, but the expected completion rates for primary school students is still at only 88 percent for boys and 75 percent for girls. Of those who complete primary school, just 30 percent continue to the secondary level, and the majority of these stop at grade ten.

2. In Pakistan, schooling is divided into five levels: primary (grades one through five), middle (grades six through eight), secondary (grades nine and ten, leading to matriculation), higher secondary/college (grades eleven and twelve, leading to an Ordinary or Advanced Level examination), and university (programs leading to graduate and advanced degrees).

3. Critics of Pakistan's public education system say that the lessons in the national curriculum "promote the goals of a government highly influenced by the military." That curriculum "instructed educators to teach that fighting India is a religious duty and that the Kashmir dispute is legitimate. . . . A recent 5th-grade Urdu textbook devoted a chapter to Pakistani soldiers killed by the Indian army. The chapter quoted religious texts emphasizing that a Muslim has no faith if he does not wish for martyrdom, and that martyrs earn a special place in heaven." Noreen S. Ahmed-Ullah and Kim Barker, "Schooled in Jihad," *Chicago Tribune*, November 28, 2004, available at www.chicagotribune.com/news/watchdog/chi-0411280298nov28,0,3991771.story.

4. Azad Kashmir (Free Kashmir) is the southernmost political entity within the Pakistani-controlled part of the former princely state of Jammu and Kashmir. It borders Indian Jammu and Kashmir in the east, North-West Frontier Province to the west, Punjab in the south, and the Federally Administered Northern Areas in the north.

Chapter 10: Setting Up Training, 1963 and 2009

1. Most of these connections, called *kunda*, tap into the main electrical grid and are illegal.

2. Money given as a tip, bribe, or charity.

3. *Dawn* is Pakistan's oldest and most widely read English-language newspaper, and one of the country's two largest English-language dailies.

4. All TCF teachers receive 120 hours of preservice training when they are hired and an additional 80-hour in-service training every year thereafter. The teachers attending our Summer Science Camp training in Karachi and Lahore had already attended their annual in-service training for 2009 and were using their summer vacation time to be trained for the camps.

5. TCF has sponsored a pilot project for adult literacy in some of its school buildings. Run by the New Century Education organization, this program, called Jugnoo, uses specially designed Urdu and math books to teach literacy. More than fifteen thousand participants, from adolescents to elderly adults, have benefited from this program.

6. "Learning by doing" is a tenet of John Dewey's progressive education philosophy, which my mother learned in her own teacher-training courses in the 1930s. Dewey (1859–1952) was an educational reformer who emphasized that learning is best accomplished when the student is actively engaged in the process and the traditional lecture format is balanced with students' actual experiences.

7. Adult literacy classes are not yet available in every TCF community.

8. Some TCF school buildings house two school units, one in the morning, the other in the afternoon. Each primary school unit has classes from kindergarten level to grade five, sometimes with two or three sections of each class, depending on the space in the school. Several schools have a nursery class as well. Secondary school units offer classes from sixth to tenth grade, and upper secondary units to grade twelve. On average, every school unit will have 180 students: 6 classrooms of up to 30 students each.

Chapter 11: Behind the Citizens Foundation

1. From 1958 to 1969, Gen. Mohammed Ayub Khan; 1977 to 1988, Gen. Muhammad Zia-ul-Haq; and 1999 to 2008, Gen. Pervez Musharraf.

2. A cluster of TCF schools is typically three primary schools and one or two secondary schools (one for boys and one for girls in Punjab Province) in close proximity to each other. The primary schools feed their graduates to the secondary schools. In some areas, a small number of upper secondary schools (grades eleven and twelve) have also been opened. The cluster plan makes it easier for area managers to distribute supplies and supervise teachers. It also ensures a small class size and teacher accountability in each school unit.

3. A smokeless *chula* is a stove made of mud or clay with a chimney to one side. It was an improvement over the open campfire used by most village women in the 1960s as it saved fuel, cooked more efficiently, and directed the smoke away from the homemaker's eyes.

4. The mentoring program, Rahbar, is a pilot program in some Karachi TCF schools. It aims to develop young people to become responsible members of their communities by linking children in grade eight with professionals who can help them develop a vision for their lives. The eight-week course is designed to build confidence between mentor and mentee. The children learn to trust their mentor and ask him or her for advice. The program has been judged as very successful by an assessment team from Karachi University and will be expanded across the TCF network.

Chapter 12: Training in Karachi, 2009

1. Volunteers are recruited from leading schools, colleges, and universities to work with various TCF adjunct programs such as Summer Camps, Eye Camps, Kidney Checkups, Fun Field Days, Motivational Sessions, Book Reading Activities, Paint-a-TCF School Days, Road Safety Programs, Summer English Camps, and Summer Science Camps. For many of the volunteers, it is their first experience working with less-privileged children in the urban and rural slums.

2. Khanewal is the site of one of the Cooperative Farming Society projects introduced by the government in 1948 to rehabilitate families uprooted at Partition and increase agricultural production by introducing better methods of cultivation and by providing credit, marketing, and supply of agricultural requirements on a cooperative basis to the immigrant and local landless peasants. Nancy was the director of the Peace Corps project in Khanewal from 1963 to 1965.

Chapter 13: Arrival in Lahore, 2009

1. Porter charges are fixed at one hundred rupees for domestic passengers, two hundred rupees for international passengers.

2. Areas for cleansing hands, feet, and mouth in preparation for prayer.

3. As Lahore expands, former residential areas are being turned into commercial centers, and the suburban population is constantly moving outward. In addition to the historic Grand Trunk Road, motorways connecting Lahore to all major cities (Islamabad, Multan, Faisalabad, Peshawar, Rawalpindi, etc.) have been built. A motorway to Sialkot is under construction.

4. The weather of Lahore is extreme during the months of May, June, and July, when the temperatures soar to 40–48°C (104–118°F). From June until August, the monsoon season starts, with heavy rainfall throughout the province.

5. Beacon and Lahore Grammar are elite private schools with reputations for excellence.

Chapter 14: Training in Lahore, 2009

1. On May 4, 2009, the Kerry-Lugar Bill authorized 1.5 billion dollars per year for five years for nonmilitary aid to Pakistan to fund roads, schools, and clinics. USAID has been given wide discretion in the dispersal of these funds.

Chapter 16: The Gymkhana Club, 2009

1. Students who enter TCF schools from government schools are frequently behind their TCF classmates and must begin at Level I (first grade). It is possible for them to work at an accelerated pace and catch up with their age-mates, but this accelerated pace creates extra work for both teacher and student, particularly in English classes.

2. Some TCF school buildings house two school units—one in the morning, the other in the afternoon—to accommodate the overflow of children. Each school unit is counted as a separate school. As of this writing, there are 730 TCF school units, enrolling 102,000 students, 50 percent of whom are female. The present goal of TCF is to build a thousand schools throughout the country.

Chapter 17: Sheikhupura and Dhamke, 2009

1. This highway, the M2, was finished in 1997. It is a modern blacktop roadway and features fuel, washroom, eating, and rest stations along its 228 miles (367 kilometers). Overhead highway signs in Urdu and English direct us toward Sheikhupura, about 17 miles north of Lahore.

Chapter 18: Khanewal and Harappa, 2009

1. Compressed natural gas (CNG) is a fossil fuel substitute for gasoline, diesel, or propane. Although its combustion does produce greenhouse gases, it is a more environmentally clean alternative to those fuels, and it is much safer than other fuels in the event of a spill. CNG is used in traditional gasoline internal combustion engine cars that have been converted into bifuel vehicles (gasoline and CNG). Natural gas vehicles are increasingly used in Europe and South America due to rising gasoline prices. Pakistan currently has the highest number of vehicles running on CNG in the world.

2. The CCFU project was a scheme introduced by the provincial government in 1948 to rehabilitate families uprooted by Partition and reclaim 147,000 acres of barren state land. The government formed 132 cooperative farming societies in the region and distributed 12.5 acres of land to each member. The cooperatives introduced limited mechanized farming by purchasing tractors to prepare the soil for seeds and by installing tube wells in areas where canal water was insufficient for cultivation.

Chapter 19: Leaving Lahore, 2009

1. The word *nautch* is an anglicized form of the Urdu word *nach*, meaning "dance." The nautch girls originally belonged to a class of accomplished singers and dancers that predated Moghul and British rule on the subcontinent. Their status changed over the years as fortunes and lavish lifestyles waxed and waned, and several classes of dancing girls emerged, ranging from strolling dancers who provided entertainment for the common man to highly accomplished dancers and courtesans who catered to the aristocracy. Pran Nevile, *Nautch Girls of the Raj* (New Delhi, India: Penguin Books, 2009).

2. The Badshai Mosque was built by Shah Jahan's son, Aurangsab, in 1673 at the height of Moghul rule on the subcontinent. It is similar in design to the Jana Mosque in Delhi and, like that and the Red Fort in Delhi, is constructed of red sandstone tiles from Rajasthan, India. The mosques' design of double domes, large prayer hall of inlaid marble, arches leading to side aisles on three sides of a vast courtyard, and four minars, give the impression of bold, cosmic, majesty. The Lahore Fort, reconstructed during the Moghul reign of Akbar (1556–1605), sits opposite the Badshai Mosque, within the walls of the Old City.

3. Sammi-Daewoo Pakistan Express Bus Service Ltd., established in 1997 and headquartered in Lahore, operates luxury bus service in thirty-one cities in Pakistan and covers more than forty destinations in the Punjab and North-West Frontier Province.

Chapter 20: Islamabad: Modern Pakistan

1. Liaquat Bagh Park, Rawalpindi is the site of the 1951 assassination of the first elected prime minister of Pakistan, Liaquat Ali Khan and the 2007 assassination of former prime minister Benazir Bhutto. Former prime minister, Zulfikar Ali Bhutto, Benazir Bhutto's father was hanged in Rawalpindi in 1979.

2. www.hdf.com/The-Foundation/About-HDF.html.

3. Razia describes pakrah as a monthlong program of prayer studies, like the hajj, the annual pilgrimage to Mecca, but without all the hajj's duties.

4. Daman-e-Koh is a popular panoramic viewing point above the zoo. Its name is a conjunction of two words in Urdu: *daman*, which means "center," and *koh*, meaning "hill." Daman-e-Koh literally means "center of the mountain," but it can also be interpreted as "hem of the mountain."

Chapter 21: Hunza: Another Pakistan

1. The Himalayas include the Hindu Kush range of Afghanistan and Tajikistan to the west and northwest and the Himalayas proper of Kashmir and Tibet to the

southeast. The Himalayan Range extends from west to east in an arc 1,490 miles long and includes over a hundred mountains exceeding 23,500 feet. Mount Everest (29,029 feet) between Tibet, Nepal, and China and K2 (28,251 feet) in Pakistan are in the Himalayan arc of mountains.

2. Rakaposhi, the twelfth highest mountain in Pakistan, the twenty-seventh highest in the world, is 25,551 feet high. Its name, in the local language, means "shining wall," and it was first climbed in 1958. Ghulmat is at the base of the mountain and commands an impressive view of Rakaposhi's grandeur from a distance.

3. Federally Administered Northern Areas (FANA) is a single administrative unit for Gilgit Baltistan Hunza, and Nagar. The administrative center is in Gilgit. Pakistan considers this territory separate from Kashmir, but India considers it as part of the larger disputed territory of Kashmir.

4. The Baltit Fort is a seven-hundred-year-old fortress, the ancestral home of Ghazanfar Ali Khan II, "given in trust as a national treasure to be restored and strengthened with new foundations and polymer mesh walls. . . . It was rebuilt, stone by stone from 1990 to 1996, using both modern and traditional methods." Described as "the most amazing fortress ever built" by a British traveler in the 1920s, "today, it would be fitting to describe it as the most amazing fort ever rebuilt." Aryn Baker, "Baltit Fort, Hunza Valley, Pakistan," *Time*, July 4, 2005; see also www.time.com/time/magazine/article/0,9171,1077216,00.html.

Chapter 22: Pakistan: Unfinished Business

1. Located on a rock near Kargah Nullah (ravine), 10 km. from Gilgit town is a beautiful rock engraving of Buddha from 7th century A.D.

Index

Abbas, Syed Qaiser, 166
Abu Dhabi, 35
Academy for Village Development,
    Peshawar, 2, 11, 12, 38
active learning, 75, 90, 146, 200n6. *See
    also under* inquiry-based instruction
Adeel, Sanober, 100–101, 111–13, 161
adult literacy, xii
Aga Khan Education Services, 176
Aga Khan Health Services, 36
Ahmad, Asad Ayub, 79, 105
Ali, Sher 174, 178–81, 183, 190
Ali, Zulfiqar, 165
Allama Iqbal International Airport, 97
Amar, 49, 57, 62
Anarkali bazaar, 159–60
Assistant Director for Basic
    Democracies, 3, 14, 24. *See also*
    Mohyddin, Ikram
Ata Mohammed, 14–15, 139–40, 142.
    See also Jerry
Awan, Col. Muhammad Anwar, 100,
    103
ayah, xiii, 46, 56, 67–68, 72–73, 75–77,
    87–88, 136, 153

Ayub, Rafique, 112–14
Azad Kashmir, 63, 104, 162, 171,
    175–76, 199

Badshai Mosque, 161, 171, 203n2
baksheesh, 68, 98, 101, 195
Baltit Fort, 180
Bangladesh, xiii, 92
bangles, 160–62
Barut Lake, 183
basic democracies, 165, 197n1
basket purses, 26–27, 29–30, 32
Benny, 19
Best Westin, 98, 107
Bhutto, Benazir, 49, 94, 203n1
Bhutto, Zulfikar Ali, 52, 92, 187, 203n1
bister, 2, 5–6, 34, 69
Bivi-gee, 15, 19, 22–25, 67, 142
Bivi, Sakina, 118–20, 122, 128, 158–59
British Raj, 6, 37, 161, 203

Carol, 19–20, 22–26, 139, 142, 197n1
cell phone: prevalence of, 35, 143, 170,
    182; use of, 36, 38, 40–41, 47, 84,
    96, 100

~

About the Author

Inspired by John Kennedy, **Leslie Noyes Mass** joined the Peace Corps one month after graduating from Gettysburg College in 1962. She was sent to a small village in West Pakistan as a community development worker, intending to help women and young girls create better lives for themselves. With little more than a liberal arts degree, a heaping dose of idealism, and exuberant youthful energy, Leslie quickly learned that the Muslim villagers had far more to teach her than she could possibly teach them.

Leslie returned to the United States at the end of her Peace Corps commitment and enrolled in graduate school to deepen her understanding of how people learn and to sharpen her skills in assisting them. She earned an MA and PhD in education from The Ohio State University, married, raised two daughters, and focused her career on teaching young children and undereducated adults how to read and write.

Leslie developed exemplary programs in early childhood education and literacy education and complemented these efforts by instructing undergraduate and graduate students and teachers in schools and early childhood programs on Native American Indian reservations, internationally, and across the United States.

At the end of her formal teaching career at Ohio Wesleyan University, Leslie returned to Pakistan with several former Peace Corps Volunteers to help Pakistani teachers learn how to implement inquiry-based science activities in their teaching. *Back to Pakistan: A Fifty-year Journey* is about the changes Leslie found—in education, in the cities and towns of Pakistan, in the Punjabi village of her first home, and in herself.

The legacy of Leslie's early commitment to Pakistan is that she is still welcome, safe, and appreciated as an American in a country that continues to struggle with its development as an independent nation. Far from the disappointment of her initial foray into teaching in Pakistan, Leslie returned from her experience in 2009 with renewed hope for Pakistan. One legacy of the Peace Corps in Pakistan, Leslie found, is a new generation of enthusiastic, competent Pakistani citizens who may have heard John Kennedy's call from Volunteers like her, and are committed to and successfully in engaged in giving back to their country.

In addition to teaching, Leslie also has a passion for long distance hiking. Her first book, *In Beauty May She Walk*, 2005, is about hiking the entire Appalachian Trail at age sixty.

Proceeds from the sale of *Back to Pakistan: A Fifty-year Journey* will be donated to educating women and children in Pakistan.